Essentials

Autodesk®
Vault Workgroup 2023

September 2022

AUTODESK
Authorized Publisher

Published by
ASCENT Center for Technical Knowledge
630 Peter Jefferson Parkway, Suite 175
Charlottesville, VA 22911

866-527-2368

www.ascented.com

Contents

Preface vii

In This Guide xi

Practice Files xiii

Chapter 1: Introduction to Autodesk Vault Workgroup 1-1

    1.1 Autodesk Vault Workgroup Overview 1-2

        Overview 1-2

        File Status 1-2

        Manage Files - Projects Feature 1-4

        Links 1-4

    Practice 1a Manage Files and Create Links 1-6

    1.2 Chapter Summary 1-18

Chapter 2: Lifecycle States in Autodesk Vault Workgroup 2-1

    2.1 Lifecycle Definitions and States 2-2

        Overview 2-2

        Lifecycle Definitions 2-3

        Viewing Lifecycle Definitions 2-6

        Creating a New Lifecycle Definition 2-6

    Practice 2a Create New Lifecycle Definition 2-11

    2.2 Configuring Lifecycle States 2-14

        Overview 2-14

        Setting Up 2-14

        Security 2-23

        Transitions 2-26

        Other Configuration Settings 2-38

    Practice 2b Configure Lifecycle Definition 2-43

    2.3 Changing Lifecycle States 2-58

        Overview 2-58

        Change State 2-58

Practice 2c Change Lifecycle States 2-64

2.4   Chapter Summary 2-75

Chapter 3: Revision Management in Autodesk Vault Workgroup 3-1

3.1   **Revisions and Versions** 3-2
     Overview 3-2
     Concept 3-2
     Default Revision Schemes and Scheme Formats 3-5

3.2   **Creating and Modifying Revision Schemes** 3-7
     Overview 3-7
     Revision Scheme and Revision Formats 3-7
     Modifying an Existing Revision Scheme 3-13

Practice 3a Create a Revision Scheme 3-18

3.3   **Revising Files** 3-24
     Overview 3-24
     Revision Controlled Documents 3-24
     Revisions and Lifecycles 3-26
     Change Revision Command 3-29

Practice 3b Revise a File 3-33

3.4   Chapter Summary 3-46

Chapter 4: Categories in Autodesk Vault Workgroup 4-1

4.1   **Categories and Rules** 4-2
     Overview 4-2
     Categories 4-2
     Change Category 4-5
     Rules 4-8

Practice 4a Changing Categories 4-9

4.2   **Managing Categories and Rules** 4-11
     Overview 4-11
     Managing Categories 4-11

Practice 4b Managing Categories 4-17

4.3   Chapter Summary 4-20

Contents

Chapter 5: Managing Properties **5-1**

5.1 **System-Defined Properties vs. User-Defined Properties** **5-2**
Overview 5-2
Learn About Terms, Data Types, and Attributes............................. 5-2
Introduction to the Property Definitions Dialog Box........................ 5-6
Change the State 5-8
Examining Usage Count 5-8
Specifying Searchable Properties 5-9
Initial Value.. 5-9
List Values... 5-10
Enforce List Values 5-10
Add or Remove a User-Defined Property 5-11

Practice 5a Create a New User-Defined Property........................... **5-12**

5.2 **The Properties Grid**.. **5-15**
Overview 5-15
Hide/Restore Properties... 5-16
Edit Properties from the Grid.. 5-16

Practice 5b Working with the Properties Grid **5-19**

5.3 **Map Properties** **5-22**
Overview 5-22
Mapping Priority 5-22
Mapping 5-23
Mapping Across Data Types 5-24
Create Option.. 5-24
Mapping AutoCAD Block Attributes 5-25
AutoCAD Mechanical 5-26
AutoCAD Electrical.. 5-26

Practice 5c Map Properties **5-28**

5.4 **Chapter Summary** **5-31**

Chapter 6: Automatic File Naming in Autodesk Vault Workgroup **6-1**

6.1 **Create Custom Numbering Schemes**...................................... **6-2**
Overview 6-2
Define Numbering Schemes 6-2

Practice 6a Define a Custom Numbering Scheme **6-9**

**Practice 6b Create a New Autodesk Inventor File
Numbering Scheme**... **6-17**

Chapter 7: Creating Reports **7-1**

   7.1 Creating Reports **7-2**
      Overview 7-2
      About Reports 7-3
      Report Templates 7-3
      Microsoft Report Viewer 7-5
      Creating Search Reports 7-6

   Practice 7a Create a Search Report **7-7**

   7.2 Creating Custom Report Templates **7-10**
      Overview 7-10
      Introduction to the Autodesk Template Authoring Utility 7-10
      Creating a New Report Template 7-12
      Including Non-property Vault Data in a Report 7-16

   7.3 Chapter Summary **7-20**

Chapter 8: Autodesk Inventor In-CAD Data Management **8-1**

   8.1 Working with Data Cards **8-2**
      Overview 8-2
      About Data Card Views 8-3
      Understanding Data Card Decks 8-6
      Editing Properties with Data Cards 8-11
      Working with Value Collectors 8-14
      Managing the Data Card Layout 8-18

   Practice 8a Manage a Card Deck **8-21**

   8.2 Data Mapping and Report Generation **8-26**
      Overview 8-26
      Introduction to the Data Mapping 8-27
      Mapping Your Data 8-28
      Creating Reports for Your Model 8-31
      Managing Chart Elements 8-33
      Managing Data Mapping Reports 8-35

   Practice 8b Map Your Data **8-38**

   8.3 Sheet Set Manager Integration **8-43**
      Overview 8-43
      Resave All Sheets 8-44
      Remove Sheet or Sheet Subset 8-44
      Move, Rename, and Copy Design in the Vault Client 8-44

   8.4 Chapter Summary **8-45**

Chapter 9: Copy Design, Job Server, Vault Revision Tables, and Backups **9-1**

9.1 **Copy Design** **9-2**
Overview 9-2
Copy Design Interface 9-2
Copy Design Procedure 9-8

Practice 9a Copy Design **9-10**

9.2 **Enable the Job Server** **9-11**
Overview 9-11
Job Server vs. Job Processor 9-11
Enable the Job Server 9-11
Job Processor 9-12
Job Server Queue 9-13
Initiate a Job 9-16

Practice 9b Run Some Jobs and Watch Them in the Job Queue **9-18**

9.3 **Configuring the Job Server** **9-20**
Overview 9-20
Configuration via Job Processor UI................................... 9-20
The Configuration File 9-21
Log File 9-22

Practice 9c Change Settings in the Job Processor **9-23**

9.4 **PDF Publishing** **9-25**
Configuring PDF Publishing Options.................................. 9-25
Publish PDF from 2D CAD Files 9-27
Create a PDF from 2D CAD Files 9-28
PDF Publish Location.. 9-29

9.5 **Vault Revision Table Administration** **9-30**
Overview 9-30
Vault Revision Table Supported Drawings and Prerequisites........ 9-30
Vault Revision Table Administration 9-31

Practice 9d Using Vault Revision Tables **9-36**

9.6 **Backup and Restore** **9-43**
Overview 9-43
Back Up the Vault 9-43
Restore a Vault 9-44
Back Up Vault Data... 9-45

Practice 9e Back Up Your Vault...................................... **9-47**

9.7 **Chapter Summary** **9-48**

Preface

The *Autodesk® Vault Workgroup 2023: Essentials* learning guide expands the Autodesk® Vault Basic functionality to working with document lifecycles and providing knowledge of advanced data organization.

This learning guide is intended for users and CAD administrators with Autodesk Vault Basic knowledge who want to expand their skills to accommodate additional engineering workflows and data organization. This learning guide focuses on the features of Autodesk Vault Workgroup. Hands-on exercises are included to reinforce lifecycle and revision management. Users are taught how to manage lifecycles, properties, categories, and revisions.

Important: Refer to the *Course and Classroom Setup* section for installing the practice files and setting up the database.

Topics Covered

- Introduction to Autodesk Vault Workgroup
- Lifecycle States
- Revision Management
- Working with Categories
- Managing Properties
- Automatic File Naming
- Creating Reports
- Job Server
- Vault Revision Table Administration

Prerequisites

- Access to the 2023 version of the software, to ensure compatibility with this guide. Future software updates that are released by Autodesk may include changes that are not reflected in this guide. The practices and files included with this guide might not be compatible with prior versions (e.g., 2022).

- It is recommended that you have a good working knowledge of Autodesk CAD programs and have working knowledge of Autodesk Vault Basic features.

Course and Classroom Setup

Classroom Environment

This guide is intended for use in an instructor-led environment. If you plan to use the guide on your own in a non-classroom environment, you must set up Autodesk Vault correctly. Before you set up your system, you should be aware of the following:

- Do not use a production vault for the practices. It is recommended that you set up a separate vault on a separate vault server.

- If you plan to repeat a practice, you must remove any files that were added to the vault when you previously completed the practice. It is recommended that you delete the entire vault and start again with a new vault.

- Do not attempt these practices on a production vault server until you are familiar with the procedures that are covered.

Note: If you have installed AutoCAD or AutoCAD-based products after installing Autodesk Vault, you might need to **Uninstall/Change** the Autodesk Vault Client installation and select **Add or Remove Features** to select the appropriate Add-In software.

You must install and run this courseware from individual computers. You cannot run the courseware from a shared server. **DO NOT install the courseware on a computer that stores working vault data.**

Overview of Installing the Courseware

The following steps describe how to install the courseware.

1. Install Autodesk Vault Client and Autodesk Vault Server on each computer. Installing Autodesk Vault Workgroup or Autodesk Vault Professional software is recommended to be able to perform all practices.

2. Install the course data sets on each computer.

3. If Autodesk Vault has been previously used on the computer, restore default settings for the user interface.

Installing Autodesk Vault

Install both Autodesk Vault Client and Autodesk Vault Server on each computer. See the Autodesk Vault installation media for installation instructions.

If you are using any of the following Autodesk® software applications in conjunction with Autodesk Vault, they must also be installed:

- Autodesk Inventor
- AutoCAD®
- AutoCAD® Mechanical
- AutoCAD® Electrical

Installing the Practice Files

To install the data files for the practices:

1. Download the practice files zip file using the link provided on the *Practice Files* page in the learning guide.

2. Unzip the zip file to the C: drive. An AOTG Vault Workgroup folder is created and contains all the files that you will need.

3. Extract the Arbor_Press.exe file to its default directory. This file is checked into the database and is required for one of the practices.

4. The remaining files are required to restore the database. The instructions for this are detailed below.

WARNING: The following procedure will overwrite the current datasets and file stores in your current Vault. Be sure to back up any necessary Vaults that might be required at a later time.

Restore the Backup

1. Click Start>All Programs>Autodesk>Autodesk Data Management>Autodesk Data Management Server Console 2023.

2. In the Log In dialog box:

   - For User Name, enter administrator.
   - Leave Password blank.
   - Click OK.
   - The Autodesk Data Management Server Console displays.

3. Select Tools>Backup and Restore.

4. Select Restore, then select Next.

5. In the Backup and Restore Wizard dialog box, in *Select backup directory for restore*, navigate to the location on your local C: drive where the AOTG Vault Workgroup files were extracted, as shown below.

- Database data location: Default Restore Location
- File Store location: Original Restore Location

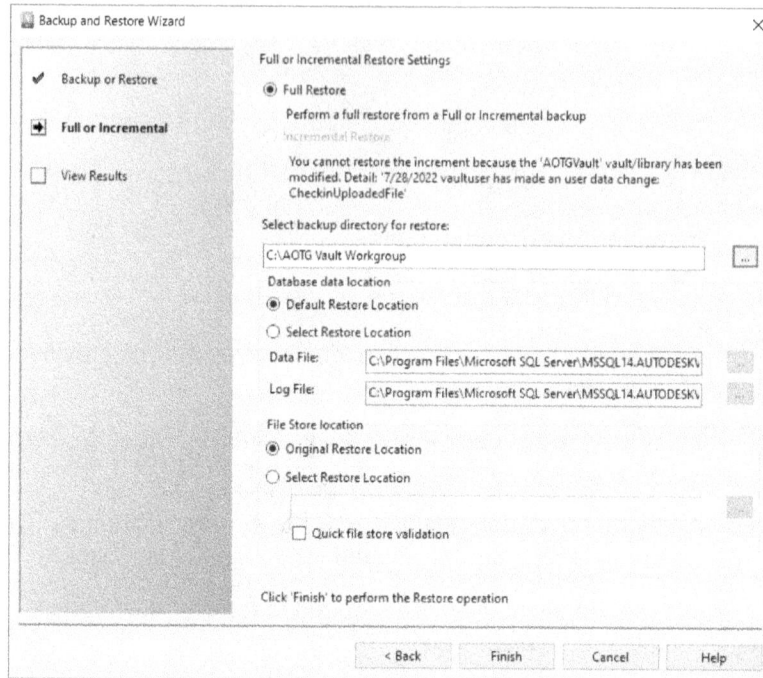

6. Click OK.

7. The Restore Progress dialog box displays the progress for restoring the database.

8. Click OK when complete.

9. In the Autodesk Data Management Server Console dialog box, click File>Exit.

In This Guide

The following highlights the key features of this guide.

Feature	Description
Practice Files	The Practice Files page includes a link to the practice files and instructions on how to download and install them. The practice files are required to complete the practices in this guide.
Chapters	A chapter consists of the following: Learning Objectives, Instructional Content, and Practices. • **Learning Objectives** define the skills you can acquire by learning the content provided in the chapter. • **Instructional Content**, which begins right after Learning Objectives, refers to the descriptive and procedural information related to various topics. Each main topic introduces a product feature, discusses various aspects of that feature, and provides step-by-step procedures on how to use that feature. Where relevant, examples, figures, helpful hints, and notes are provided. • **Practice** for a topic follows the instructional content. Practices enable you to use the software to perform a hands-on review of a topic. It is required that you download the practice files (using the link found on the Practice Files page) prior to starting the first practice.

Practice Files

To download the practice files for this guide, use the following steps:

1. Type the URL *exactly as shown below* into the address bar of your Internet browser to access the Course File Download page.

   Note: If you are using the ebook, you do not have to type the URL. Instead, you can access the page simply by clicking the URL below.

https://www.ascented.com/getfile/id/sahyadriaPF

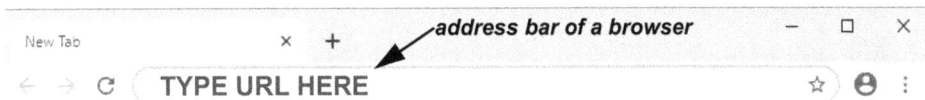

2. On the Course File Download page, click the **DOWNLOAD NOW** button, as shown below, to download the .ZIP file that contains the practice files.

3. Once the download is complete, unzip the file and extract its contents.

   The recommended practice files folder location is:
   C:\AOTGVault Workgroup

   Note: It is recommended that you do not change the location of the practice files folder. Doing so may cause errors when completing the practices.

Introduction to Autodesk Vault Workgroup

This chapter gives an overview of Autodesk® Vault Workgroup.

Learning Objectives in This Chapter

- Describe some differences between Autodesk Vault Basic and Autodesk Vault Workgroup.
- Identify the user interface elements and navigate the user interface.

1.1 Autodesk Vault Workgroup Overview

Overview

When moving from Autodesk Vault Basic to one of the higher end Autodesk Vault products, there are a few differences in functionality a user should be aware of.

Objectives

After completing this lesson, you will know:

- Differences in Autodesk Vault Basic and Autodesk Vault Workgroup.

File Status

Icons and the font color used for the filename indicate the status of files in the vault. The icons indicate whether you have a local copy, if your copy is up-to-date, if you have a current version, and so on. The font color will indicate if the file is not checked out, is checked out to you, or is checked out to another user.

Status Fonts

Font Color/ Weight	Description
Black/Normal	The file is not checked out.
Blue/Bold	The file is checked out to you.
	Note: Files which are checked out to you and have changes in memory that have not been saved will have an asterisk appended to the filename (e.g., Fork-Damper.dwg*).
Gray/Italic/ Strikethrough	The file is checked out to another user.
Vault Status Modifier (+)	Local copy has saved edits.

Status Icons

Option	Description
No icon	If no icon displays, the file is in the vault, but you do not have a local copy of the file on your computer. You can quickly identify which files are new to the vault. Use Get/Checkout to retrieve a copy of the file.
○	The file is in the vault and available for check out. This is the leading version of the leading revision of the file. Use Get/Checkout to retrieve a copy of the file.
⊘	The file is checked out to you and the local version is the same as in the vault, which is also referred to as the latest version of the leading revision. Use Check In to check the file back into the vault or select Undo Checkout to cancel any changes and check the file back into the vault.
●	The local file is newer than the file in the vault.
◉	The file is checked out by you and the local copy is newer than the latest version in the vault. This typically means that you made changes to the file since it was checked out but have not checked it back in.
◑	The local copy of the file is the released version of the latest revision, but it is not the latest version of the latest revision. This typically happens when you have a local copy of the released version but a quick change has been executed by another user.
⁺↻	The file is not in the vault. You can add the file by using the Check In feature.
△	The local copy is a historical revision of the leading revision in the vault.
⟳	The local copy of the file does not match the latest version in the vault. Use the Refresh from Vault feature to obtain the latest version of the file.
🔒	The file is locked and the local copy is up-to-date.
🔒	The file is locked and the local copy is not up-to-date.
ⓘ	There has been an unexpected result with the file (e.g., the local file has been changed without being checked out). See the tooltip for more information.

Manage Files - Projects Feature

The Projects feature is available in Autodesk Vault Workgroup and Autodesk Vault Professional.

Autodesk Vault projects enable you to organize and manage all project related data in one seamless interface.

Links

The Links feature is available in Autodesk Vault Workgroup and Autodesk Vault Professional.

A link enables you to organize and manage all project related data in one place. Links can be created for files, folders, items, and change orders. A link is a direct representation of an object that can reside anywhere in the Project Explorer. While the link can reside in many places, the object represented by the link, the target object, resides in only one place.

Most commands executed against a link are executed against the target object. This enables the user to perform actions, such as Check Out and Check In, on all data types from one location. The two exceptions to this rule are the Delete Command and the Move command. These commands affect the link only and not the target file.

Since a link is a direct representation of a target object, it has all of the properties of the target and will appear to be almost identical to the target. Since the link has the same name as the target, the defining difference between a link and a target is the shortcut overlay on the link's icon.

Procedure: Create a Link

Follow these steps to create a link.

1. Select the target object that you would like to link to.
2. In the Edit menu, select Copy.

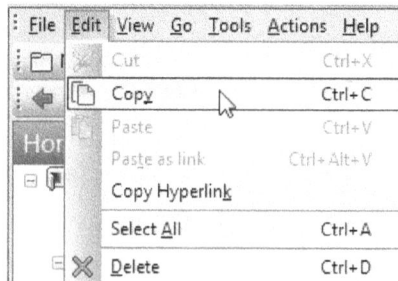

© 2022, ASCENT - Center for Technical Knowledge®

3. Select the destination folder of the link.
4. In the Edit menu, select Paste as link.

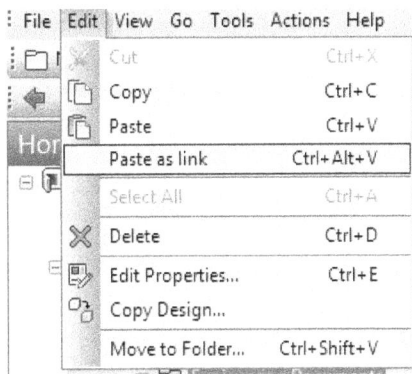

File	Edit	View	Go	Tools	Actions	Help
	Cut					Ctrl+X
	Copy					Ctrl+C
	Paste					Ctrl+V
	Paste as link					Ctrl+Alt+V
	Select All					Ctrl+A
	Delete					Ctrl+D
	Edit Properties...					Ctrl+E
	Copy Design...					
	Move to Folder...					Ctrl+Shift+V

The right mouse button drags & drops. The <Ctrl>+<C>/<Ctrl>+<Alt>+<V> techniques can also be used to Copy and Paste the target objects into a new location thereby creating a link.

5. The link is created in that folder.

Practice 1a

Manage Files and Create Links

In this practice, you will assign two different categories to two different sets of files. One set of files will be categorized as Engineering files and the other set as Office files. You will also set a project category to a folder and create links in the new project folder.

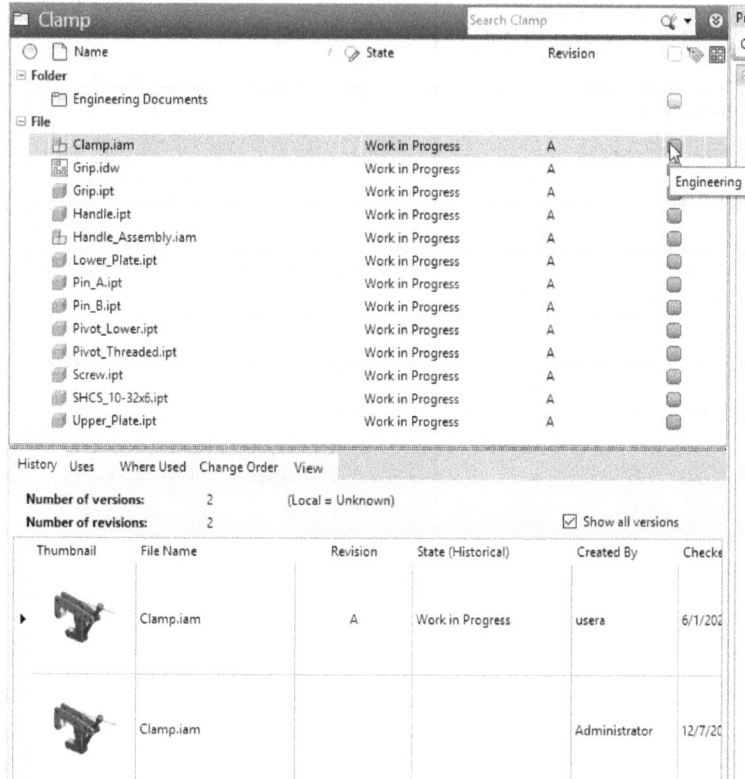

The completed practice

Task 1 - User setup.

Note: Steps 1 through 16 are only required if the users do not yet exist. If using the database provided with the course, steps 1 through 16 can be skipped.

1. Log in to Vault Workgroup as an Administrator by doing the following:

- For User Name, enter **Administrator**.
- Leave the password field blank.
- Select AOTCVault from the Vault drop-down list.

2. Select the Tools menu then Administration>Global Settings to display the Global Settings dialog box.

3. In the Security tab, select Manage Access... from the Users and Groups section to display the User and Group Management dialog box.

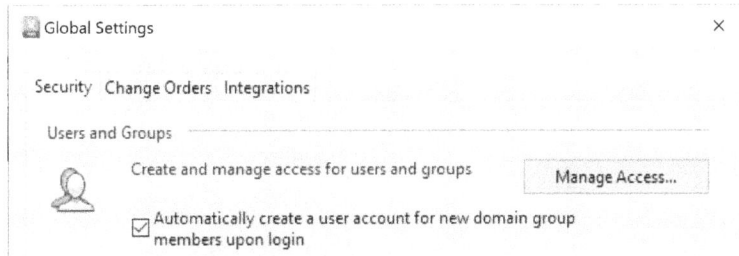

4. Select usera and then select Actions>Edit. Select Accounts... For Vault Account, enter **vault** as the password and confirm it. Select OK.

5. Select Roles to display the Add Roles dialog box for this user.

6. Clear Administrator. Ensure that the checkboxes are selected next to the entries for Document Editor (Level 2), Document Manager (Level 2), and Item Editor (Level 2).

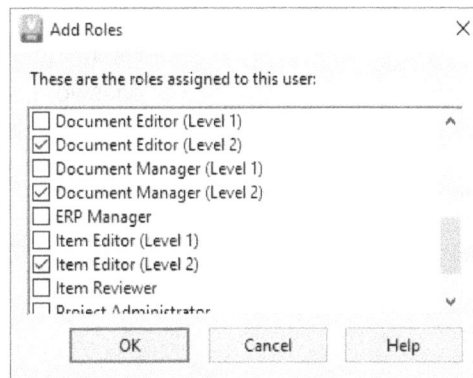

7. Select OK to close this dialog box and return to the User Profile.

8. Select Vaults to display the Add Vaults dialog box for this user.

9. Select the checkbox next to the AOTCVault and the Data Card and Mapping Vault.

10. Select OK to close this dialog box and return to the User Profile.

11. Select OK to close this dialog box and return to the User and Group Management dialog box.

12. Create a userb, userc, and userd using the same vault password as usera.

13. Repeat Steps 6 through 12 for the following users:

  • userb
  • userc
  • userd

14. When finished, close the User Management dialog box.

15. Select Close to close the Global Settings dialog box.

16. Select the File menu then Log Out to log out of Autodesk Vault Workgroup.

Task 2 - Change category.

1. Log in to Autodesk Vault Workgroup with the following information:

  • For User Name, enter **usera**.
  • For password, enter **vault**.
  • For the Vault choose AOTCVault.

2. In the Navigation Pane, select Project Explorer ($).

3. In the File menu, select Set Working Folder to display the Browse for folder dialog box.

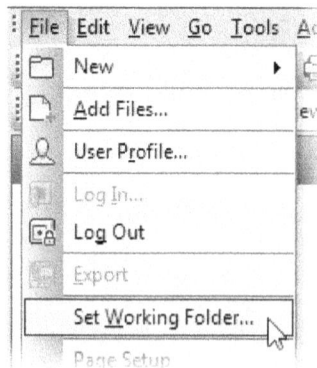

4. Browse to the following location:
   C:\AOTCVaultPro\VaultWorkingFolder.

   Note: If this folder does not exist, then use the Make New Folder command to create it in the specified location.

5. Select Select Folder to set the working folder and return to Vault Workgroup.

6. In the Navigation Pane, expand the root (Project Explorer ($)) folder, and then expand the Designs folder.

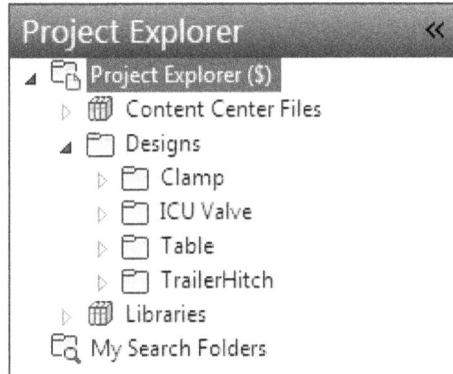

7. Select the Clamp folder to display the Clamp folder files in the Main pane.

8. Note the status of the files. The files are in the vault, but you do not have local copies of the files on your computer. The files are assigned to the Base category after migration. There is no Revision or State assigned to the files.

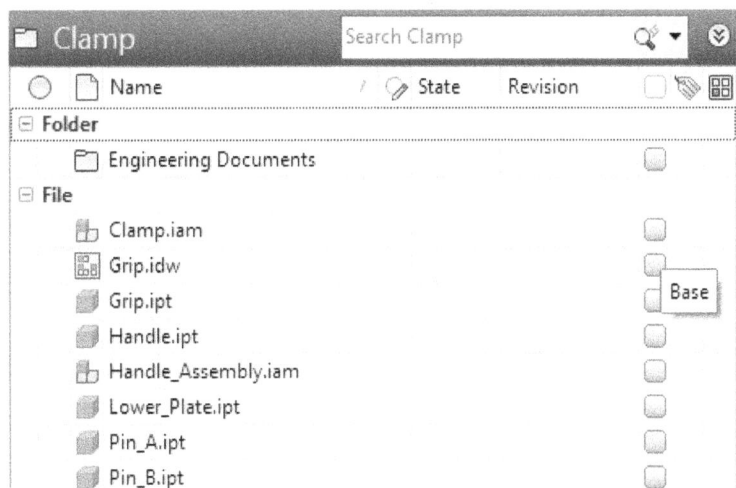

9. Select the top-level assembly Clamp.iam in the file list and then select Actions>Change Category.

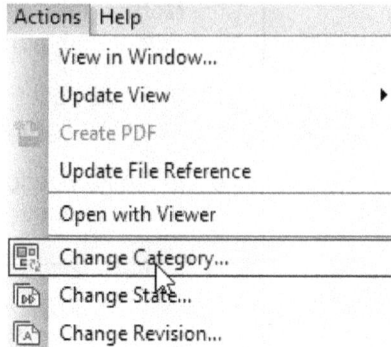

Actions	Help
View in Window...	
Update View	▶
Create PDF	
Update File Reference	
Open with Viewer	
Change Category...	
Change State...	
Change Revision...	

10. The Change Category dialog box displays. Select the first icon in the row just below the file list to include the dependent files.

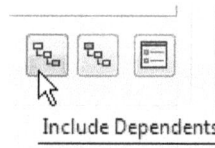

Include Dependents

11. All of the children files representing the whole design are now selected.

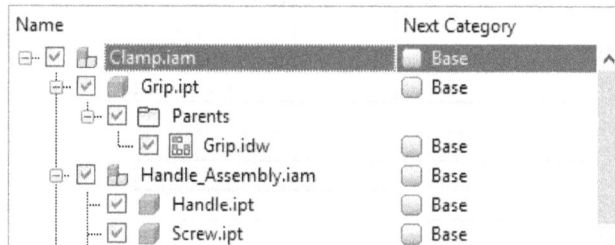

Name	Next Category
☑ Clamp.iam	Base
☑ Grip.ipt	Base
☑ Parents	
☑ Grip.idw	Base
☑ Handle_Assembly.iam	Base
☑ Handle.ipt	Base
☑ Screw.ipt	Base

12. In the Select a new category drop-down list, select Engineering.

Select a new category:

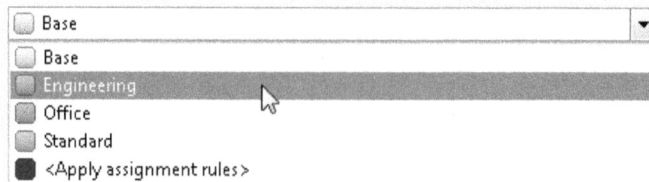

Base	▼
Base	
Engineering	
Office	
Standard	
<Apply assignment rules>	

13. Note the Next Category is now set to Engineering.

Name	Next Category
☑ 🖧 Clamp.iam	🔲 Engineering
☑ 📦 Grip.ipt	🔲 Engineering
☑ 📁 Parents	
☑ 📇 Grip.idw	🔲 Engineering
☑ 🖧 Handle_Assembly.iam	🔲 Engineering
☑ 📦 Handle.ipt	🔲 Engineering
☑ 📦 Screw.ipt	🔲 Engineering

14. In the Enter Comments text box, enter a comment or accept the default comment. Select OK.

Enter comments:

Set Engineering category

OK	Cancel	Help

15. View the results in the list of files.

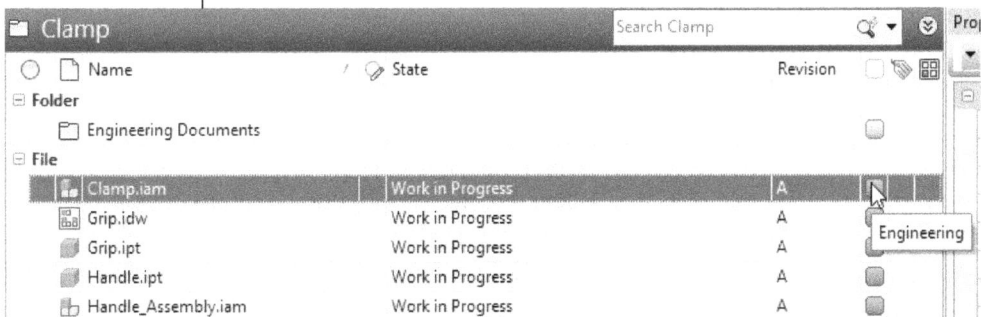

Name	State	Revision	
Folder			
📁 Engineering Documents			
File			
📇 Clamp.iam	Work in Progress	A	Engineering
📇 Grip.idw	Work in Progress	A	
📦 Grip.ipt	Work in Progress	A	
📦 Handle.ipt	Work in Progress	A	
🖧 Handle_Assembly.iam	Work in Progress	A	

- The Category Glyph is now set to Engineering.
- The Engineering Category specifies the default Lifecycle State for the files to be Work In Progress which you can see in the State column.
- The rules for changing to the Work In Progress Lifecycle State specify the Revision be bumped based on the Primary Revision with the Standard Alphabetic Revision Scheme. The first value in this revisions scheme's sequence is A which you can see in the Revision column.
- Because a new file version is created when a new Revision is made the files are all at Version 2.

16. In the Navigation Pane, expand the Clamp folder to reveal the Engineering Documents folder.

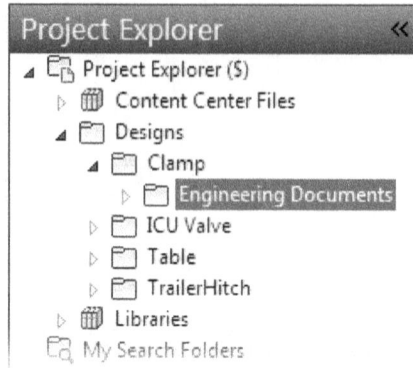

17. In the Engineering Documents folder, note the current state of the single document. This is a Microsoft Word document and like the CAD files was migrated into the Base Category which has no Lifecycle state or Revision associated with it.

18. Select the file and select Actions>Change Category to once again display the Change Category dialog box.

19. Select Office from the Select a new category and enter a comment.

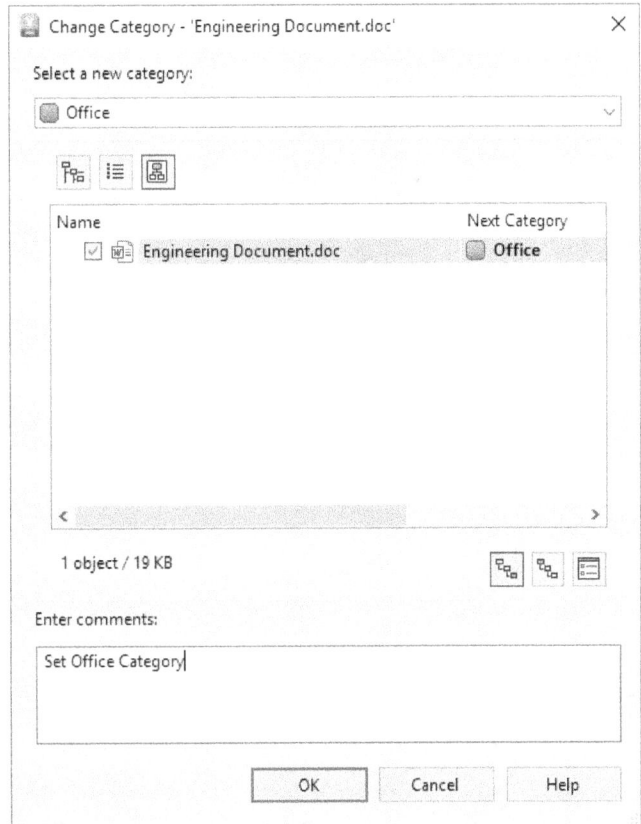

20. Select OK to dismiss the dialog box and complete the category change.

21. View the results.

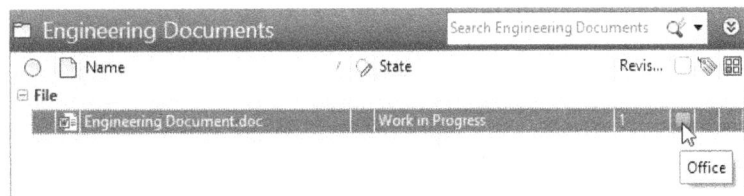

- The Category Glyph is now set to Office.
- The Office Category specifies the default Lifecycle State for the files to be Work In Progress which you can see in the State column.

- The rules for changing to the Work In Progress Lifecycle State specify the Revision be bumped based on the Primary Revision with the Standard Numeric Scheme. The first value in this revision scheme's sequence is 1 which you can see in the Revision column.
- Because a new file version is created when a new Revision is made the files are all at Version 2.

Task 3 - Create a project folder.

1. Log in to Autodesk Vault Workgroup as an Administrator by doing the following:

   - Set the User Name as **Administrator**.
   - Leave the password field blank.
   - Select AOTCVault in the Vault drop-down list.

2. In the Tools menu, select Administration>Vault Settings to display the Vault Settings dialog box.

3. Select the Behaviors tab and then select Categories in the Categories section.

4. Select New.

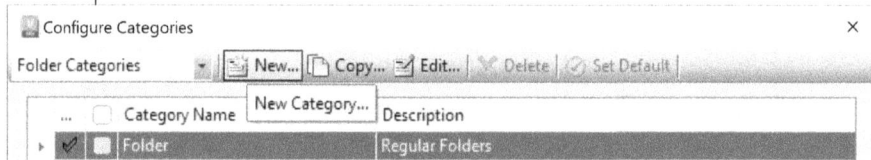

5. Set Name as Project. For Description, enter **Project Folder** and for Color, select Blue.

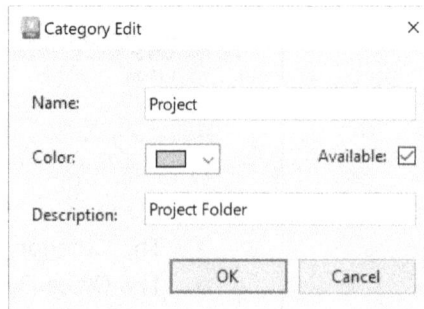

6. Click OK and then Close twice.

7. Click Project Explorer.

8. Right-click on Project Explorer ($) and select New Folder.

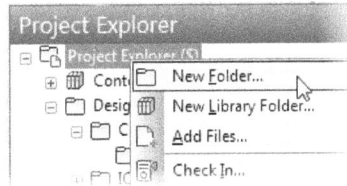

9. Create a new folder called Projects.

10. Click OK.

11. Right-click on Projects and select New Folder to create a new subfolder called 10-A-111. Change Category to Project.

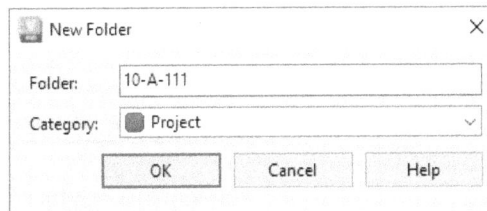

12. Click OK.

Task 4 - Create a link.

---

1. In the Navigation Pane, click *Designs\ICU Valve*.

2. Select all the files in the folder and subfolders using <Ctrl>+<A>.

3. In the Edit menu, select Copy.

4. Navigate to the 10-A-111 projects folder.

5. In the Edit menu, select Paste as link. The folders and files display as links as shown by the shortcut overlay on the link's icon.

Task 5 - Make change to link.

1. Select the link for ICU Valve Main Assembly.iam and then select Actions>Change Category.

2. In the Select a new category drop- down list, select Engineering.

3. In the Enter Comments text box, enter a comment.

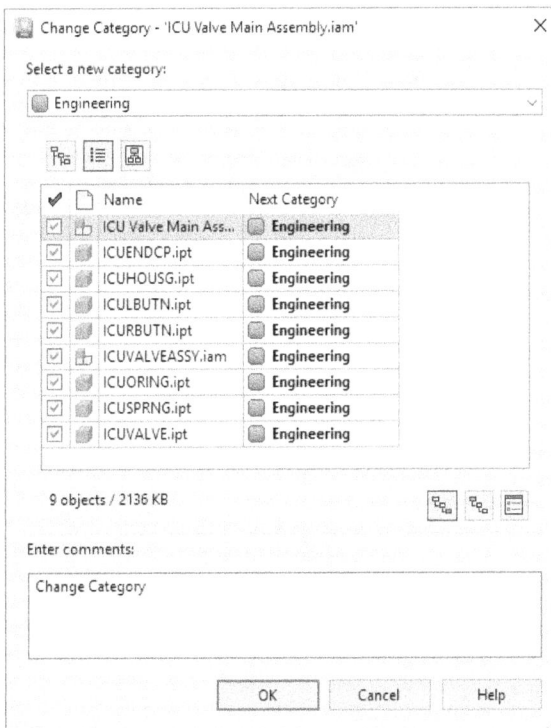

Change Category - 'ICU Valve Main Assembly.iam'

Select a new category:

Engineering

✔	🗋 Name	Next Category
☑	ICU Valve Main Ass...	Engineering
☑	ICUENDCP.ipt	Engineering
☑	ICUHOUSG.ipt	Engineering
☑	ICULBUTN.ipt	Engineering
☑	ICURBUTN.ipt	Engineering
☑	ICUVALVEASSY.iam	Engineering
☑	ICUORING.ipt	Engineering
☑	ICUSPRNG.ipt	Engineering
☑	ICUVALVE.ipt	Engineering

9 objects / 2136 KB

Enter comments:

Change Category

OK   Cancel   Help

4. Click OK.

5. Navigate to the target of the link, *Designs\ICU Valve*.

6. Note that the target files are now all set to the Engineering category.

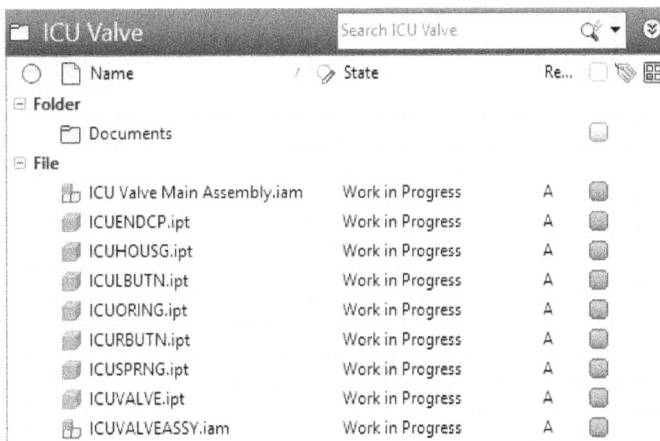

🗋 Name		🖉 State	Re...		
Folder					
🗂 Documents					
File					
🏭 ICU Valve Main Assembly.iam		Work in Progress	A		
ICUENDCP.ipt		Work in Progress	A		
ICUHOUSG.ipt		Work in Progress	A		
ICULBUTN.ipt		Work in Progress	A		
ICUORING.ipt		Work in Progress	A		
ICURBUTN.ipt		Work in Progress	A		
ICUSPRNG.ipt		Work in Progress	A		
ICUVALVE.ipt		Work in Progress	A		
🏭 ICUVALVEASSY.iam		Work in Progress	A		

ICU Valve

Search ICU Valve

1.2 Chapter Summary

Autodesk Vault Workgroup provides product lifecycle management to your designs. A common interface provides access to files, folders, revisions, and categories.

Having completed this chapter, you can:

- Describe some differences between Autodesk Vault Basic and Autodesk Vault Workgroup.

- Identify the user interface elements and navigate the user interface.

- Create a project folder and a link and describe their benefits.

Lifecycle States in Autodesk Vault Workgroup

Lifecycle management refers to the process a company uses to track its products from inception through retirement. As a product is conceived, defined, designed, tested, revised and produced, it will transit various stages that are often quite specific to a particular company. Autodesk® Vault Workgroup enables lifecycle management by applying a uniform set of behaviors to project data in the lifecycle management process. Along with uniformity, Autodesk Vault Workgroup is a tool that enables configuration of states, transitions, and other aspects of lifecycle management so that companies can tailor the tool to best fit their processes. In this chapter, you will learn about Autodesk Vault Workgroup Lifecycle Management, what default Lifecycle Definitions and States are available out-of-the-box and how to configure them or a new Lifecycle Definition and set of States to meet your organization's needs. You will learn how to change the lifecycle state of a Vault object using the lifecycle definitions and states.

Learning Objectives in This Chapter

- Describe the default out-of-the-box Lifecycle Definitions and how they could be applied for different situations.
- Describe the default out-of-the-box Lifecycle States and how they could be used to control data access.
- Create a new Lifecycle Definition and set of associated Lifecycle States.
- Plan for the configuration of Lifecycle Definitions and associated States.
- Configure the States of a Lifecycle Definition.
- Apply the Lifecycle Definition to project data.
- Change the lifecycle state of a file.
- Understand how the lifecycle state settings affect the ability to read and modify files.

2.1 Lifecycle Definitions and States

Overview

A lifecycle definition is an engine that can be configured to automatically assign security, behaviors, and properties to Vault objects based on where the object is in the life of the design process. This functionality enables you to streamline your work environment by removing the overhead involved in managing groups of files, custom objects, or an entire project. Several lifecycle definitions are included with the "out-of-the-box" installation. These range from a simple release process where project data is either editable or locked for editing to a more complex process involving long-lead time manufacturing, the review of project data before it is released, and the ability to short cut the formal release process for simple project data changes. They are designed to fit those processes seen in many companies from small shops to large corporations.

Each of these lifecycle definitions are comprised of two or more lifecycle states. A lifecycle state represents a certain point in the lifecycle of vault data. Common lifecycle states include: work-in-progress, review, and released. Lifecycle states control the ability to view and modify project data. Transitions from one state to the next control how new versions are created and other activities. There are controls for specifying required conditions before a transition can be made.

These set of Lifecycle Definitions and States cover many possible processes. If one does not fit your organization, a new definition with its unique set of states can be created.

Objectives

After completing this lesson, you will be able to:

- Describe the out-of-the-box Lifecycle Definitions and how they could be applied for different situations.

- Describe the predefined Lifecycle States and how they could be used to control project data access.

- Create a new Lifecycle Definition and set of associated Lifecycle States.

Lifecycle Definitions

A lifecycle definition uses states to identify the state of an object in the project lifecycle. Examples of states are: Work in Progress, For Review, and Released. An object moves from one state to another based on the lifecycle definition transition rules. These transition rules determine when the state change occurs, and whether the change can occur manually or automatically (or both), based on criteria determined by the administrator. The lifecycle definition also determines if any other automatic behaviors occur based on a state change.

For example, a lifecycle definition can be configured to automatically revise a file when it moves from a Work in Progress state to a Review state. Alternatively, if a user changes a folder's status to Obsolete, the lifecycle definition can automatically apply security settings to the folder so that only an administrator can modify the folder and its contents, or reinstate the folder for use.

Note: You must have administrative access to perform these tasks.

Lifecycles can be used with files, project folders, items, and custom objects.

Default Definitions

Several lifecycle definitions are included with the "out-of-the-box" installation that will assist administrators in assigning definitions to Vault content without having to create them. The Lifecycle Definitions are located in the Vault Settings dialog box, in the Behaviors tab. The following table lists the various lifecycle definitions.

Lifecycle Definition	Description
Basic Release Process	Basic manufacturing lifecycle process for release control. This definition can be used with most manufacturing project content.
Item Release Process	For use with the Vault Professional software. Basic item lifecycle process for release control. This definition can be used with all items and includes the following states: Work in Progress In Review Released Quick-Change Obsolete

Flexible Release Process	Flexible manufacturing lifecycle process for release control. This definition includes all of the Basic Release Process states and a Quick Change state for editing released data.
Simple Release Process	A generic lifecycle process for many different types of project data. This definition consists of a Work in Progress state and a Released state.
Long Lead Time Release Process	Best suited for long lead time manufacturing projects. This definition includes a Pre-Release state indicating that the project data has been sent to manufacturing but is still in a state of change.
Long Lead Time Release Process with Change Order	Best suited for long lead time manufacturing projects directed by change orders. This definition includes the Work in Progress, Review, and Pre-Release states. The Pre-Release state indicates that a file has been sent to manufacturing but is still in a state of change. When there are no more change orders for the file, it moves to a released state. From there, the file can return to the Pre-Release state through a Quick Change.
Design Representation Process	All PDF files created for document control are automatically assigned to the Design Representation category. A dedicated category enables administrators to manage their rules, lifecycles, and properties independent of the associated design files.
<None>	This definition enables any category to assign a null definition to opt out of using a lifecycle definition but to still retain category behavior.

Lifecycle States

The following table lists the various predefined Lifecycle States.

State Name	Description
Work In Progress	Sometimes known by the abbreviation "WIP", this is the state most commonly associated with the editing of the files. The editing, and often viewing of files in this state are usually restricted to a small group of individuals, usually in the Engineering function.
For Review	This is the state that usually precedes the release of a design to manufacturing. In this state, more users can interact with the data, but generally no editing is permitted. This state enables users to evaluate new designs and changes to existing designs, before they are re-released to manufacturing.

Released	In this state a broad range of groups in the organization now can read the data but usually editing is not permitted or at a minimum restricted to a very small group under controlled conditions.
Obsolete	This state is associated with designs that are no longer active. The products they are associated with are no longer being manufactured or are in a maintenance state. Access to these designs is more restricted and usually no edits can be made to them.
Quick Change	This state is common in processes where there needs to be a quick yet controlled method of updating files without going through a formal review to release process. For example, files with typographical errors but no fundamental form, fit, or function, changes. Modifications are generally permitted by a very small group of people.
Pre-Release	In processes where there are a large number of files, for example large assemblies or a product, this state enables the organization to approve the design or changes to the design but not designate them as released to manufacturing. Access can be permitted to a large group, but modification is usually prohibited and the ability to move them to the Released State also restricted.

In addition to edit ability, there is a set of rules regarding what happens to object revisions when an object is transitioned from one state to the next, who can make these transitions, and other considerations.

Considerations Using the Predefined Definitions

Each of the Predefined Lifecycle Definitions use one or more of the default States. There are a minimum set of rules governing transitions between states and object editing or viewing in a given State. These form the basic rules of the definition and can be adequate for your organization.

It is likely that you will need to configure the Lifecycle Definitions and States. This could range from minor tuning to major changes in the default states. Alternatively, you might need to create your own Lifecycle Definitions with their associated States, transitions, rules and actions.

Viewing Lifecycle Definitions

Viewing Lifecycle Definitions is an administrative task done through the Vault Settings dialog box. The dialog box can be opened using the Tools menu>Administration>Vault Settings and then selecting the Behaviors tab of this dialog box. The Lifecycle Definitions dialog box is accessed by selecting Lifecycles in the Lifecycles and Revisions section. From here you can choose to create new definitions, copy an existing definition, and edit or delete a definition from the Lifecycle Definition toolbar.

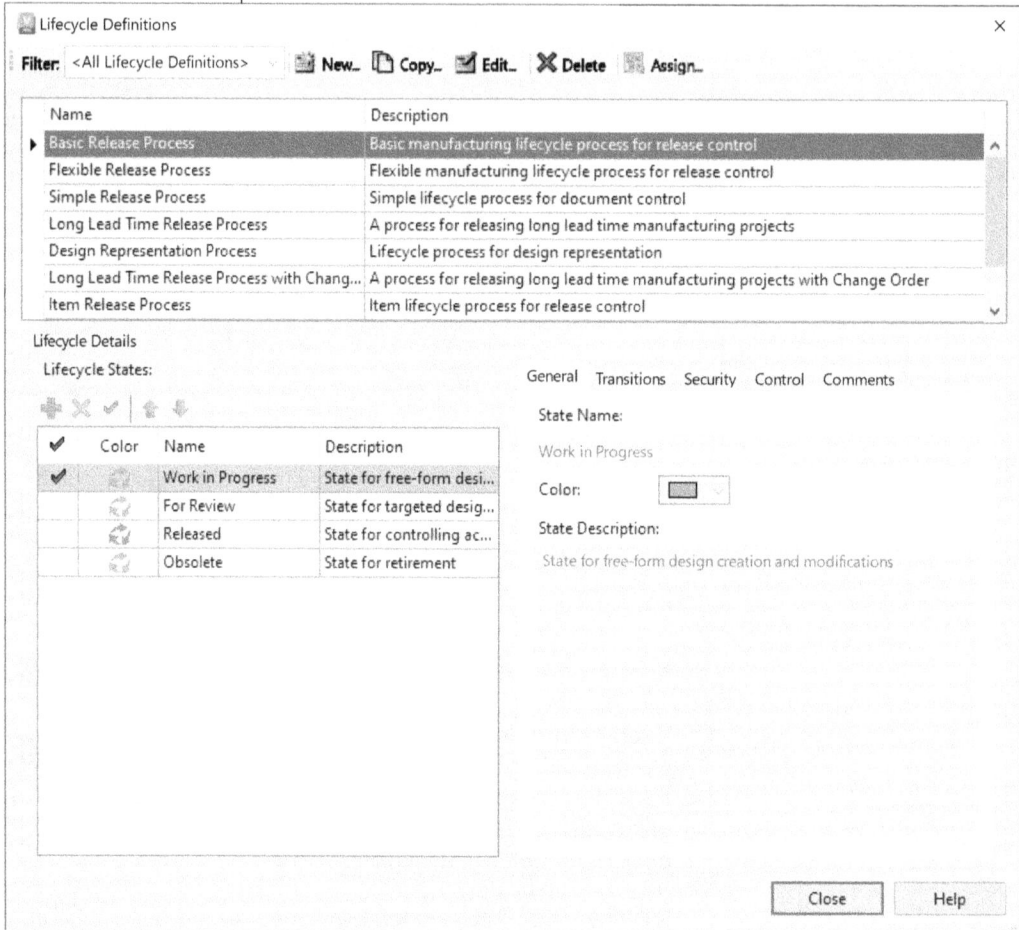

Creating a New Lifecycle Definition

In some cases, it might be desirable to create a new Lifecycle Definition and set of states. For example, in a small organization there have been three states traditionally used to describe the files used to manufacture the product:

- Development

- Manufacturing

- Out of Production

This is a simple but effective process for the organization and they want to use these lifecycle states rather than one of the defaults.

Procedure: Create New Lifecycle Definition

Follow these steps to create a new lifecycle definition called Company Default.

1. In the Vault Settings dialog box, select the Behaviors tab followed by selecting Lifecycles in the Lifecycles and Revisions section to display the Lifecycle Definitions dialog box.
2. In the Lifecycle Definition dialog box, click New to display the Lifecycle Definitions dialog box.

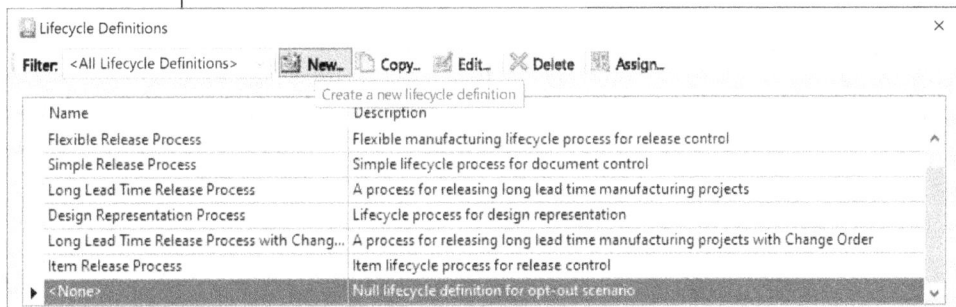

3. Enter a name and description for the new lifecycle definition.
4. In the Category list, select the categories you want to assigned to the new lifecycle definition.
5. In the Lifecycle Details section, select Plus (+) to display the New Lifecycle State dialog box.

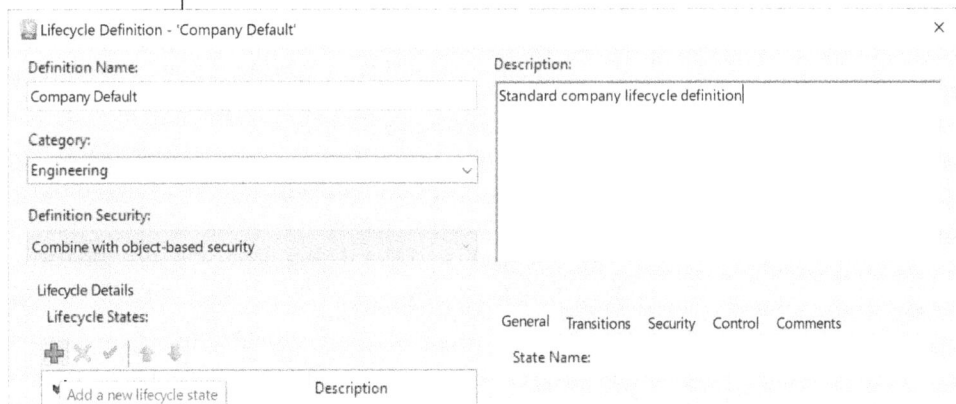

6. Enter a name and description for this state and select a color, then click OK to close this dialog box and return to the Lifecycle Definition dialog box.

7. Note that the first state defined is assigned the default state.
8. Repeat the previous step for the remaining states. If a different default state is required, select it and select the checkmark to set it as the default state for the lifecycle definition.

9. Reorder lifecycle states by selecting a state in the Lifecycle Details view and clicking the up or down arrow. The order of the lifecycle states determines the order in which they display in the Change State dialog box.
10. Click Apply to apply the new states for the new definition.
11. Click OK to close this dialog box and return the Lifecycle Definitions dialog box.
12. Before closing this dialog box, look through each tab in the right to see the default information for a given lifecycle state. Specifically, for a given state there is no lifecycle state security and every lifecycle state can transition to every other lifecycle state.
13. Click Close to close this dialog box and return to the Vault settings dialog box.

Scope of Configuration

Each Lifecycle Definition has a set of Lifecycle States. From the illustration below you can see the states associated with the Basic Release Process Lifecycle Definition.

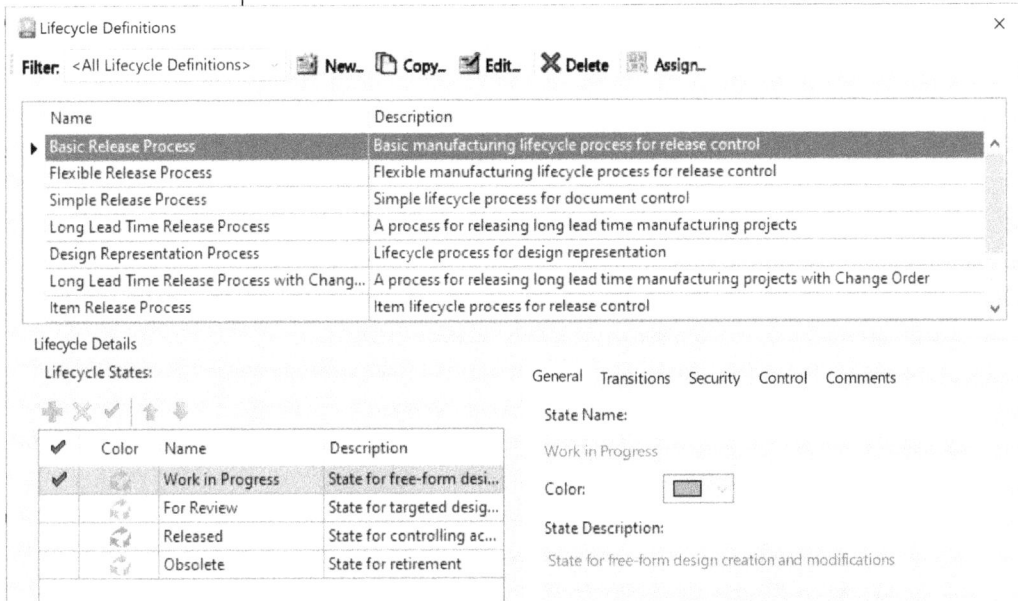

You can see that this Lifecycle Definition has a Lifecycle State called Work In Progress associated with it. The second illustration below shows the states associated with the Flexible Release Process Lifecycle Definition.

This Lifecycle Definition too has a Lifecycle State called Work In Progress associated with it. While they can have the same name, these are two independent Lifecycle States and the rules and actions associated with the customization of one of them does not affect the other.

Practice 2a | Create New Lifecycle Definition

In this practice, you will create a new lifecycle definition named Standard Process with three states: Development, Manufacturing, and Out of Production.

The completed practice

1. Log in to Autodesk Vault Workgroup using the following information:

   - User Name: **Administrator**
   - Leave password blank
   - Vault: AOTCVault

2. In the Tools menu, select Administration>Vault Settings to display the Vault Settings dialog box.

3. Select the Behaviors tab and then select Lifecycles in the Lifecycles and Revisions section.

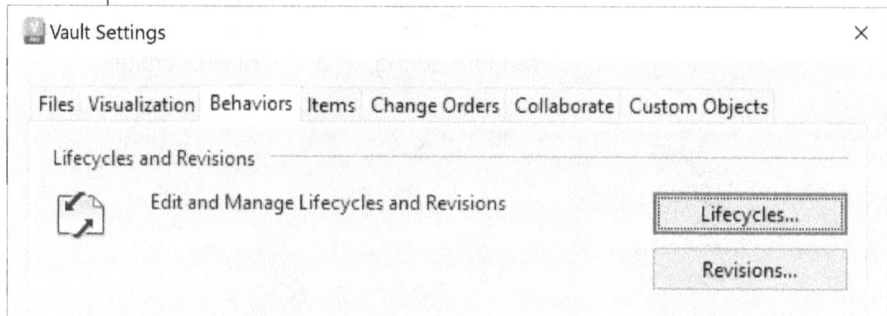

The Lifecycles Definitions dialog box displays.

4. In the toolbar, select New to display the Lifecycle Definition – 'New Definition' dialog box.

5. Do the following:

   - For Definition Name, enter **Standard Process**.
   - For Description enter **Company Standard Process.**
   - For Category, leave as None selected.

6. In the Lifecycle Details section, click Plus (+).

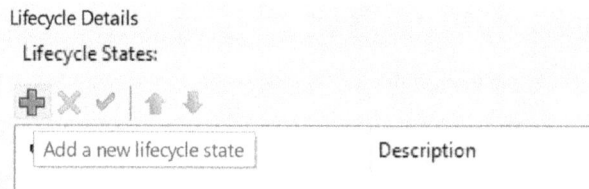

The New Lifecycle State dialog box opens.

7. Do the following:

   - For State Name, enter **Development**.
   - For Color, select **Green**.
   - For State Description, enter **Design development**.
   - Select OK to return to the previous dialog box.

8. Repeat the previous step using the following information:

   - For State Name, enter **Manufacturing**.
   - For Color, select **Blue**.
   - For State Description, enter **Released designs**.
   - Select OK to return to the previous dialog box.

9. Again, repeat the previous step using the following information:

- For State Name, enter **Out of Production**.
- For Color, select **Black**.
- For State Description, enter **Archived designs**.
- Select OK to return to the previous dialog box.

10. Examine the three states. Note that they display in blue text, which means they have not yet been applied.

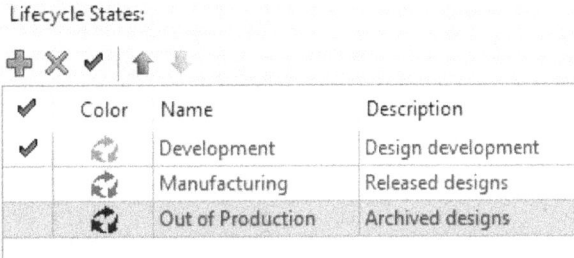

Lifecycle States:

✔	Color	Name	Description
✔	♻	Development	Design development
	♻	Manufacturing	Released designs
	♻	Out of Production	Archived designs

Note that the next step would be to configure the three lifecycle states. This will be done in the next practice.

11. Click Apply to apply the three new lifecycle states and then OK to dismiss the Lifecycle Definition dialog box. Note that the new Lifecycle Definition named Standard Process has been added.

Name	Description
Flexible Release Process	Flexible manufacturing lifecycle process for release co
Simple Release Process	Simple lifecycle process for document control
Long Lead Time Release Process	A process for releasing long lead time manufacturing
Long Lead Time Release Process with Change Order	A process for releasing long lead time manufacturing
<None>	Null lifecycle definition for opt-out scenario
▶ Standard Process	Company Standard Process

Lifecycle Details

12. Click Close to close the dialog box and return to the Vault Settings dialog box. Click Close again to close this dialog box.

2.2 Configuring Lifecycle States

Overview

The ability to define lifecycle definitions and behaviors enables you to customize your workflow environment to classify data based on their lifecycle status in the work process.

Objectives

After completing this lesson, you will be able to:

- Configure the lifecycle state to specify which users and groups can read, modify and delete files which are in that state.

- Specify which actions should be taken when a file transitions from one lifecycle state to another.

- Specify which users and groups can transition a file from one lifecycle state to another or if the transition should be permitted by anyone.

- Specify which files versions for a given revision should be removed in a Purge operation.

- Configure the default comments added when a lifecycle state transition occurs.

Setting Up

In order to effectively configure a Lifecycle Definition's Lifecycle States, it is critical to do some up-front planning. For example, different users can have different abilities to read or modify files in a given lifecycle state. One lifecycle state can transition to any other lifecycle state but some of these transitions might not make sense in your process and should not be permitted.

The following diagram shows an example of a Lifecycle Definition and the important considerations that must be planned before configuring one of the default lifecycle definitions or creating a new one.

Regardless of how you do this planning, it is important to review the following considerations before embarking on configuring the lifecycle definition.

Vault Workgroup Lifecycle Definition - Flexible

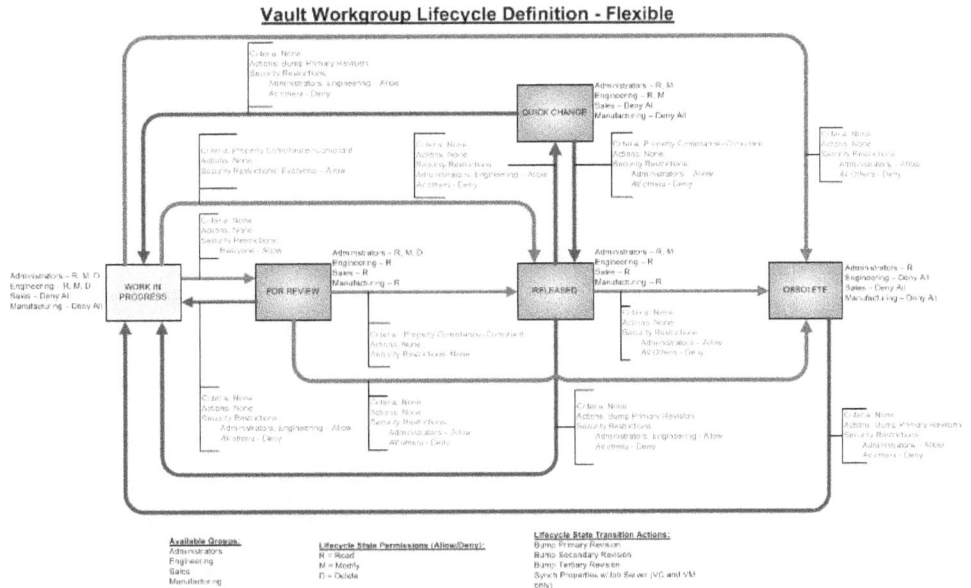

Groups

It is important to think of the different groups in your organization and what access you will want them to have for files in different lifecycle states. For example, in the Work In Progress State you probably only want the Engineering group and a few special users to be able to read or edit files. This special group of users can be administrators or department managers. In the Released State, it is common to grant access to all users but permit none, or a small group, the ability to modify them.

Similarly, different groups of users will have different ability to transition between the lifecycle states. For example, you will likely have only a small group of users that can release a set of new or revised files to manufacturing. It is unlikely you will permit the users in the marketing or sales team to have this ability.

Access Control Lists (ACLs)

The Access Control List enables you to add and remove members to control who has access to certain files, folders, items, and custom objects. You can also control whether the member can only view the content, modify the content, or delete the content.

Note: Custom Objects are available in Vault Professional.

A file, folder, or custom object that does not have an Access Control List defined uses object-based security.

Object-based security can be overridden. An override of security means that the ACL still exists on the object but it is being overridden by a newly defined ACL. This is called an Override Access Control List or an Override ACL.

As long as an override ACL exists, the object-based security is ignored. If the user removes the override ACL, then the object-based security becomes the new security. If an override ACL is active, only members and users in the ACL list have permissions to modify the object.

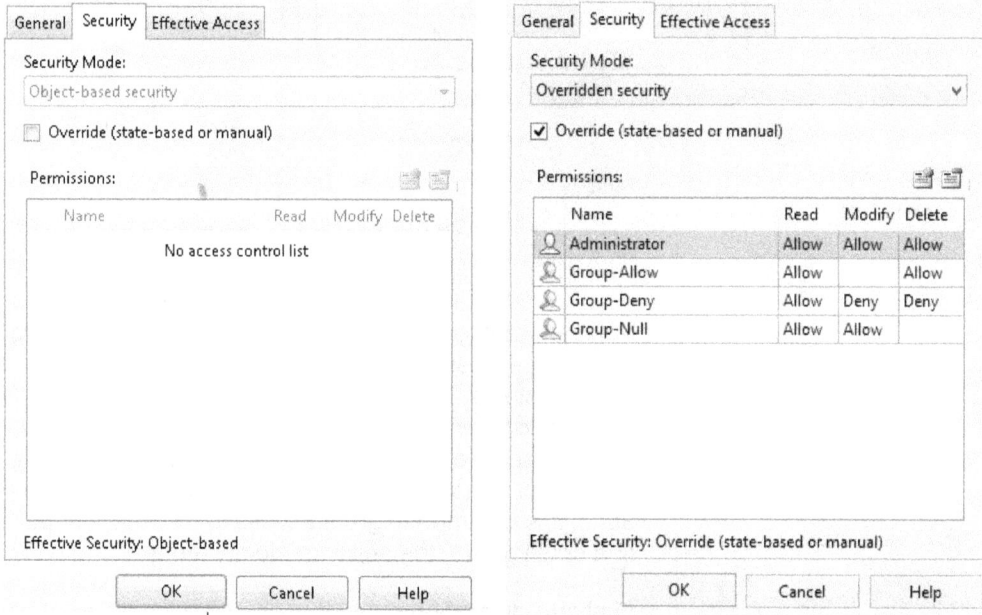

General	Security	Effective Access

Security Mode:

Object-based security

☐ Override (state-based or manual)

Permissions:

Name	Read	Modify	Delete
No access control list			

Effective Security: Object-based

[OK] [Cancel] [Help]

General	Security	Effective Access

Security Mode:

Overridden security

☑ Override (state-based or manual)

Permissions:

Name	Read	Modify	Delete
Administrator	Allow	Allow	Allow
Group-Allow	Allow		Allow
Group-Deny	Allow	Deny	Deny
Group-Null	Allow	Allow	

Effective Security: Override (state-based or manual)

[OK] [Cancel] [Help]

View Object Security

Examine file, folder, Item, and custom object security through the context menu.

Note: Items and custom objects are available in Vault Professional.

You must be an administrator to view object security.

1. Right-click on a file, folder, item, or custom object in Vault and select Details.
2. In the Details dialog box, select the Security tab.

General | **Security** | Effective Access

Security Mode:

Overridden security ⌄

☑ Override (state-based or manual)

Permissions:

Name	Read	Modify	Delete
Administrator	Allow	Allow	Allow
Group-Allow	Allow		Allow
Group-Deny	Allow	Deny	Deny
Group-Null	Allow	Allow	

Effective Security: Override (state-based or manual)

OK | Cancel | Help

- **Security Mode:** Shows the security precedence for the selected object.

  - **Object-based security:** Security derived from the object. This is the default option and is the only option available if no other security is defined.

  Note: Items do not have object-based security.

  - **State-based security:** Security available when a state-based Access Control List (ACL) exists and is combined with object-based security.

  - **Overridden security:** Security available when a state-based ACL is overriding object-based security, or when the administrator sets a manual override on the object.

- **Permissions:** The ACL shows which groups and users are granted access to the selected object and their respective permissions.

  Note: See Access Control Lists for more information.

- **Effective Security:** Security currently in use by the object (found at the bottom of the dialog box). In the example above, Override (state-based or manual) security is in effect.

3. Select the Effective Access tab to view user permissions for the object.

Name	Read	Modify	Delete
User1	Allow	Deny	Allow
User2	Allow	Deny	Deny
User3	Allow	Allow	Deny
User4	Allow	Deny	Allow
User5	Allow	Deny	Deny
User6	Allow	Allow	Deny
User7	Allow	Deny	Allow
User8	Allow	Deny	Deny
User9	Allow	Allow	Deny

General | Security | Effective Access

Select the security type to see permissions per user for different types:

Effective Access

Permissions:

OK | Cancel | Help

Security Type

Select a security type to see a user's effective permissions for that security mode. This is primarily useful when both object-based security and state-based security are applied, and the administrator wants to finder a user's effective permissions.

Note: Only individual user permissions can be viewed. Groups cannot be added in the Effective Access tab.

Permissions

The permissions list in the Effective Access tab is empty by default. Add 📄 and remove 📄 members to the list to view the type of access they have to the object under the selected security type. Change the security type to see how permissions are impacted.

Note: The Effective Access tab is for viewing security permissions only. Adding and removing members does not change security permissions for the object. Permission changes must be performed in the Security tab.

Lifecycle Transitions

There are several considerations dealing with the ability for a lifecycle state to be changed or transitioned to another state. These are:

- Criteria: Are there Property considerations governing the state transition? Criteria could also include a condition, such as not permitting a transition to In Review if the file is not associated to a change order.

- Actions: What actions, if any, should be performed when making the state transition. The actions include checking that the dependent child files, dependent child folders, contained files, linked files, linked folders, or linked custom objects are released. Actions can also include incrementing revision values, synchronizing properties, and creating visualization representation files.

- Custom Job Types: What custom jobs should be assigned to the transition?

- Security: Which user or groups are permitted the ability to transition from one state to the next?

Criteria

Criteria primarily deal with the Properties that are associated with the file. These can be either System or User Defined properties. Generally, you can prohibit a state transition if one or more of the properties do not meet specified criteria. Examples are:

- The value of a property contains a phrase like 'Default' or 'Unknown'.

- The value of a property falls outside a certain range.

- The properties associated with a file do not meet the compliance criteria established for those properties.

The list example of property compliance is very important and will be discussed in a later lesson. This gives the Administrator the ability to require the values for a group of properties must be filled in and conform to requirements unique for each member of the property set.

Actions

The next step in the planning involves the following considerations:

- When transitioning from one state to another, is a new revision of the file created and of what kind?

- When making the transition, are there system level tasks that should be initiated? When transitioning to a released state, are checks on the state of the dependent children, content, or linked data required?

There are a number of default revision schemes that can be applied to a file. For each revision scheme there is a primary increment, secondary bump and tertiary bump. A primary bump can be represented by moving from revision 'A" to "B". A secondary revision bump can be represented by moving from revision "B" to revision "B.1.' For each scheme it is possible to specify what, if any, action will be taken to increment (or 'Bump') the revision.

It is also possible to specify:

- If mapped property values should be synchronized by the Job Server.

- If both property values should be synchronized and visualization files updated by the Job Server.

This is helpful if you have a large number of files or properties that need to be updated on a lifecycle state transition.

In some organizations it is not permitted to release a file to manufacturing if all of the children of that file (if any) are not released. This is especially true of Inventor assemblies and AutoCAD files that have externally referenced file.

In the following illustration, an Inventor assembly has two children and is in the Work In Progress State.

```
⊟ Assembly.aim    State = Work In Progress
  ┊┄ Part1.ipt    State= Work In Progress
  ┊┄ Part2.ipt    State = Released
```

One of the children is also in the Released State but the other is still in the Work In Progress State. Specifying the check that dependent child files are released prohibits the user from changing the lifecycle State of the assembly file Assembly.iam to the Released State before changing the lifecycle state of the Part1.ipt to the Released State first. Specifying that the dependent children of a parent file must be released before the parent itself can be released is a method to ensure that manufacturing is not producing a product or component while some of the files that define that product or component are not yet ready for production.

The administrator can choose to restrict the transition to the release state of files, project folders, and custom objects based on the state of the dependent children, content, and linked data. Any data that is not in a released (consumable) state, causes a restriction and prevents the transition of the select object(s). The checks that can be performed are listed in the table below.

Action	Description
Check that dependent child files are released	This will check the state dependent children to ensure that they are in a released state.
Check that dependent child folders are released	This will check the subfolders of a project folder to ensure that they are in a released state.

Check that contained files are released	This will check the state of all files contained in a project folder to ensure that they are in a released state.
Check that links to files are released	This will check the state of all linked files in a project folder or custom object to ensure that they are in a released state.
Check that linked folders are released	This will check the state of all linked folders in a project folder or custom object to ensure that they are in a released state.
Check that linked custom objects are released	This will check that all links to custom objects in a project or custom object are in a released state.

Security Restrictions

The final consideration for the lifecycle state transition is which group of users, if any, is permitted to perform the state change. These are the important considerations for this topic:

- Does the state transition make sense for your process?

- If so, which set of users and groups can perform the transition?

For example, in the default state In Review is it permitted to change the state to Obsolete? If so, who can do it? If not then no one user or group can perform the transition.

Creating the Guidelines

Once these questions have been answered for every lifecycle state and every transition between state, it will be much easier to accomplish the configuration. The illustration below shows how a tool like Microsoft Visio can be used to diagram this.

Lifecycle Definition – Company Default

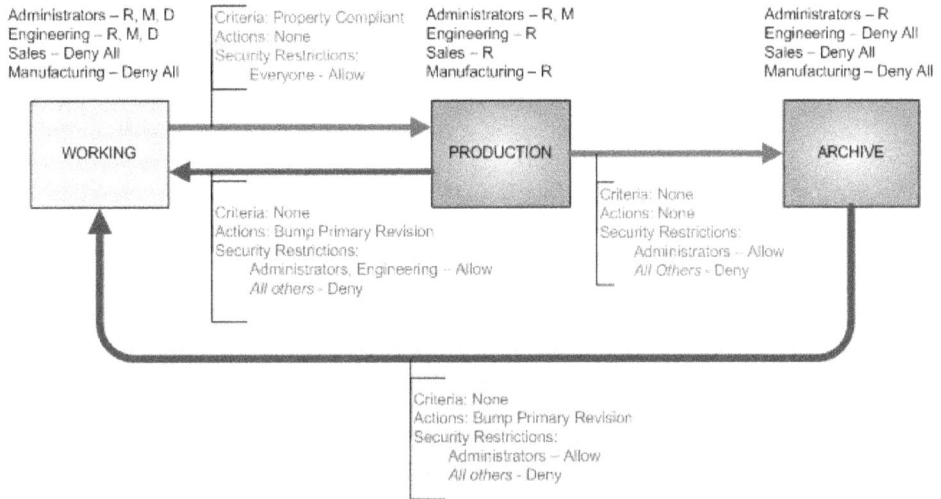

Administrators – R, M, D
Engineering – R, M, D
Sales – Deny All
Manufacturing – Deny All

Criteria: Property Compliant
Actions: None
Security Restrictions:
    Everyone - Allow

Administrators – R, M
Engineering – R
Sales – R
Manufacturing – R

Administrators – R
Engineering – Deny All
Sales – Deny All
Manufacturing – Deny All

WORKING

PRODUCTION

ARCHIVE

Criteria: None
Actions: Bump Primary Revision
Security Restrictions:
    Administrators, Engineering – Allow
    All others - Deny

Criteria: None
Actions: None
Security Restrictions:
    Administrators – Allow
    All Others - Deny

Criteria: None
Actions: Bump Primary Revision
Security Restrictions:
    Administrators – Allow
    All others - Deny

Available Groups:
Administrators
Engineering
Sales
Manufacturing

Lifecycle State Permissions (Allow/Deny):
R = Read
M = Modify
D = Delete

Lifecycle State Transition Actions:
Bump Primary Revision
Bump Secondary Revision
Bump Tertiary Revision
Synch Properties w/Job Server (VC and VM only)

Security

Configuring security is an important step in the configuration. By default, no security beyond that which is determined by permissions assigned to each individual object is enforced for files in a given lifecycle state, as shown in the illustration below.

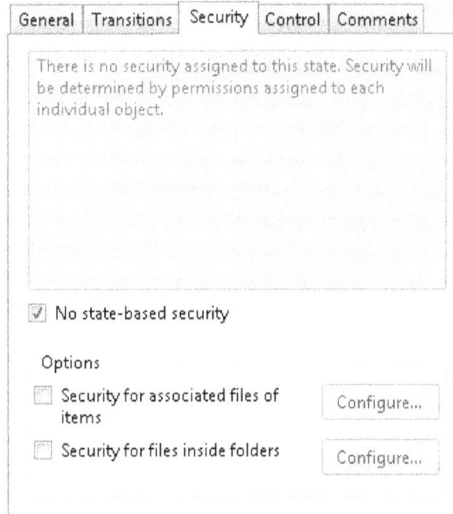

| General | Transitions | Security | Control | Comments |

There is no security assigned to this state. Security will be determined by permissions assigned to each individual object.

☑ No state-based security

Options

☐ Security for associated files of items   [Configure...]

☐ Security for files inside folders   [Configure...]

For Lifecycle definitions created in the 2017 software release and greater, Autodesk Vault uses a dual-gate security model that combines object security with state security. Users must have role permission and combined object and state-based permissions to access a Vault object. Administrators can control individual access to a Vault object based on organizational area or business line. For example, an administrator can ensure that a group has read, write, and delete permissions and at the same time, deny permissions to certain members of the group while in various lifecycle states.

For Definition Security, as shown in the image below, select one of the following options:

- **Combine with object-based security:** Any state-based security defined for individual states within this lifecycle definition combine with the object-based security set on the object. In other words, the combined security becomes the effective security for the entity.

- **Override object-based security:** Any state-based security defined for individual states within this lifecycle definition override the object-based security set on the object. In other words, state-based security becomes the effective security for the entity.

Note: Vaults migrated from Vault 2016 or earlier use **Override object-based security** as the default setting so that legacy (single-gate) security is maintained. However, all new vaults use **Combine with object-based security** as the default security setting, which is a dual-gate security setting. Change this setting at any time to mimic legacy (single-gate) security.

Define State-Based Security

Access Security for a Lifecycle State:

1. Click Tools>Administration>Vault Settings.
2. In the Vault Settings dialog box, click the Behaviors tab> Lifecycles.
3. In the Lifecycle Definition dialog box, select the name of the life cycle definition and click Edit. The selected definition name displays in the title bar.
4. Select the state for which you want to define security.
5. Select the Security tab to display the current security settings for that state.

Disable State-Based Security:

1. Click No state-based security if you don't want to assign security for the state. Security is determined by the permissions assigned to the object.

Add a Member or Group Permission to a Lifecycle State

1. In the Security tab, clear the No state-based security checkbox if it is selected.
2. Click Add.
3. In the Add Members dialog box, select the member or group from the Available Members list, and then click Add. The selected name is moved to the Current Members list.

   Note: Filter the Available Members list by selecting a qualifier from the Select Members From list.

   From the Current Members list, select one or more members, and then click Remove to modify the current members list.

4. Click OK.

Edit Member or Group Permissions

1. In the Lifecycle Definition dialog box, select the state from the Lifecycle States list.
2. In the Security tab, select the member or group to edit.

3. In the Permissions box, enable or disable the Allow and Deny checkboxes for each permission.

Permission	Access
Read	**Allow:** States can be viewed.
	Deny: States cannot be viewed. If a member is denied read access, then they are not permitted Modify or Delete access either.
	None: State cannot be viewed.
Modify	**Allow:** States can be modified.
	Deny: State cannot be modified.
	None: State cannot be modified.
Delete	**Allow:** State can be deleted
	Deny: State cannot be deleted.
	None: State cannot be deleted.

4. Click OK.

Transitions

Each lifecycle state has the ability to transition to every other lifecycle state. In some cases there is no reason to ever have one state transition to another. In other cases, you might want to control who can make the transition, if there are any conditions that must be fulfilled before making the transition and what actions take place when a transition is made.

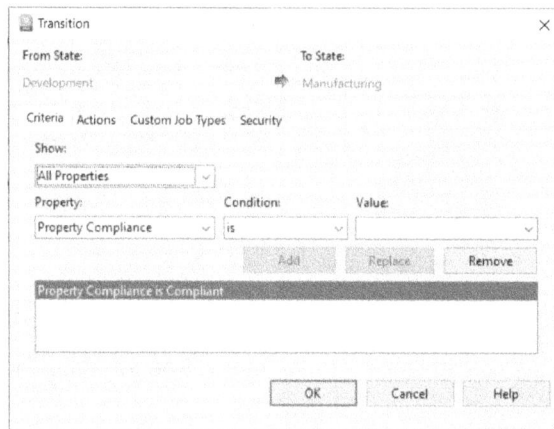

Criteria

Specifying Criteria is much like the Advanced Find capability. You can specify if one or more of the system or user defined properties associated with the file meet specific criteria. If all of the criteria are met the transition can take place. If one or more of the criteria are not met then the user is warned and cannot make the transition until the criteria are met or the lifecycle definition is changed.

The only default criteria that are set for some of the lifecycle state transitions in the default lifecycle definitions are property compliance. A property is said to be compliant if its value meets one or more criteria itself.

For example, the property Description must have a value between 10 and 20 characters long and the property Cost must have a numeric value greater than zero. If the individual conditions are true then the two properties are compliant. All properties that have compliance criteria must be compliant in order for the Property Compliance property to be Compliant. This is a useful way of making sure that the important properties associated with a file are filled out correctly before the lifecycle state can be transitioned.

Procedure: Configure Criteria

To configure the criteria that must be met before a file can transition into a new lifecycle state do the following:

1. In the Vault Settings dialog box, select the Behaviors tab.
2. Select Lifecycles in the Lifecycles and Revisions section to display the Lifecycle Definitions dialog box.
3. Select the lifecycle definition to be customized.
4. Select Edit to display the Lifecycle Definition dialog box for the selected definition.
5. Select the lifecycle state from the list of Lifecycle States to be configured.

6. Select the *Transitions* tab to display a list of all of the lifecycle transitions for the selected lifecycle definition.

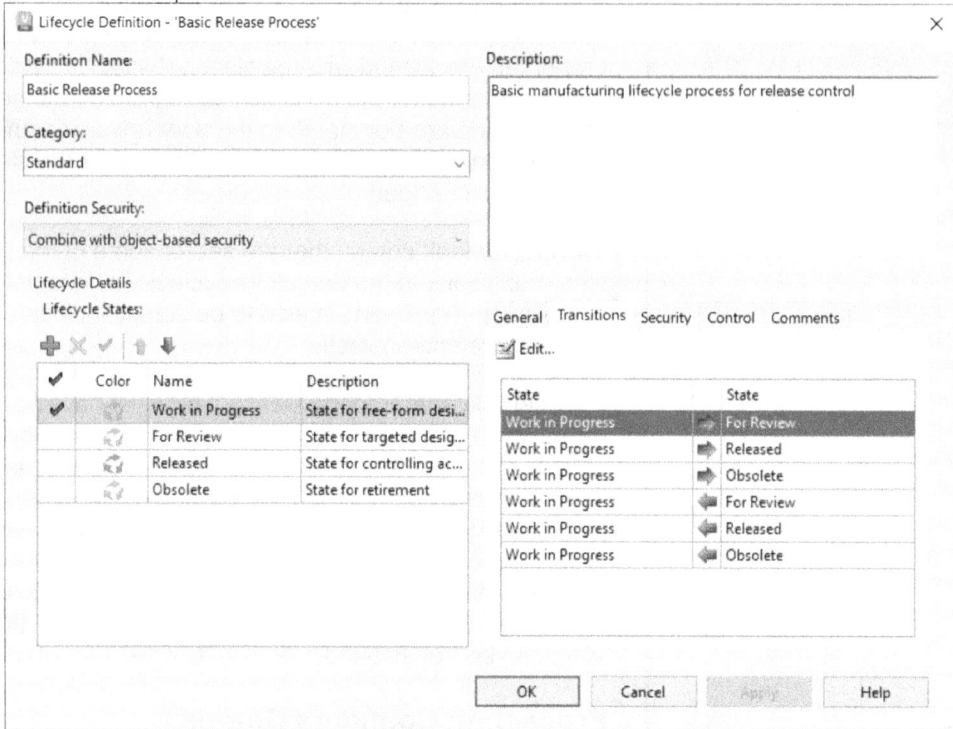

7. Select the transition to edit.
8. Select Edit to display the Transition dialog box.

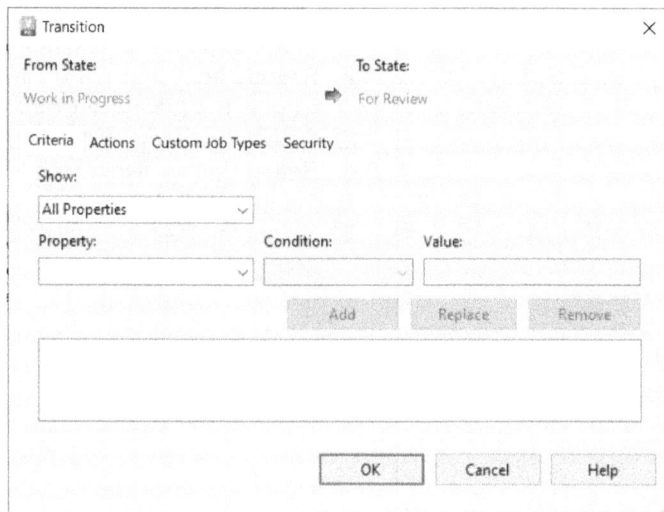

9. If required, filter which properties display based on a certain entity class using the Show drop-down list. For example, you can configure it so that only File Properties are shown in the Property drop-down list.

10. In the Property drop-down list, select the property to evaluate.

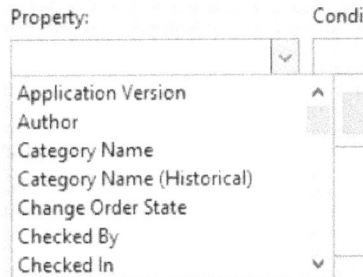

Property: Condi

| Application Version |
| Author |
| Category Name |
| Category Name (Historical) |
| Change Order State |
| Checked By |
| Checked In |

11. Specify the condition and value for that property.

12. Select Add to add it to the list of all properties to evaluate.

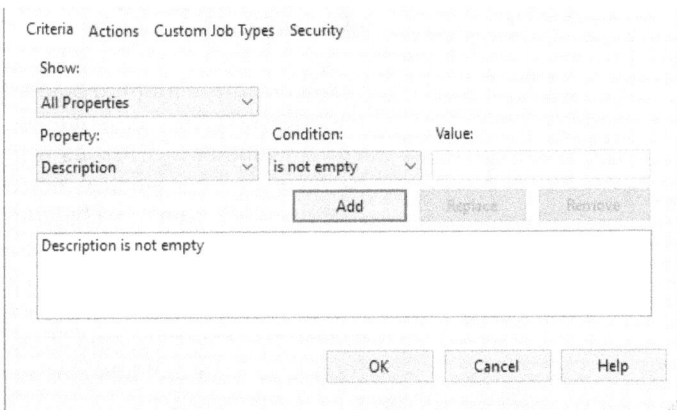

Criteria   Actions   Custom Job Types   Security

Show:

All Properties

Property: Condition: Value:

Description   is not empty

Add   Replace   Remove

Description is not empty

OK   Cancel   Help

13. Repeat the previous three steps to add additional criteria.

14. Select OK to dismiss this dialog box and return to the Lifecycle Definition dialog box for the selected lifecycle definition.

15. Configure the remaining transitions for the selected lifecycle state.

Note: Every transition is shown for a given lifecycle state. For example, if you select State 1 your will find a transition from State 1 to State 2 and a transition from State 2 to State 1. Similarly, if you select State 2 you will find a transition from State 2 to State 1 and from State 1 to State 2. You only need to configure a particular state transition once. You do not need to configure it for every possible state transition. They are shown on every state transition for convenience.

16. Select OK to dismiss this dialog box and return to the Lifecycle Definitions dialog box.
17. Select Close to dismiss this dialog box and return to the Vault Settings dialog box.

Actions

Actions are method of both automating process and enforcing rules associated with changing a file revision when moving from one lifecycle state to the other.

When a file changes from one lifecycle state to another, User Defined and System Properties associated with the file might need to be updated from their mapped file property values. Conversely, if System and User Defined file properties have been updated in Vault Workgroup, the property values need to be written back to the mapped file property values. If there are many properties and many files changing state this can reduce system performance. Specifying that these property values are updated in a separate process can help improve this performance.

Revisions are a method of identifying major form, fit and function changes to a file. For example, a set of files representing a shaft has a diameter of 2 inches is in the Released State and is at Revision A. After several months in production it is discovered that the shaft cannot withstand the loads it experiences in operation. The decision is made to re-design the shaft, increasing its diameter to 2 ¼ inches. The file is put in a Work In Progress State and engineering updates the models and drawings. When it comes time, the files are once again set to the Released State but this time at Revision B.

Revision Scheme Definition - 'Standard Alphabetic Format'   ✕

Definition Name: Description:

Standard Alphabetic Format   Only characters are permitted within the primary format

Category:

Design Representation, Engineering, Standard, Assembly... ⌄

Scheme Details

Scheme Values: Preview   Scheme Format   Comments

Type	Value
▶ Delimiter	.
Primary Scheme Format	Alphabetic
Secondary Scheme Format	Numeric
Tertiary Scheme Format	Numeric

Revision primary sequence values:

```
A                                    ^
B
C
D
E
F
G
H                                    ⌄
```

Example Revision Formats

Delimiter Character: .
Primary: A
Secondary: A.1
Tertiary: A.1.1

[OK]   [Cancel]   [Help]

There are different default revision schemes and you can make custom revisions schemes. All schemes can be defined to have a primary, secondary and tertiary format. For example, revision A has a primary revision number only whereas A.1 has a primary and secondary revision number.

The example in the illustration below shows the actions that are performed in a lifecycle definition where the state transition is from the Released State to the Work In Progress State. In this case the primary revision is bumped. So if the file were released at revision A its revision would change to B when the state transition occurs. No properties would be synchronized by the Job Server and no release state checks would be performed.

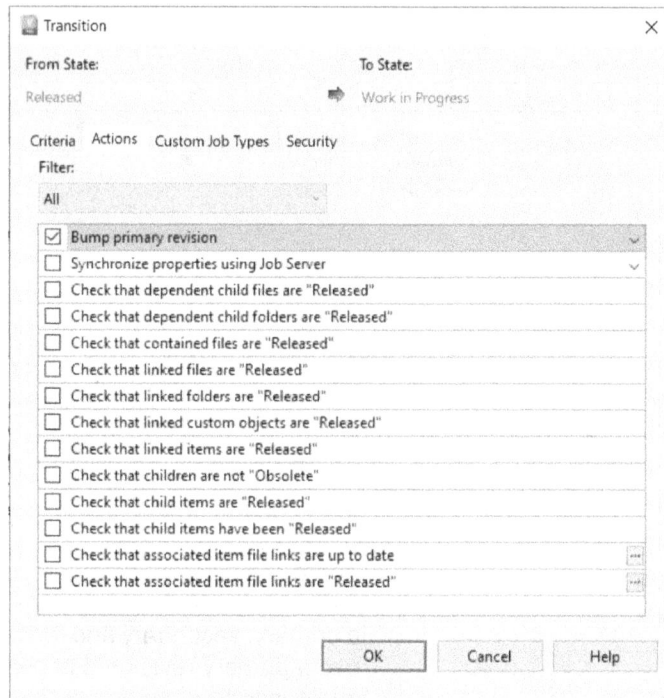

Procedure: Configure Actions

The following steps enable you to configure the actions that take place when a lifecycle state transition occurs:

1. In the Vault Settings dialog box, select the Behaviors tab.
2. Select Lifecycles in the Lifecycles and Revisions section to display the Lifecycle Definitions dialog box.
3. Select the lifecycle definition to be customized.
4. Select Edit to display the Lifecycle Definition dialog box for the selected definition.
5. Select the lifecycle state from the list of Lifecycle States to be configured.
6. Select the Transitions tab to display a list of all of the lifecycle transitions for the selected lifecycle definition.
7. Select the required state transition.

8. Select Edit to display the Transition dialog box.
9. Select the Actions tab to display the actions initiated by the selected state transition.

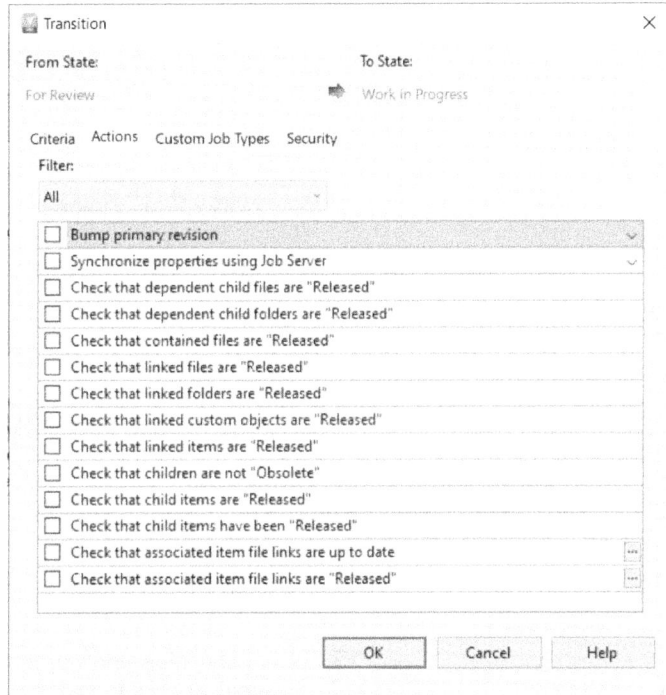

10. The default actions are shown. None are selected.
11. If required, select an entity class in the Filter drop-down list to show only the actions available for that entity class (e.g., select Folders to only see actions available for folder state transitions).
12. To specify a revision bump action, select the drop-down list to see the possible actions. Select the required action.

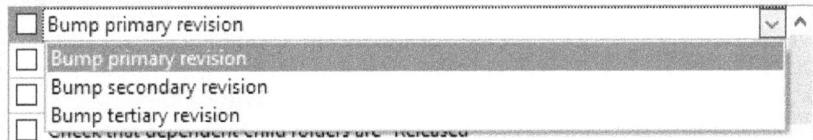

13. To specify a Job Server action, select the drop-down list to see the possible actions. Select the required action.

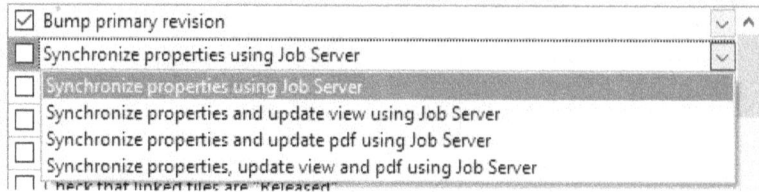

☑ Bump primary revision	⌄ ∧
☐ Synchronize properties using Job Server	⌄
☐ Synchronize properties using Job Server	
☐ Synchronize properties and update view using Job Server	
☐ Synchronize properties and update pdf using Job Server	
☐ Synchronize properties, update view and pdf using Job Server	
☐ Check that linked files are "Released"	

14. Review the final choices.

Criteria   Actions   Custom Job Types   Security

Filter:

All	⌄

☑ Bump primary revision	⌄ ∧
☑ Synchronize properties using Job Server	⌄
☐ Check that dependent child files are "Released"	
☐ Check that dependent child folders are "Released"	
☐ Check that contained files are "Released"	
☐ Check that linked files are "Released"	
☐ Check that linked folders are "Released"	⌄

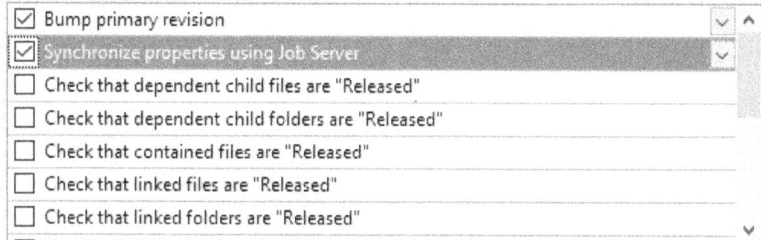

15. To specify release restrictions, select one or more of the options that check that the state of the dependent children, content, or linked data is set to released.
16. Select OK to dismiss this dialog box and return to the Lifecycle Definition dialog box for the selected lifecycle definition.
17. Configure the remaining transitions for the selected lifecycle state.
18. Select OK to dismiss this dialog box and return to the Lifecycle Definitions dialog box.
19. Select Close to dismiss this dialog box and return to the Vault Settings dialog box.

Transition Security

The last consideration for lifecycle transitions is which set of users and groups can initiate a state transition, if any. For example, the ability to initiate a transition from the For Review state to the Released state is generally restricted to a certain group or a few individuals that understand the impact of issuing a new set of designs and drawings into manufacturing. In other cases, there is no logical reason for a lifecycle state to transition from one lifecycle state to another.

Take the case of the Quick Change, a state often used to by-pass the formal review process. It might not make sense to let anyone transition from the Quick Change State to the For Review state since the whole point of a quick change is to bypass this step. However, in some organizations this can be a valid lifecycle state change.

The illustration below shows that when releasing a new design or major design change, only the Administrator group has the ability to initiate the transition.

From State:		To State:
Work in Progress	➡	Released

Criteria Actions Custom Job Types Security

Add... Remove ⓘ

Name	Permission
Administrator	Allow

☐ No restrictions on this transition

OK	Cancel	Help

Procedure: Configure Transition Custom Job Types

Two steps are necessary to create a custom job. First, a programmer must create the custom job and install it within the vault extensions. Then, an administrator adds it to the transition.

The following steps enable you to associate a custom job with a state transition:

1. Click Tools>Administration>Vault Settings.
2. In the Vault Settings dialog box, click Behaviors tab>Lifecycles.
3. In the Lifecycle Definitions dialog box, select a Lifecycle Definition (e.g., Basic Release Process) and click Edit. The selected definition name displays in the title bar.
4. From the Lifecycle States list, select the lifecycle state to edit and then click the Transitions tab.
5. Select the desired Transition, then click Edit to open the Transitions dialog box. Select the Custom Job Types tab.

6. Click Add and enter a name in the Add to Input New Custom Job Type Name field. Click OK.

   Note: A typical naming convention is to add as a prefix your company name to any job types.

7. Click OK to exit the Transition dialog box.
8. This Custom Job Type will initiate whenever an object transitions through this lifecycle.

   To enable this Custom Job on other transitions, repeat steps 3 to 5 and specify an existing Custom Job Type instead of creating a new Custom Job.

Procedure: Configure Transition Security

The following steps enable you to specify which users and groups can initiate a state transition:

1. In the Vault Settings dialog box, select the Behaviors tab.
2. Select Lifecycles in the Lifecycles and Revisions section to display the Lifecycle Definitions dialog box.
3. Select the lifecycle definition to be customized.
4. Select Edit to display the Lifecycles Definition dialog box for the selected definition.
5. Select the lifecycle state from the list of Lifecycle States to be configured.
6. Select the Transitions tab to display a list of all of the lifecycle transitions for the selected lifecycle definition.
7. Select the required state transition.
8. Select Edit to display the Transition dialog box.
9. Select the Security tab to display the default security.

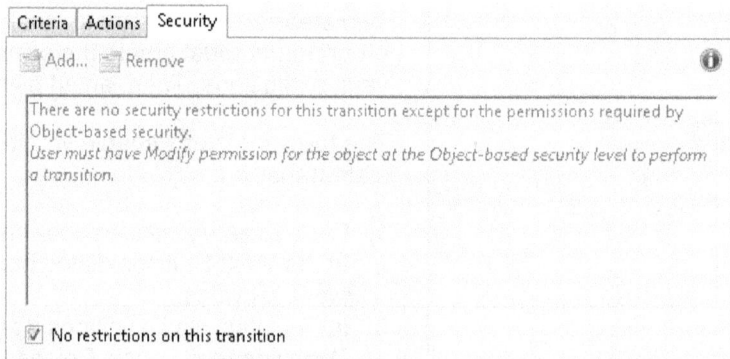

| Criteria | Actions | Security |

🔲 Add... 🔲 Remove   ⓘ

There are no security restrictions for this transition except for the permissions required by Object-based security.
User must have Modify permission for the object at the Object-based security level to perform a transition.

☑ No restrictions on this transition

10. To configure security, first clear the checkbox for No restrictions on this transition option.

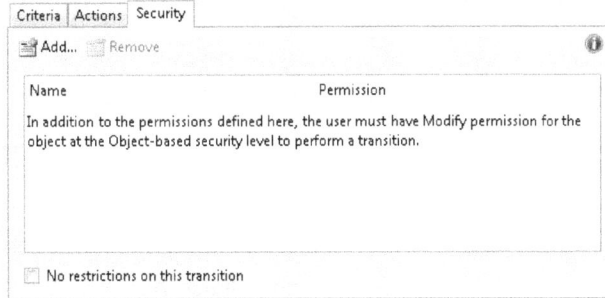

Criteria	Actions	Security	

Add... Remove ⓘ

Name	Permission
In addition to the permissions defined here, the user must have Modify permission for the object at the Object-based security level to perform a transition.	

☐ No restrictions on this transition

The tab changes enable you to specify which users and groups can perform the transition.

11. Select Add to display the Add Members dialog box.
12. From the list select the users and groups from the Available Members that are to granted or denied permission to perform the lifecycle change. Select Add to add them to the Current Members list.

Current Members:

Name
▶ 👤 Engineering
👤 Manufacturing
👤 Sales
👤 Administrators

13. Select OK to close this dialog box and return to the Transition dialog box with the selected members.

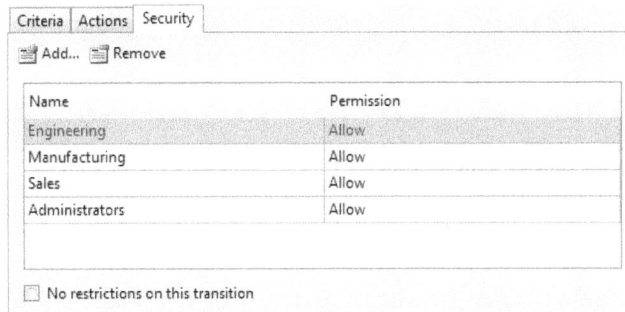

Criteria	Actions	Security	

Add... Remove

Name	Permission
Engineering	Allow
Manufacturing	Allow
Sales	Allow
Administrators	Allow

☐ No restrictions on this transition

By default, all members are permitted rights to change the file's lifecycle state. However, anyone who is not a member of a group or explicitly added as a member will be denied the ability to perform the state transition.

14. For each user or group specify if they are permitted or denied the ability to change the file's state.

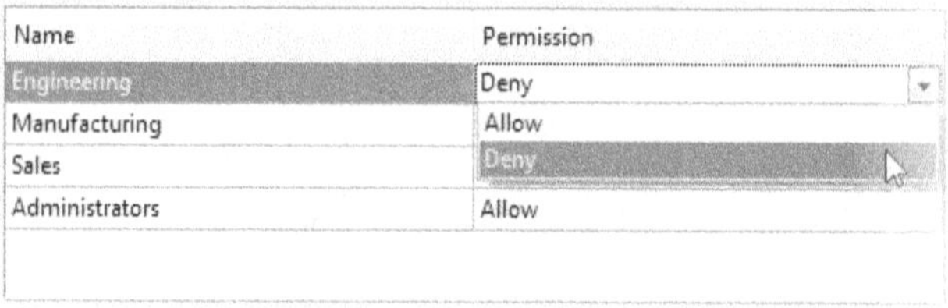

Name	Permission
Engineering	Deny
Manufacturing	Allow
Sales	Deny
Administrators	Allow

15. When done review the final selections. Select OK to dismiss this dialog box and return to the Lifecycle Definition dialog box for this state transition.
16. Configure the remaining transitions for the selected lifecycle state.
17. Select OK to dismiss this dialog box and return to the Lifecycle Definitions dialog box.
18. Select Close to dismiss this dialog box and return to the Vault Settings dialog box.

Other Configuration Settings

There are two more settings that can be configured for a given lifecycle state.

Control

The control setting specifies what happens during a Purge operation. The tab is illustrated below.

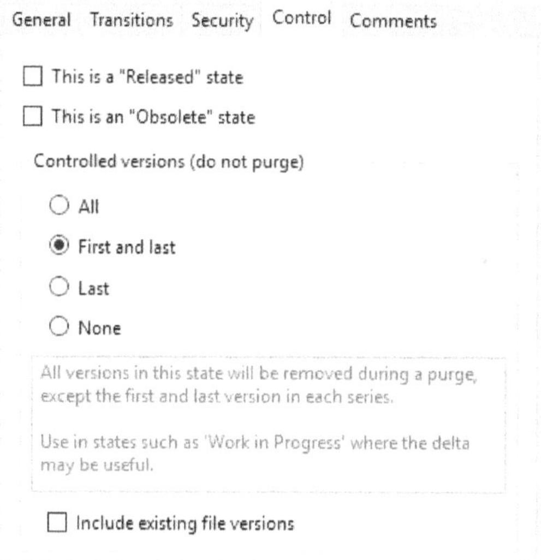

General Transitions Security Control Comments

☐ This is a "Released" state

☐ This is an "Obsolete" state

Controlled versions (do not purge)

○ All

◉ First and last

○ Last

○ None

All versions in this state will be removed during a purge, except the first and last version in each series.

Use in states such as 'Work in Progress' where the delta may be useful.

☐ Include existing file versions

As you learned earlier, file versions are created every time you check a file in after being edited. File versions mark major milestones, for example release of a set of files representing a new product, or the subsequent major modification of one of those files for form, fit, and function purposes. For each revision, there can be many versions as files are checked out, modified, and checked in on a daily basis, a new user makes a modification to a files, etc. For the selected state, the radio buttons (All, First and Last, Last, None) control which versions of a file will be kept if a purge occurs.

Comments

When an object is transitioned from one lifecycle state to another a comment is added. This tab controls what comment is added. The example below shows the dialog box that is presented to the user when transitioning to the For Review state.

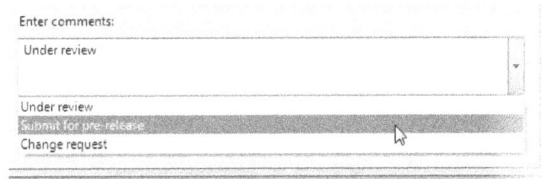

The Comment tab has a list of suggested text strings to use as a default. The user is free to add or replace this comment with one of their own. The illustration below shows the suggested and default comment for a state transition to For Review.

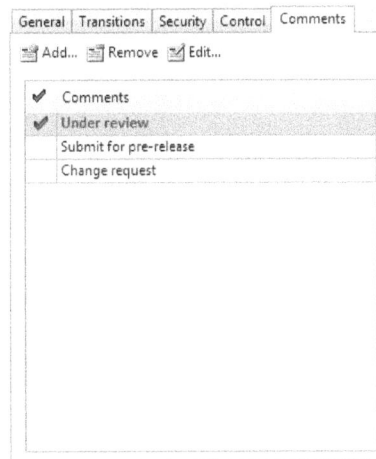

Procedure: Configuring Control and Comments

The following steps enable you to specify which objects are removed during a purge operation and the default comment text for the state being transitioned to:

1. In the Vault Settings dialog box, select the Behaviors tab.
2. Select Lifecycles in the Lifecycles and Revisions section to display the Lifecycle Definitions dialog box.
3. Select the lifecycle definition to be customized.
4. Select Edit to display the Lifecycles Definition dialog box for the selected definition.
5. Select the lifecycle state from the list of Lifecycle States to be configured.
6. Select the Control tab to display the settings for controlled versions.

General   Transitions   Security   Control   Comments

☑ This is a "Released" state

☐ This is an "Obsolete" state

Controlled versions (do not purge)

◉ All

◯ First and last

◯ Last

◯ None

No versions in this state will be removed when a purge is performed.

Use in states where not many versions will be created or where each version is critical.

☐ Include existing file versions

7. First, determine whether this state represents a released or obsolete condition. If it is a "Released" or "Obsolete" state, select the appropriate checkbox.
8. Determine which versions should not be purged. Select the different radio buttons to get details about each selection.

   - **All:** No versions in this state are removed when a purge is performed. This option is recommended for states where not many versions are created or where each version is critical.

   - **First and Last:** All versions in this state are removed during a purge, except the first and last version in reach series. Use this option for states where the changes between the first and last versions are not important.

- **Last:** All versions in this state are removed during a purge, except the last version in each series. This option is recommended for states where a record that the file was in the state is important.
- **None:** No version in this state will be retained after the purge has been performed.

Important: No record of the file being in this state will exist after the purge.

General Transitions Security Control Comments

☐ This is a "Released" state

☐ This is an "Obsolete" state

Controlled versions (do not purge)

○ All

○ First and last

○ Last

◉ None

No version in this state will be retained after the purge has been performed.

Warning: No record of the version being in this state will exist after the purge.

☐ Include existing file versions

9. Next select the Comments tab to display the list of default comments (if any) prepopulated for this state.
10. Select the comment to set as default, or select Add to add a new comment.

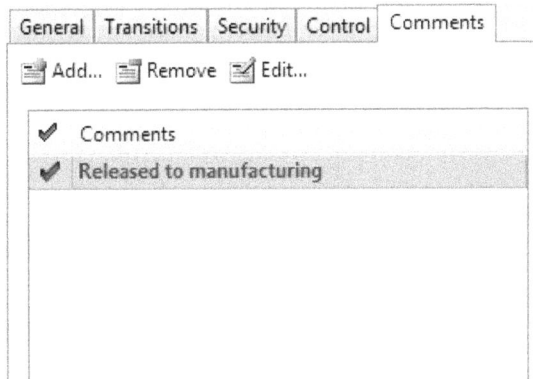

General	Transitions	Security	Control	Comments

📝 Add... 📝 Remove 📝 Edit...

✔ Comments
✔ **Released to manufacturing**

11. To create a new default comment, enter the text in the Comment. Click OK to close this dialog box.

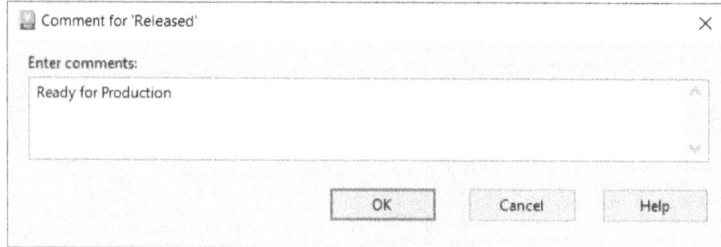

12. Double-click on the new comment if one was added to make it the new default.

    Note that you could also edit an existing comment rather than add a new one or remove a current one so it no longer displays in the drop-down list.

13. Configure the remaining transitions for the selected lifecycle state.
14. Click OK to close this dialog box and return to the Lifecycle Definitions dialog box.
15. Click Close to dismiss this dialog box and return to the Vault Settings dialog box.

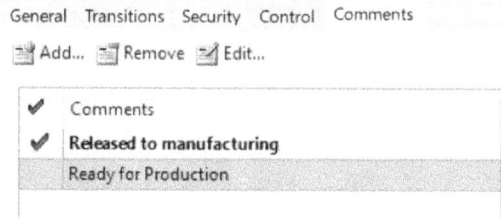

Practice 2b | Configure Lifecycle Definition

In this practice, you will customize the Standard Process lifecycle definition that you created in Lesson 1.

Lifecycle Definition – Standard Process

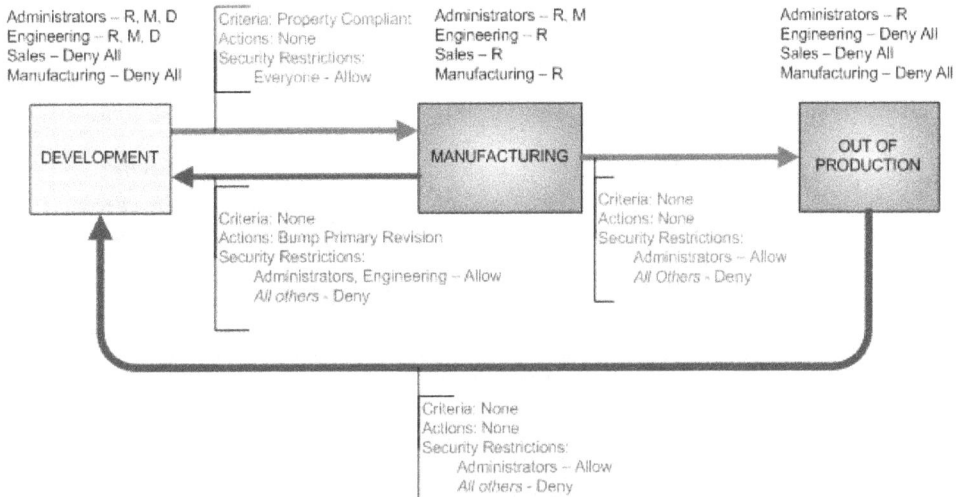

Administrators – R, M, D
Engineering – R, M, D
Sales – Deny All
Manufacturing – Deny All

Criteria: Property Compliant
Actions: None
Security Restrictions:
    Everyone - Allow

Administrators – R, M
Engineering – R
Sales – R
Manufacturing – R

Administrators – R
Engineering – Deny All
Sales – Deny All
Manufacturing – Deny All

DEVELOPMENT

MANUFACTURING

OUT OF PRODUCTION

Criteria: None
Actions: Bump Primary Revision
Security Restrictions:
    Administrators, Engineering – Allow
    All others - Deny

Criteria: None
Actions: None
Security Restrictions:
    Administrators – Allow
    All Others - Deny

Criteria: None
Actions: None
Security Restrictions:
    Administrators – Allow
    All others - Deny

Available Groups:
Administrators
Engineering
Sales
Manufacturing

Lifecycle State Permissions (Allow/Deny):
R = Read
M = Modify
D = Delete

Lifecycle State Transition Actions:
Bump Primary Revision
Bump Secondary Revision
Bump Tertiary Revision
Synch Properties w/Job Server

The completed practice

Task 1 - Create groups.

---

1. Open the Global settings dialog by selecting from the Tools menu>Administration>Global Settings.

2. Select Manage Groups in the Groups section of the Security tab to display the Group Management dialog box.

3. Create a group called Administrators defined with a role of Administrator.

4. In the Group dialog box, do the following:

    • Select Vaults and select AOTCVault from the Add Vaults dialog box.
    • Select OK to dismiss the dialog box.

5. Select Add to display the Add Members dialog box.

6. Select usera from the Available Members list and then select Add to add this to the list of Current Members.

7. Select OK to dismiss this dialog box and return to the Group dialog box.

8. Select OK to dismiss this dialog box and return to the Group Management dialog box.

9. Select New Group from the toolbar.

10. The Group dialog box opens. Do the following:

   • For Group Name, enter **Engineering**.
   • For Roles, select Document Editor Level 2 and Document Manager Level 2.
   • For Vaults, select AOTCVault box.

11. Select Add to display the Add Members dialog box.

12. Select userb from the Available Members list and select Add to add this to the list of Current Members.

13. Select OK to dismiss this dialog box and return to the Group dialog box.

14. Select OK to dismiss this dialog box and return to the Group Management dialog box.

15. Select New Group from the toolbar.

16. The Group dialog box opens. Do the following:

   • For Group Name enter **Manufacturing**.
   • For Roles, select Document Editor Level 2 and Document Manager Level 2.
   • For Vaults, select AOTCVault.

17. Select Add to display the Add Members dialog box.

18. Select userc from the Available Members list and select Add to add this to the list of Current Members.

19. Select OK to dismiss this dialog box and return to the Group dialog box.

20. Select OK to dismiss this dialog box and return to the Group dialog box.

21. Select New Group from the toolbar.

22. The Group dialog box displays. Do the following:

- For Group Name, enter **Sales**.
- For Roles, select Document Editor Level 2 and Document Manager Level 2.
- For Vaults, select AOTCVault.

23. Select Add to display the Add Members dialog box.

24. Select userd from the Available Members list and select Add to add this to the list of Current Members.

25. Select OK to dismiss this dialog box and return to the Group dialog box.

26. Select OK to dismiss this dialog box and return to the Group Management dialog box.

Group Name	Enabled
Administrators	Yes
Engineering	Yes
Manufacturing	Yes
Sales	Yes

27. Select the File menu then Exit to close this dialog box and return to the Global Settings dialog box.

28. Select Close to dismiss this dialog box.

Task 2 - Configure lifecycle security.

1. Open the Vault Settings dialog by selecting the Tools menu then Administration>Vault Settings.

2. Select the Behaviors tab, then select Lifecycles in the Lifecycles and Revisions section to display the Lifecycle Definitions dialog box.

3. Select the lifecycle definition Standard Process.

4. Select Edit to display the Lifecycle Definition - 'Standard Process' dialog box.

5. In the Lifecycle Details section, ensure that the Development lifecycle state is selected in the list.

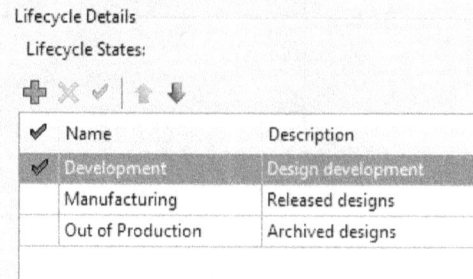

Lifecycle Details

Lifecycle States:

✔	Name	Description
✔	Development	Design development
	Manufacturing	Released designs
	Out of Production	Archived designs

6. Select the Security tab.

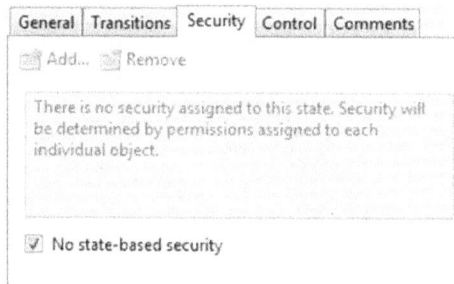

General | Transitions | Security | Control | Comments

Add... Remove

There is no security assigned to this state. Security will be determined by permissions assigned to each individual object.

☑ No state-based security

By default there is no state-based security set.

7. Clear the No state-based security checkbox to enable state-based security.

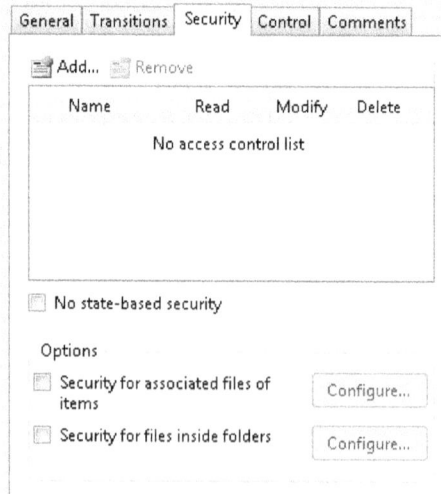

General | Transitions | Security | Control | Comments

Add... Remove

Name	Read	Modify	Delete
	No access control list		

☐ No state-based security

Options

☐ Security for associated files of items   Configure...

☐ Security for files inside folders   Configure...

8. Select Add to display the Add Members dialog box.

9. In the Select Members From drop-down list, select Groups.

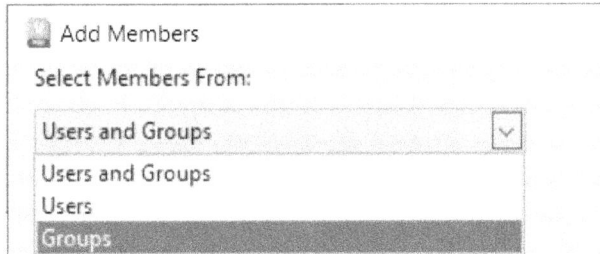

10. In the Available Members list, press <Ctrl> + select Administrators, Engineering, Manufacturing, and Sales groups.

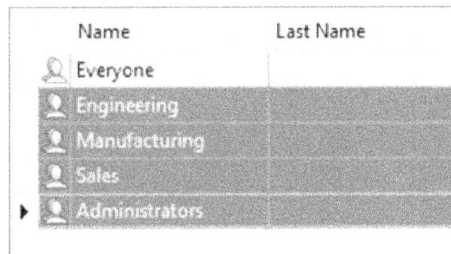

11. Select Add to add the selection to the Current Members list.

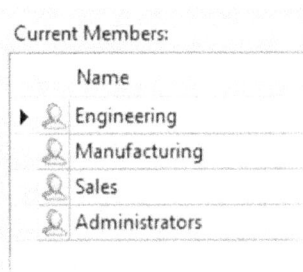

12. Select OK to dismiss this dialog box and return to the Lifecycle Definition dialog box.

13. Do the following for the Development state:

- For Engineering, set Read/Modify/Delete/Download to Allow.
- For Manufacturing, set Read/Modify/Delete/Download to Deny.
- For Sales, set Read/Modify/Delete/Download to Deny.
- For Administrators, set Read/Modify/Delete/Download to Allow.

General	Transitions	Security	Control	Comments

Add...   Remove

	Name	Read	Modify	Delete	Download
👤	Administrators	Allow	Allow	Allow	Allow
👤	Engineering	Allow	Allow	Allow	Allow
👤	Manufacturi...	Deny	Deny	Deny	Deny
👤	Sales	Deny	Deny	Deny	Deny

☐ No state-based security

Options

☐ Security for associated files of items   Configure...

☐ Security for files inside folders   Configure...

14. Select Apply to apply the settings to the selected lifecycle state.

15. Select the next lifecycle state Manufacturing from the Lifecycle States list.

16. Clear the No state-based security checkbox to enable state-based security.

17. Do the following for the Manufacturing state:

- For Engineering, set Read to Allow, Modify and Delete to Deny.
- For Manufacturing, set Read to Allow, Modify and Delete to Deny.
- For Sales, set Read to Allow, Modify and Delete to Deny.
- For Administrators, set Read and Modify to Allow, Delete to Deny.

18. Select Apply to apply the settings to the selected lifecycle state.

19. Do the following for the Out of Production state:

    - For Engineering, set Read/Modify/Delete to Deny.
    - For Manufacturing, set Read/Modify/Delete to Deny.
    - For Sales, set Read/Modify/Delete to Deny.
    - For Administrators, set Read to Allow, Modify and Delete to Deny.

20. Select Apply to apply the settings to the selected lifecycle state.

Task 3 - Configure transitions: Security.

In our example there are 3 lifecycle states and 6 possible transitions that can occur. Some of these transitions are not permitted by anyone and will be configured first.

1. In the Lifecycles States list, select the Development State.

2. Select the Transitions tab to display a list of all possible transitions from and to this state.

3. Select the entry that specifies from Development and to Out of Production. Select Edit to display the Transition dialog box.

4. Select Edit to display the Transition dialog box.

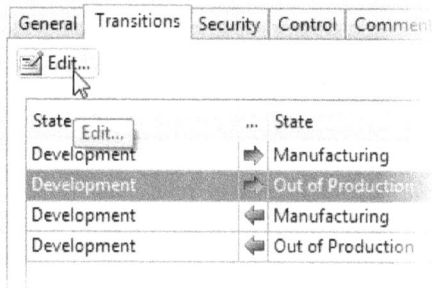

5. Select the Security tab and clear the checkbox for No restrictions on this transition option.

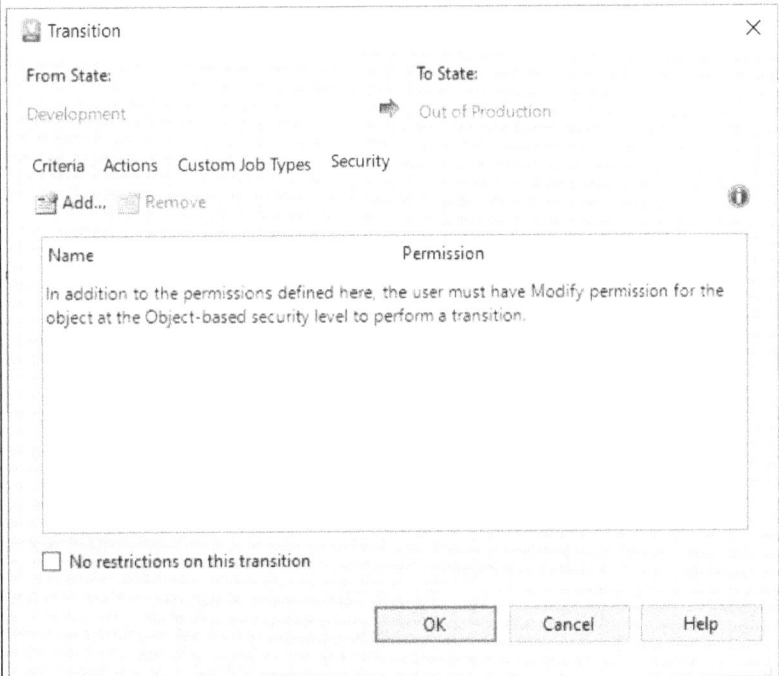

6. Select Add to display the Add Members dialog box.

7. In the Select Members From drop-down list, select Groups.

8. In the Available Members list, select Everyone.

9. Select Add to add Everyone to the list of Current Members.

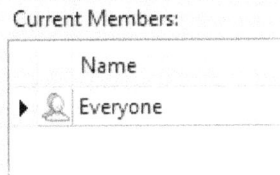

10. Select OK to dismiss this dialog box and return to the Transition dialog box.

11. The group Everyone has been added to the Security list with the default permission Allow.

12. Select the default permission to open the drop-down list and select Deny.

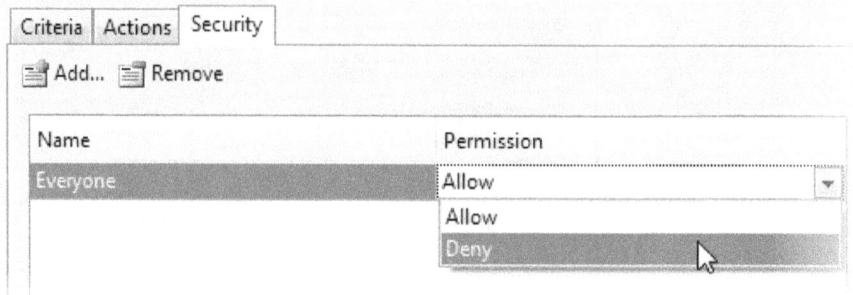

13. Select OK to dismiss this dialog box and return to the Lifecycle Definition dialog box.

14. In the Lifecycles States list, select Out of Production.

15. In the Transitions tab, select the from State Out of Production and to State Manufacturing entry from the list.

16. Select Edit to display the Transition dialog box.

17. Select the Security tab and clear the No restrictions on this transition checkbox.

18. Select Add to display the Add Members dialog box.

19. In the Select Members From drop-down list, select Groups.

20. In the Available Members list, select Everyone.

21. Select Add to add Everyone to the list of Current Members.

22. Select OK to dismiss this dialog box and return to the Transition dialog box.

23. The group Everyone has been added to the Security list with the default permission Allow.

24. Select the default permission to open the drop-down list and select Deny.

25. Select OK to dismiss this dialog box and return to the Lifecycle Definition dialog box.

26. In the Lifecycles States list, select Development.

27. In the Transitions tab, select the from State Manufacturing and to State Development entry from the list.

State	...	State
Development	➡	Manufacturing
Development	➡	Out of Production
Development	⬅	Manufacturing
Development	⬅	Out of Production

28. Select Edit to display the Transition dialog box.

29. Select the Security tab and clear the No restrictions on this transition checkbox.

30. Select Add to display the Add Members dialog box.

31. In the Select Members From drop-down list, select Groups.

32. In the Available Members list, press <Ctrl> + select Administrators, Engineering, Manufacturing, and Sales.

33. Select Add to add the selected entries to the list of Current Members.

Current Members:

	Name
▶ 👤	Engineering
👤	Manufacturing
👤	Sales
👤	Administrators

34. Select OK to dismiss this dialog box and return to the Transition dialog box.

35. The four groups have been added to the Security list with the default permission Allow.

36. Select Manufacturing and then select the default permission to open the drop-down list and select Deny.

37. Repeat the previous step with the group Sales.

Name	Permission
Engineering	Allow
Manufacturing	Deny
Sales	Deny
Administrators	Allow

38. Select OK to dismiss this dialog box and return to the Lifecycle Definition dialog box.

39. In the Lifecycles States list, select Manufacturing.

40. In the Transitions tab, select the from State Manufacturing and to State Out of Production entry from the list.

41. Select Edit to display the Transition dialog box.

42. Select the Security tab and clear the No restrictions on this transition checkbox.

43. Select Add to display the Add Members dialog box.

44. In the Select Members From drop-down list, select Groups.

45. In the Available Members list, press <Ctrl> + select Administrators, Engineering, Manufacturing, and Sales.

46. Select Add to add the selected entries to the list of Current Members.

47. Select OK to dismiss this dialog box and return to the Transition dialog box.

48. The four groups have been added to the Security list with the default permission Allow.

49. Select Manufacturing and then select the default permission to open the drop-down list and select Deny.

50. Repeat the previous step with the group Sales and Engineering.

Name	Permission
Engineering	Deny
Manufacturing	Deny
Sales	Deny
Administrators	Allow

51. Dismiss the Transition dialog box by selecting OK.

Task 4 - Configure states: Criteria.

In our example there is only one state transition which has criteria. This is from Development to Manufacturing. The lifecycle state Manufacturing should still be selected in the Lifecycle States list.

1. In the Transition tab, select the from State Development to State Manufacturing transition.

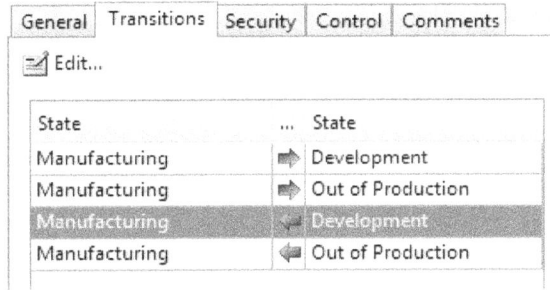

2. Select Edit to display the Transition dialog box. The Criteria tab should be displayed.

3. In the Property drop- down list, find the attribute Property Compliance and select it.

4. In the Value drop-down list, select Compliant.

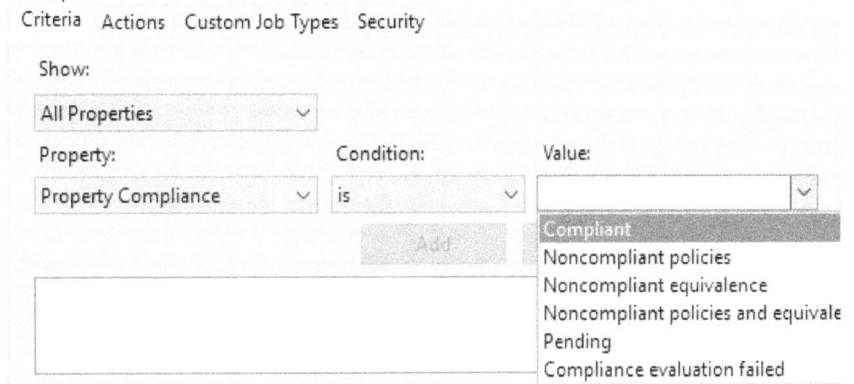

5. Select Add to add it to the list.

Task 5 - Property configuration: Actions.

In this case, there are two state transitions that have actions. One action is from Development to Manufacturing state transition and the other is from Manufacturing to Development state transition. The Development to Manufacturing state transition should already be selected.

1. Select the Actions tab.

2. Select the checkbox next to Check that dependent child files are released.

3. Select OK to dismiss this dialog box and return to the Lifecycle Definition dialog box.

4. In the Transitions tab, select the from State Manufacturing and to State Development transition.

5. Select Edit to display the Transition dialog box.

6. Select the Actions tab.

7. Select the checkbox next to Bump primary revision.

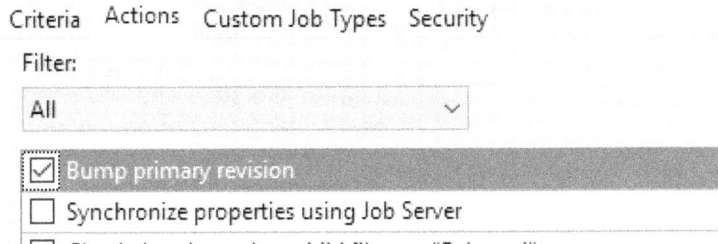

8. Select OK to dismiss this dialog box and return to the Lifecycle Definition dialog box for the selected lifecycle definition.

Task 6 - Control: Released state.

The final step is to specify that the Manufacturing State is the 'Released' State. This is important to check that dependent child files with 'Released' criteria know what state to enforce. The lifecycle state Manufacturing should still be selected in the Lifecycle States list.

1. Select the Control tab.

2. Select This is a "Released" State checkbox.

3. Select Apply to apply the change.

4. Select OK to dismiss this dialog box and return to the Vault Settings dialog box. Close all open dialog boxes.

2.3 Changing Lifecycle States

Overview

The Change State dialog box changes the state of files, folders, items, and custom objects. Before the state is changed the criteria, if any, are first checked. The user must have the ability to change the state and any conditions are evaluated. When the state change is performed, any actions specified are then performed. The user has the option of specifying a comment to inform others why the state was changed.

Objectives

After completing this lesson, you will be able to:

- Describe the way a Vault object's state can be changed.

- Change the state of a set of related files.

- Describe how the criteria and security can restrict lifecycle state changes.

- Understand how the new lifecycle state can impact the ability to read, modify and delete data.

Change State

There are several ways that a file can change state:

- Adding a new file to the vault: New files can be added to the vault using different methods: Manually adding a file, adding a file through the application add-in, migrating from Autodesk Vault to Autodesk Vault Workgroup and using the Autoloader to add Autodesk® Inventor files. In a later lesson you will learn how assignment rules and categories can be setup to automatically assign a lifecycle definition and default state to a file.

- Change Category: Vault Workgroup enables you to create and assign files to different categories. The action of doing so can also assign a default lifecycle definition and initial state to the file. This will also be covered in a later lesson.

- The Change State Command: This is the manual method of changing a state and is based on some significant lifecycle event like revising a set of files that represent products in production or archiving a set of deign files that is no longer in production.

Change State Command

The Change State command is available in three locations:

- Right-click on a file in the main pane.

- In the Actions menu.

- In the Behaviors toolbar.

This command enables the authorized user to:

- Specify the Lifecycle Definition to use: It is possible to change lifecycle definitions during a state change. This is helpful if the file needs to be managed differently. For example, your organization can manage files in the prototyping phase of product development differently from those that are in production and undergoing revision. Another example could be when one company acquires another and changes the way one of the company's file are lifecycle managed.

- Specify the Lifecycle State: Once the definition is chosen, a set of valid lifecycle state transitions is presented. It is up to the user to specify which lifecycle state to change to based on the reason for making the lifecycle change.

- Select the effected files. Because the files can have many different relationships, it is possible to select which of the related files will also undergo the state change. This includes parent and children files and attached, library and related documentation.

- Enter a comment to inform other users why the change was made. The lifecycle state transition can be configured to present a list of options or the user can enter their own reason.

Hint: Change State Dialog Box

The Change State dialog box can change the state of files, folders, items, and custom objects. Multiple instances of any of those entity types can be acted on at one time. However, the Change State dialog box does not support more than one entity type at a time. For example, the user cannot change state on a file and folder at the same time.

Procedure: Change State

To change the state of a set of related files do the following.

1. Before you attempt to change state you should determine whether you are a user or member of a group that can make the required lifecycle state change. You saw earlier how security is set on lifecycle transitions. If you attempt to make the state change and do not have permission to do so, you will not be informed until after you dismiss the Change State dialog box (e.g., there is no precheck).

2. Select the file or group of files from the main pane that are to be changed. If you need to change a set of related files you can use the options in the dialog box to select these for you. If the files are not related use <Shift> + select or <Ctrl> + Select option to select the files from the list.

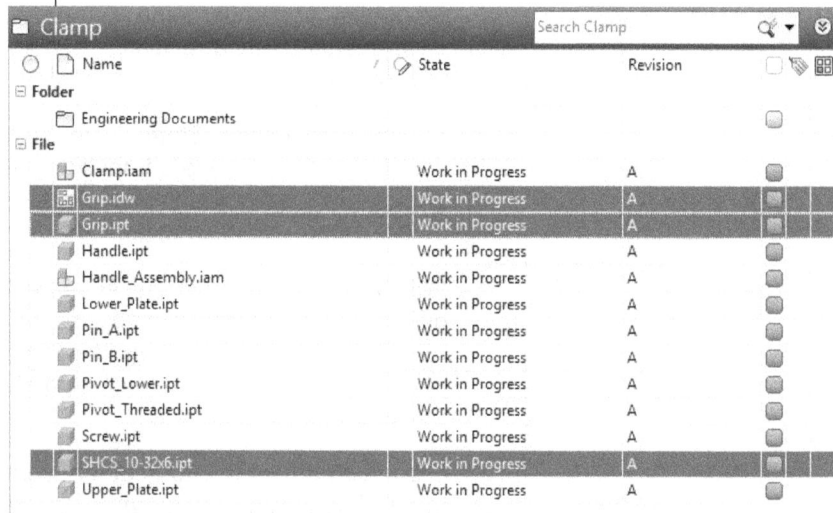

3. Select the Change State command to display the Change State dialog box.

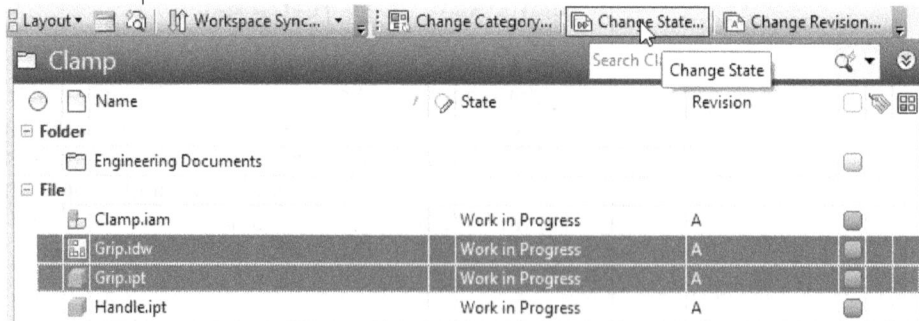

4. In the Select a new lifecycle state section, select the lifecycle definition from the drop-down list.

Select a new lifecycle state:

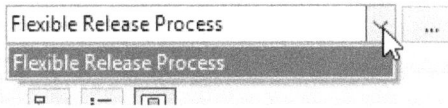

| Flexible Release Process | ... |

Flexible Release Process

5. To select a different lifecycle definition, select the button next to the field to display the Change Lifecycle Definition dialog box. Select a different lifecycle definition and then select OK to dismiss this dialog box.

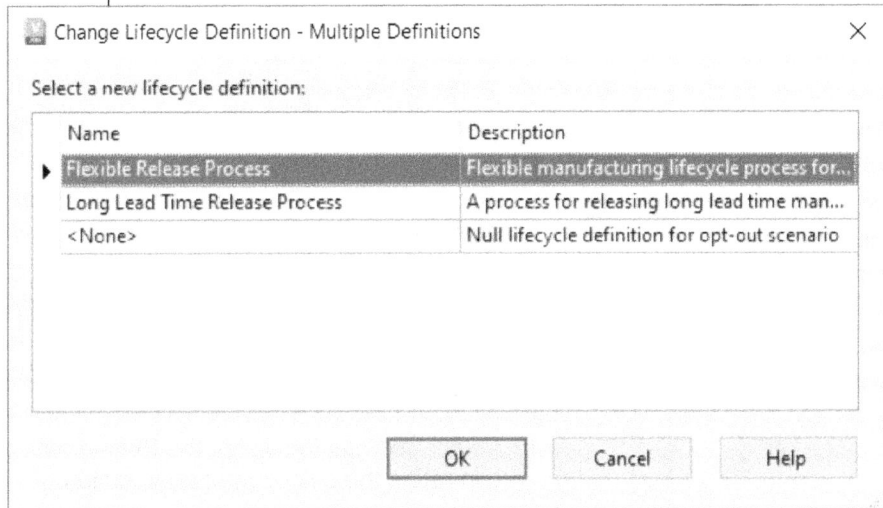

Change Lifecycle Definition - Multiple Definitions ✕

Select a new lifecycle definition:

Name	Description
Flexible Release Process	Flexible manufacturing lifecycle process for...
Long Lead Time Release Process	A process for releasing long lead time man...
<None>	Null lifecycle definition for opt-out scenario

OK   Cancel   Help

6. Once the definition is selected, select the state from the drop-down list.

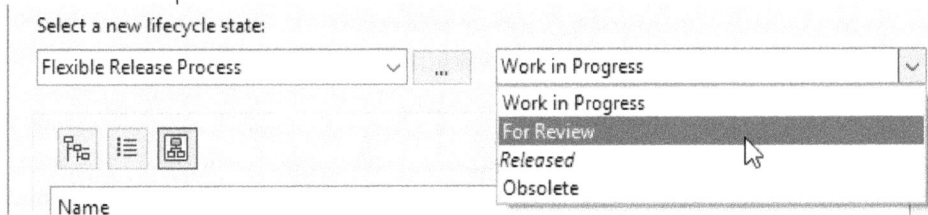

Select a new lifecycle state:

| Flexible Release Process | ... | | Work in Progress | ⌄ |

Work in Progress
For Review
Released
Obsolete

Name

7. When a new definition or state is chosen the columns in the file list update to show the new selection.

Name	State	△	Lifecycle Definition
Grip.idw	For Review		Flexible Release Process
Grip.ipt	For Review		Flexible Release Process
Grip.ipt	For Review		Flexible Release Process
SHCS_10-32x6.ipt	For Review		Flexible Release Process

8. Use View to change the view to help understand file relationships.

Folder View   Name   List View   Name   Design View

9. Use the Parent / Child selection buttons to modify the selection.

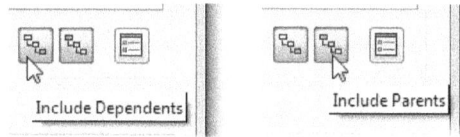

Include Dependents   Include Parents

10. Select Settings to display the Setting dialog box. Here you can refine the selection of related files.

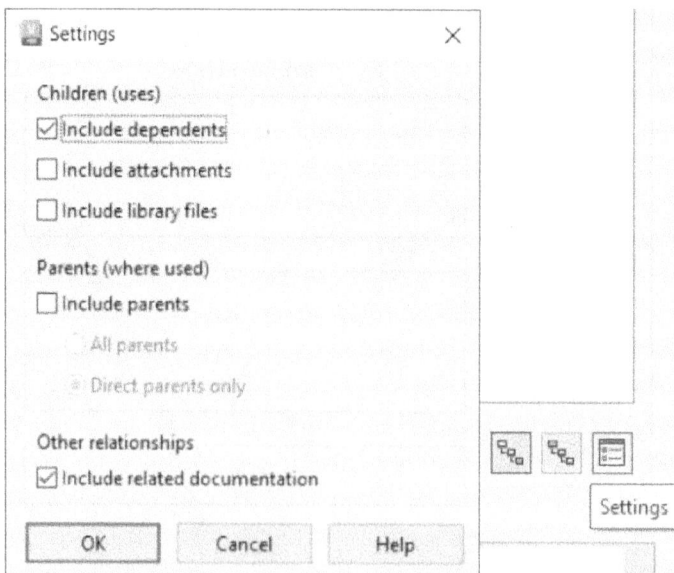

Settings ✕

Children (uses)
☑ Include dependents
☐ Include attachments
☐ Include library files

Parents (where used)
☐ Include parents
  ○ All parents
  ○ Direct parents only

Other relationships
☑ Include related documentation

Settings

OK   Cancel   Help

11. Select the related files that will also change lifecycle state.
12. Enter a comment or select a predefined comment from the drop-down list.

Enter comments:

Under review	▼

Submit for pre-release
Change request

13. Select OK to complete the procedure.

Practice 2c | Change Lifecycle States

In this practice, you will change the state of the Table files to release them to manufacturing. You will create a new category named Design and assign the Standard Process Lifecycle Definition to it. In a later chapter, you will learn how Categories can be used to help control your files.

The completed practice

Task 1 - Create new category.

1. Log in to Vault Workgroup using the following information:

    • For User Name, enter **Administrator**.
    • Leave the Password field blank
    • For Vault select AOTCVault from the drop-down list.

2. Select the Tools menu then Administration>Vault Settings to display the Vault Settings dialog box.

3. Select the Behaviors tab and then select Categories in the Categories section to display the Configure Categories dialog box.

4. Select File Categories from the drop-down list.

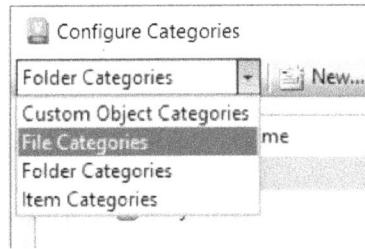

5. Select New in the toolbar to display the Category Edit dialog box.

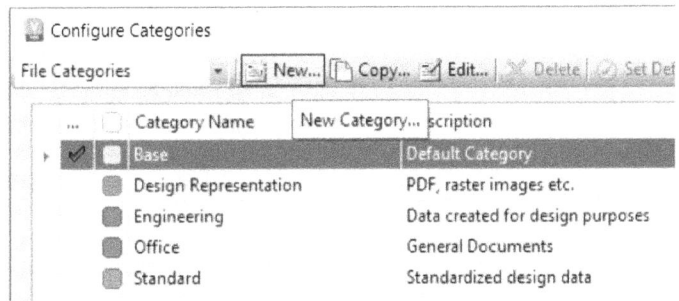

6. In the Category Edit dialog box, enter the following information:

- For Name, enter **Design**.
- In the Color drop-down list, choose orange as shown below.
- For Description, enter **Design Files**.
- Ensure that the Available checkbox is selected.

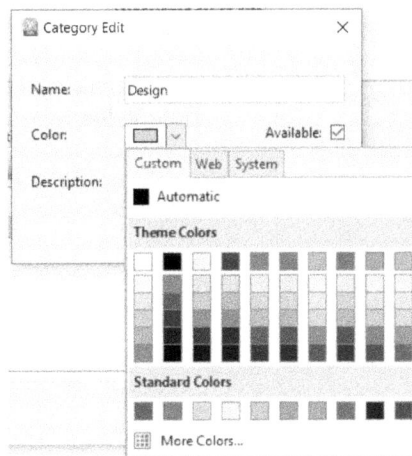

7. Select OK to return to the Configure Categories dialog box.

8. Ensure that the new Design category is selected in the list.

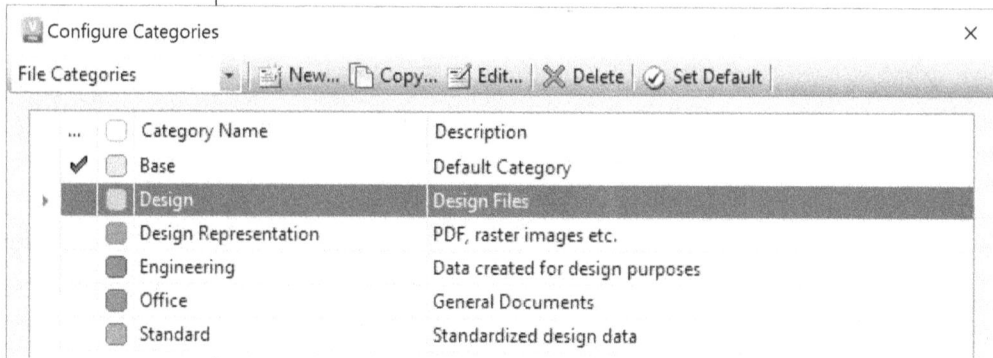

9. In the Behaviors section of the Configure Categories dialog box, select the Lifecycles tab.

10. In the toolbar, select Assign.

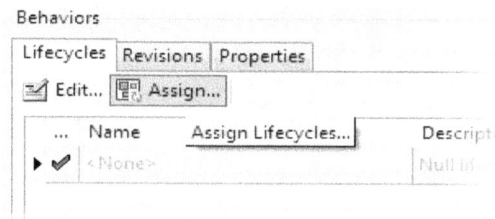

11. The Assign Category – Design dialog box displays.

12. In the All Lifecycle Definitions list, select the Standard Process entry.

13. Select Add to add it to the Assigned Lifecycle Definitions list.

14. Double-click on the Standard Process entry to make it the default lifecycle definition to use for the Design category.

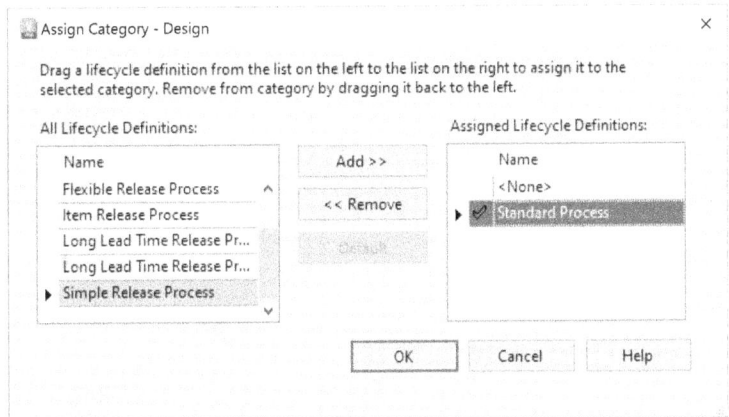

15. Select OK to dismiss this dialog box and return to the Configure Categories dialog box.

16. Select the Revisions tab in the Behaviors section.

17. Select Assign to display the Assign Category – Design dialog box.

18. In the All Revision Schemes list, select the Standard Numeric Format.

19. Select Add to add it to the Assigned Revision Schemes list.

20. Double-click on the new entry to make it the default.

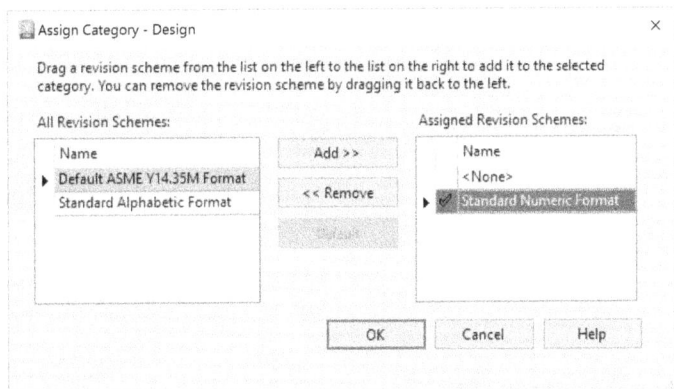

21. Select OK to close the dialog box and return to the Configure Categories dialog box.

22. Select Close to dismiss this dialog box and return to the Vault Settings dialog box. Select Close to dismiss this dialog box and return to Vault Workgroup.

23. Log out of Autodesk Vault Workgroup software.

Task 2 - Change category.

1. Log in to Autodesk Vault Workgroup using the following information:

   - For User Name, enter **usera**.
   - For Password, enter **vault**.
   - For Vault, select AOTCVault from the drop-down list.

2. In the Navigation Pane, expand the Project Explorer ($) folder and then expand the Designs folder. Double-click on the Table folder to display the table assemblies and parts in the Main Pane.

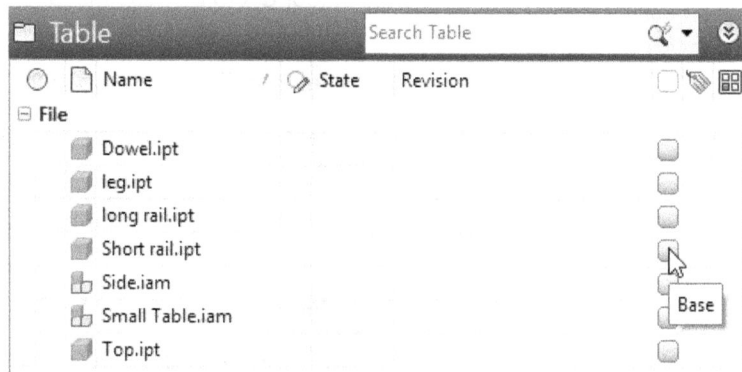

Note that all of the files are assigned to the Base category during the migration and have no Revision or State values.

3. Select the file Small Table.iam and then select the Actions>Change Category.

4. In the dialog box, select Design from the Select a new category drop-down list.

5. All of the children for the table should also be selected. If not, select Include Dependents in the row of buttons below the file list.

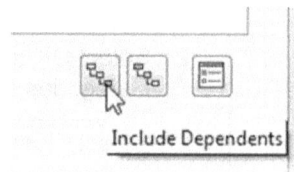

6. In the Enter comments text box, enter the comment Design files. Review the dialog box entries. Select OK to finish the Change Category workflow.

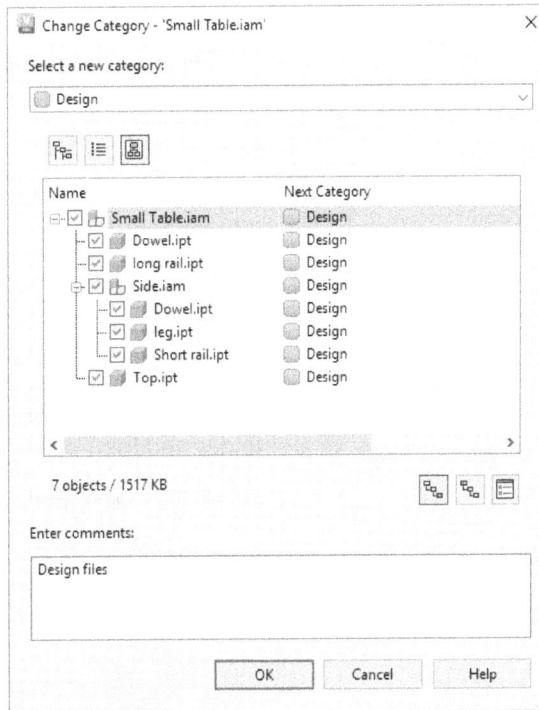

7. Return to the Main pane and review the file list.

- The Category Glyph is now set to Design.
- The Design Category specifies the default Lifecycle State for the files to be Development which you can see in the State column.

- The rules for changing to the Development Lifecycle State specify the Revision be bumped based on the Primary Revision with the Standard Numeric Revision Scheme. The first value in this revisions scheme's sequence is 1 which you can see in the Revision column.
- Because a new file version is created when a new Revision is made the files are all at Version 2.

8. Log out of Autodesk Vault Workgroup.

9. Log in to Autodesk Vault Workgroup using the following information:

    - For User Name, enter **userd**.
    - For Password, enter **vault**.
    - For Vault, select AOTCVault from the drop-down list.

10. In the Navigation Pane, expand the Project Explorer ($) folder and then expand the Designs folder.

11. Select the Table folder.

    Note that the files are not displayed. In the Lifecycle Definition State "Development, the Sales group (which userd is a member of) has no Read, Modify or Delete permission.

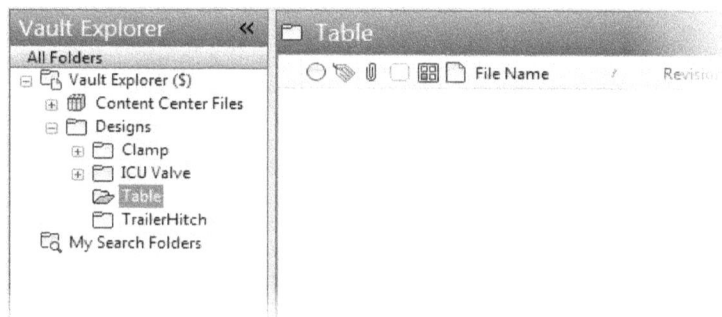

12. Log out of Vault Workgroup.

13. Log in to Autodesk Vault Workgroup using the following information:

    - For User Name, enter **userb**.
    - For Password, enter **vault**.
    - For Vault, select AOTCVault from the drop-down list.

14. In the Navigation Pane, expand the Project Explorer ($) folder and then expand the Designs folder.

15. Select the Table folder.

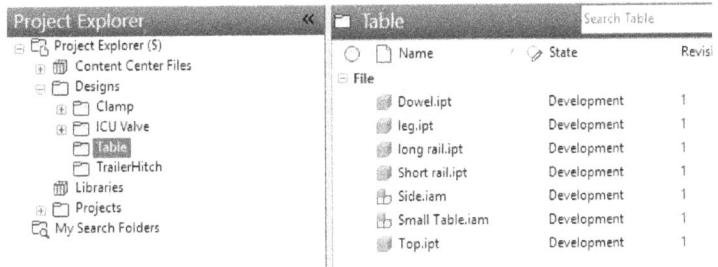

Since userb is part of the Engineering group, and this group has Read permission in the Development State the files display.

Task 3 - Change lifecycle state.

---

1. Select the Small Table.iam file.

2. In the Behaviors toolbar, select Change State.

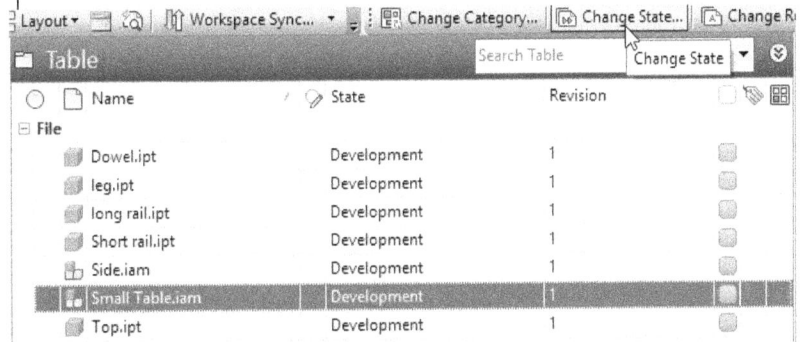

3. The Change State – 'Small Table.iam' dialog box displays. Ensure that only the main assembly Small Table.iam is checked as shown below.

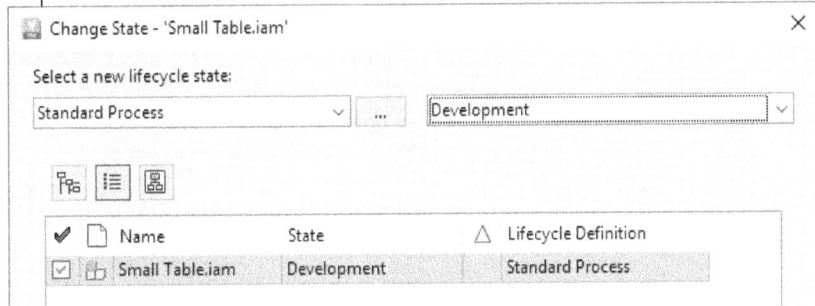

4. In the Select a new Lifecycle State field, in the right side drop-down list, select Manufacturing.

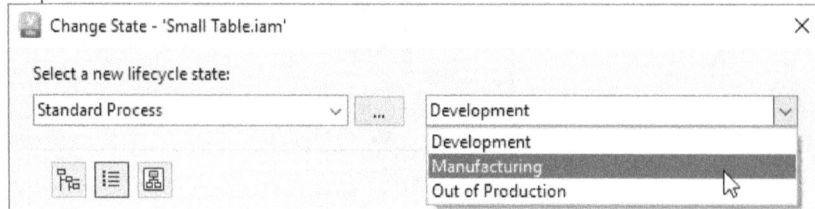

5. In the Enter comments field, enter the comment **Release to production**.

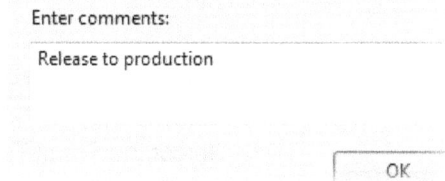

6. Select OK to finish the lifecycle state change.

7. An error message displays: Select Details to see the complete error message.

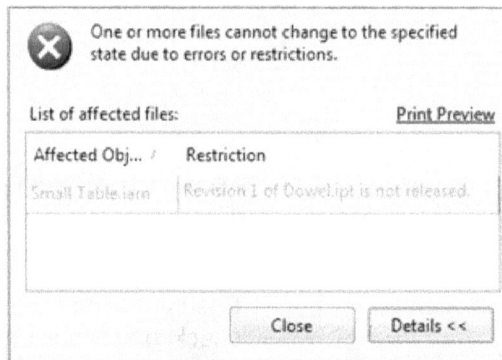

In the Control setting for the Manufacturing state, you specified that the state was a released state. In the transition from Development to Manufacturing lifecycle state change, you set the criteria that 'Check that dependent child files are released'. So you must first release the children. To do this, select all the children in the Change State - 'Small Table.iam' dialog box

8. Repeat Step 1 to 6. In the Change State dialog box, include dependents to set new state to Manufacturing for all children as well.

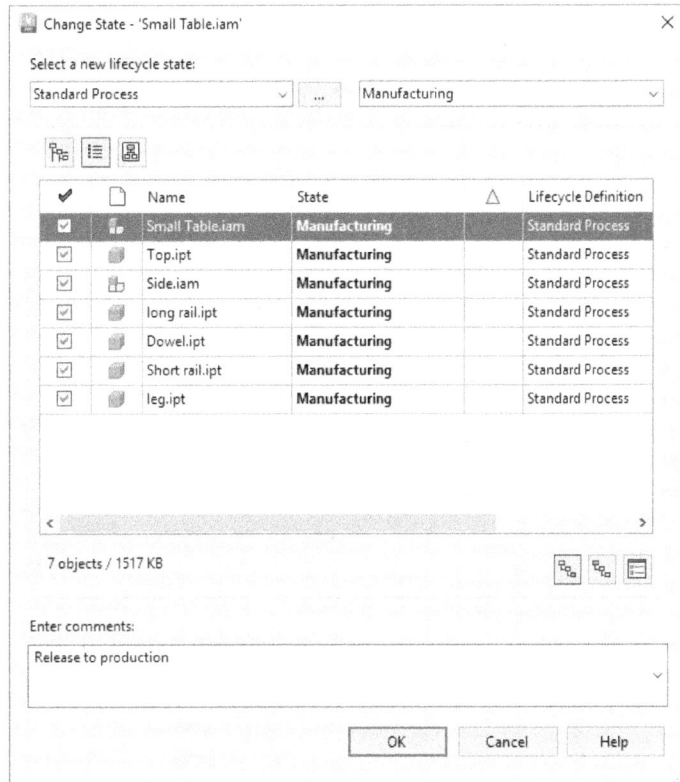

9. Review the results.

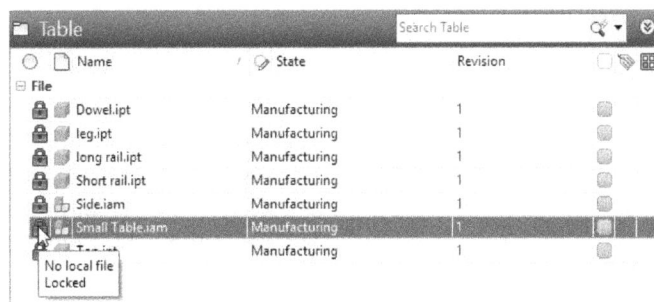

- The files are locked and cannot be edited.
- The Lifecycle State is now set to Manufacturing.
- The state change did not create a new Revision or Version for any of the files.

10. Log out of Autodesk Vault Workgroup.

11. Log in to Autodesk Vault Workgroup using the following information:

- For User Name, enter **usera**.
- For Password, enter **vault**.
- For Vault, select AOTCVault in the drop-down list.

12. In the Navigation Pane, expand the Project Explorer ($) folder and then expand the Designs folder. Select the Table folder.

13. Review the files.

The files do not show as being locked. This is because usera is part of the Administrators group which has Modify permission in the Manufacturing (Released) State. This enables the Administrators to make minor changes to the files without taking them out of production.

2.4 Chapter Summary

Lifecycle Management for files is one of the foundational aspects of Autodesk Vault Workgroup. It provides uniform set of behaviors to files in the lifecycle management process. In this chapter the default Lifecycle Definitions and States were reviewed. The chapter described in detail how to create a new Lifecycle Definition and set of states and how to configure it as well as the default Lifecycle Definitions and States to meet the unique needs of your organization.

Having completed this chapter, you can:

- Describe the default Lifecycle Definitions and how they could be applied for different situations.

- Describe the default Lifecycle States and how they could be used to control file access.

- Create a new Lifecycle Definition and set of associated Lifecycle States.

- Plan for the configuration of Lifecycle Definitions and associated States.

- Configure the States of a Lifecycle Definition.

- Apply the Lifecycle Definition to a set of files

- Change the lifecycle state of a file

- Understand how the lifecycle state settings affect the ability to read and modify files.

Revision Management in Autodesk Vault Workgroup

Products have defined lifecycles from inception through production. Product development and enhancement introduces changes to the product files. These changes must be tracked and managed to provide a complete history of the changes and modifications as the product develops. Revision management provides consistency throughout the product lifecycle by applying a common definition and behavior to files in a vault.

Learning Objectives in This Chapter

- Describe the difference between a Revision and a Version and why both are important.
- Explain what Revision Schemes and Revision Scheme Formats are.
- Know the details of the Default Revision Schemes and Revision Scheme Formats supplied with Autodesk® Vault Workgroup software.
- Know how to modify an existing Revision Scheme.
- Create new Revision Scheme.
- Describe the different ways a file or item can be revised.
- Explain the concepts of revision controlled documents and describe what released biased means.
- Understand how the concept of released biased revisions gives the designer increased flexibility in the design process.
- Use the Change State command to automatically revise a group of files or items.
- Use the Change Revision command to manually revise a file or item.

3.1 Revisions and Versions

Overview

Revision management is functionality available in Vault Workgroup that enables a user to label a significant change or set of changes to a document and its related files. The label itself is the revision and the collection of files affected in that revision are considered a revision level. A revision level can be retrieved later so that a document and the version of the related files associated with that particular revision are preserved.

Objectives

After completing this lesson, you will be able to:

- Describe what a Version is and why they are useful.

- Describe what a Revision is and why they are useful.

- Describe the relationships between Revisions and Versions.

Concept

When editing documents in a vault, the changes are saved as versions history on the server using the default file settings. The history has little information that can be used to identify significant events.

The engineering industry has standards used for labeling significant changes to data. This is typically called the document revision. The revision is usually marked with one or more characters, and the document is given a new character string for any significant changes that are done after the document has been released.

The Revision Management feature in Autodesk Vault Workgroup gives the ability to mark any point in time as a significant change to a document and its related files. A revision level of a document can be retrieved along with the correct revision level of any related documents. When used in combination with lifecycles, a revision level is created automatically during predefined events. The revision will also be marked as 'Released' when the document is placed into certain lifecycle states identified as released states. During open and download procedures, the user can choose to retrieve released or non-released revisions of the document and its related files.

Definition: Versions

A version is an iteration of a document and its meta-data that has been committed to the system.

Autodesk Vault is designed to help you manage different versions of a file. You can get a previous version or revert to a previous version.

Definition: Revision

A revision is a collection of file versions rolled up into one object that displays to the user. After a revision is created, document edits are contained in that revision until a new revision is created. This means that as changes are made and committed to the system, the user sees no change to the revision label.

For example: a document is created and assigned the revision level "A". As the user makes changes and those versions are committed, the revision label remains "A". Only when the user performs a revision bumping action will a new revision be created. One way to do this in Vault Workgroup is by using the Change Revision command to iterate the revision. This will cause a new revision of the document to be created with the label "B". Any subsequent edits would then be collected in revision "B". The illustration shows the results for a CAD file that is revised four times, a new revision B is created and then revised four more times. The underlined version is the latest version for a given revision.

When you create a new revision of a file, a version of the file is also created. The last file version 4 for revision A in the illustration is the same as the first file version 5 for revision B.

Once the revision objects have been created, any revision can be downloaded or opened. When a revision is downloaded, only one version in that revision is used to represent the revision. If lifecycles are not used, then that version is always the latest version in that revision.

In general, it is up to the user to create a new revision of a file (or set of files) when some milestone is met. As part of a lifecycle transition, actions can be setup to automatically increment the revision based on a set of lifecycle state rules.

For the case of a lifecycle state change, the most common example is when a file that represents a part or component that is being manufactured needs to be changed to address form, fit, or function, problems. In this example, Revision A represents the manufactured part before the change is made and revision B represents the revised revision. However, revisions can be used to signify any notable event where it is important to keep a history of the files and its metadata at that point in time.

You can manually create a new revision using the Change Revision command. The command enables you to specify the next revision from a specified Revision Definition and add a comment as to the nature of the revision.

The Revision Definition is a formula that will automatically calculate the next revision character in a sequence.

The next image shows the effect of changing the lifecycle state of the file. The lifecycle rules, as you saw in the last lesson, can be defined to 'bump' (create) a new revision for certain state changes.

For both manual and lifecycle-based revision changes, a set of revision schemes with its associated revision scheme formats are used to specify the next character or set of characters in the next revision.

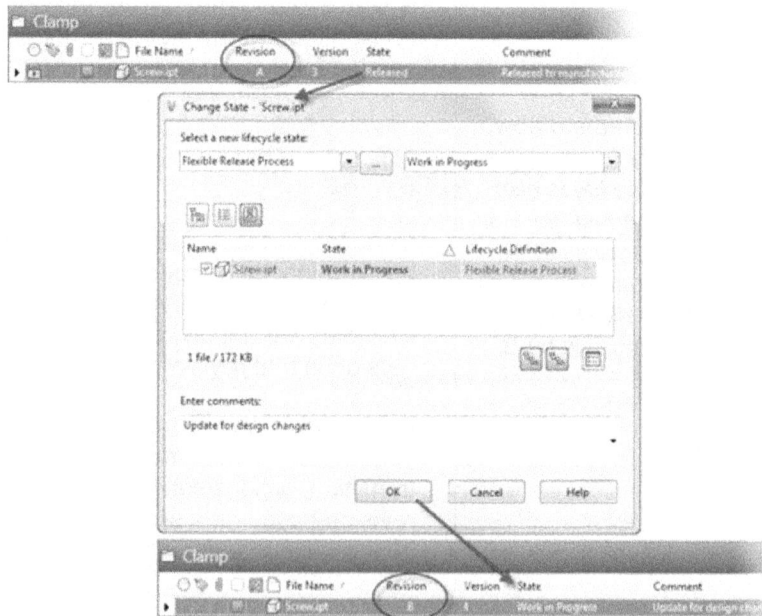

For both manual and lifecycle-based revision changes, a set of revision schemes with its associated revision scheme formats are used to specify the next character or set of characters in the next revision.

Default Revision Schemes and Scheme Formats

Definition of Terms

The following table defines the terms for revision schemes.

Term	Description
Revision Scheme	A formula used to calculate the initial revision characters for a file and the subsequent revision characters as that file is revised.
Revision Scheme Format	A defined sequence of characters used to create a revision scheme.
Revision Scheme Format Type	Enables multiple levels of incrementing a revision. The three types are: Primary Scheme Format Secondary Scheme Format Tertiary Scheme Format
Delimiter	A single character that separates the revision scheme format types.

There are three default revision scheme formats, ten delimiter characters, and four default revisions scheme definitions included with Autodesk Vault Workgroup.

Default Revision Scheme Formats

Autodesk Vault Workgroup has three predefined Revision Scheme Formats. A format simply specifies the progression of characters as a revision is bumped. They are listed in the following table.

Name	Description
Alphabetic	Only alphabetic characters [1] are permitted in the primary format. The first revision is A.
Numeric	Only numeric characters [2] are permitted in the primary format. The first revision is 1.
Default ASME Y14.35M	Only alphabetic characters with some characters omitted [3] are permitted in the primary format. The first revision is '-'.

Notes:

1. Alphabetic Formats: Include alphabetic characters starting at A through Z and then AA through ZZ.
2. Numeric Formats: Include the numeric sequence from 1 to 99.
3. Default ASME Y14.35M: Include alphabetic characters starting at A through Y and then AA through YY, excluding any character or combination of characters containing the following letters: I, O, Q, S, X, and Z as these could be confused with numbers.

For example, as the primary revision is bumped for the Alphabetic sequence the progression is:

A, B, C, D...

For a Numeric format the progression is:

1, 2, 3, 4, 5...

Default Revision Scheme Definitions

From these three default revision scheme formats, 4 different revisions schemes are provided.

Name	Delimiter	Primary	Secondary	Tertiary
Standard Alphabetic	Period (.)	Alphabetic	Numeric	Numeric
Standard Numeric	Period (.)	Numeric	Numeric	Numeric
Default ASME Y14.35M	Period (.)	Default ASME Y14.35M	Numeric	Numeric
None	Null Revision Scheme for opt out scenario			

These revision schemes and revision scheme formats are designed to cover a wide range of the revision practices in industry. If either a format or scheme does not meet your needs new ones can be created.

3.2 Creating and Modifying Revision Schemes

Overview

The Autodesk Vault Workgroup software comes with multiple revisions schemes. These represent common revision practices found in a cross section of the manufacturing industry. They can be used with or without modification.

It is possible to modify one of the provided schemes to adapt it to your environment. In some cases a new revision scheme needs to be created.

Objectives

After completing this lesson, you will be able to:

- Create a new revision scheme.

- Create a new revision scheme format.

- Modify an existing revision scheme.

Revision Scheme and Revision Formats

A revision scheme is defined by two basic entities: the delimiter and the revision scheme format. For every revision scheme there are three revision scheme formats separated by two delimiters. Revision scheme formats can be different but you can only use one type of delimiter per revision scheme.

Delimiter

This is a character that separates the three revision scheme formats. The permitted characters for delimiters are:

- Single quote (')

- Hyphen (-)

- Double quote (")

- Comma (,)

- Period (.)

- Forward slash (/)

- Colon (:)

- Semi-colon (;)

- Back slash (\)

- Underscore (_).

Revision Scheme Format

As discussed earlier these can be alphabetic or numeric sequences. There must be three revision scheme formats for every revision scheme:

- Primary Format

- Secondary Format

- Tertiary Format

Building a Revision Sequence

The illustration below shows how the delimiter and the three revision scheme formats are used to build a complete revision scheme.

> <Primary Format><Delimiter><Secondary Format><Delimiter><Tertiary Format>

Several examples of revision sequences are shown below using different delimiters and different alphabetic and numeric revision scheme formats:

A, A.1, A.1.1, A.1.2, B…

1, 1/A, 1/B, 1/B/1, 1/B/2, 2…

A, A-A-1, A-A-2, A-B, C…

Creating a New Revision Scheme

An organization can use secondary or tertiary formats if they desire, but they must be used in conjunction with a primary format.For each revision scheme, all three formats must be present.

Creating a new revision scheme involves importing a simple text file that has all of the possible characters for the primary revision scheme format. For example, the primary revision scheme format looks like the following sequence:

> R1, R1, R3 …

This is not one of the supplied formats so one will need to be created.

Procedure: Create a New Revision Scheme and Format using Import

The following steps show how a new revision scheme is created.

1. The first step does not involve Vault Workgroup at all. In a plain text editor like Microsoft Notepad, create a file where each row represents a revision character. The first row will be the first character in the sequence, the second row the second character in the sequence and so on.

    Note: You will need to enter as many rows as you expect to use when creating different revisions. If you get to the last character in the sequence then the bump primary revision command will start incrementing the secondary revision and so on with the tertiary until all possible characters are used. This is not likely to happen unless you build all three formats with very few characters.

2. Save this file on your local file system.

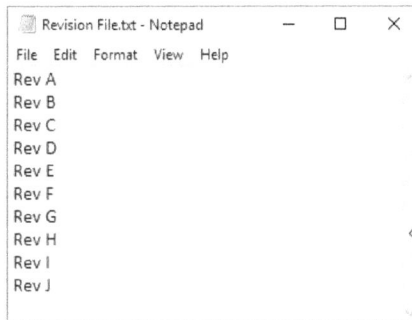

3. Return to Autodesk Vault Workgroup logging in as an Administrator. Open the Vault Settings dialog box and go to the Behaviors tab.
4. Select Revisions to open the Revision Schemes Definitions.
5. In the toolbar, click Import.

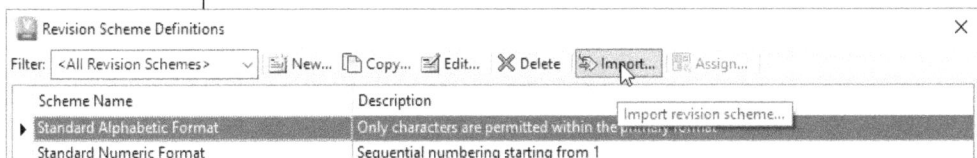

6. The Import Revision Scheme Definition dialog box displays.

7. Select the button next to the Name field and browse to the file you created. Select the file from the file browser.

8. The scheme represented by the values in the file is created. By default the secondary and tertiary formats are set to the numeric format.

9. The default name used is the same as the filename. This should be changed to reflect the true name of the new sequence.

10. In the Delimiter drop-down list, select the delimiter to use.

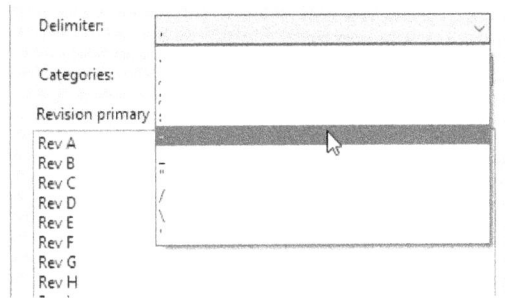

11. Enter a Description and leave the Category field blank.

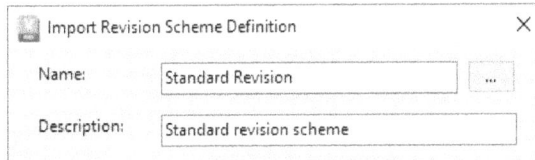

12. Select OK to dismiss this dialog box and return to the Revision Scheme Definitions dialog box.

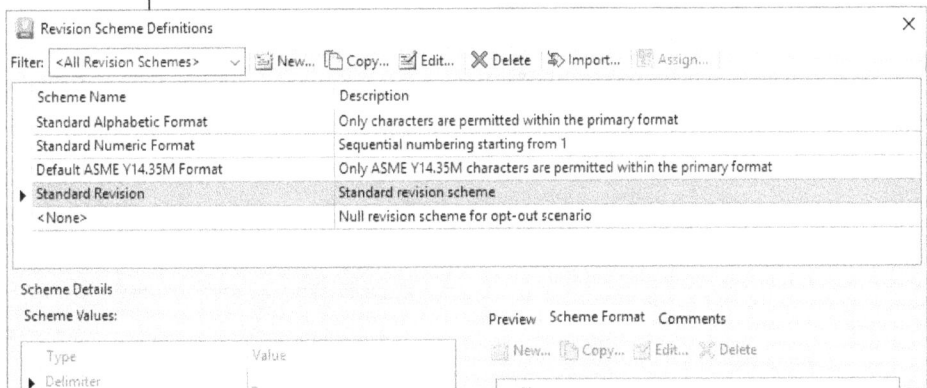

13. Review the new revision scheme. Note the default values for the secondary and tertiary formats. If this is acceptable then select Close to dismiss this dialog box.

14. To change the secondary or tertiary formats, select Edit from the toolbar.

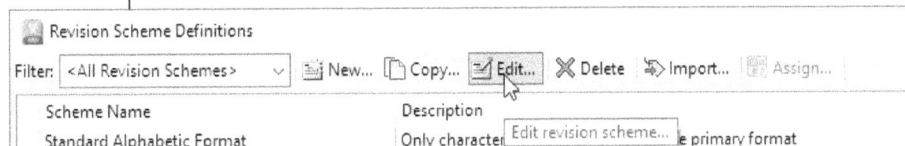

15. The Revision Scheme Definition dialog box for the selected sequence displays.

16. In the Scheme Values list select the scheme you want to change. Note that you could also change the primary value at this point.

In the process of creating a new revision scheme, a revision scheme format was also created. You can use this new revision scheme format in other custom revision schemes you might need.

17. Review the examples of the new revision sequence in the Preview tab.

Example Revision Formats

Delimiter Character:	-
Primary:	Rev A
Secondary:	Rev A-1
Tertiary:	Rev A-1-1

18. Select OK to close the dialog box and return to the Revision Scheme Definitions dialog box.
19. Select Close to return to the Vault Settings dialog box.

Modifying an Existing Revision Scheme

In some cases, modifying an existing revision scheme will enable it to conform to your existing practices or process design.

Procedure: Modify an Existing Revision Scheme

The following steps show an example of how an existing revision scheme can be modified:

1. In the Vault Settings dialog box, select the Behaviors tab.
2. Select Revisions in the Lifecycles and Revisions section to display the Revision Scheme Definitions dialog box.
3. Select Edit in the toolbar.

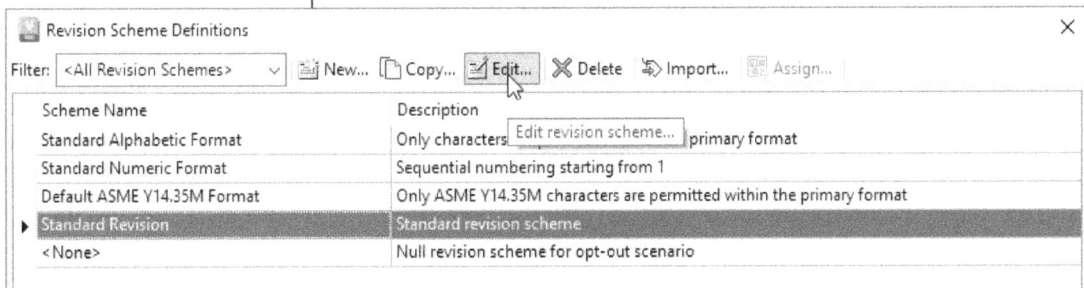

Revision Scheme Definitions   ×

Filter: `<All Revision Schemes>`   New...   Copy...   Edit...   Delete   Import...   Assign...

Scheme Name	Description
Standard Alphabetic Format	Only characters Edit revision scheme... primary format
Standard Numeric Format	Sequential numbering starting from 1
Default ASME Y14.35M Format	Only ASME Y14.35M characters are permitted within the primary format
Standard Revision	Standard revision scheme
`<None>`	Null revision scheme for opt-out scenario

4. The Revision Scheme Definition dialog box for the selected revision scheme displays.

5. Change the Definition Name, Category, and Description to better reflect the purpose for this scheme.

6. In the Scheme Details area, select the Value column for the Delimiter and select a new value in the drop-down list.

7. In the Scheme Details area, select the Value column for the revision scheme format that you want to change and select the new value.

Scheme Values:

Type	Value
Delimiter	-
I Primary Scheme Format	Numeric
Secondary Scheme Format	Alphabetic
Tertiary Scheme Format	Default ASME Y14.35M
	Numeric

Scheme Values:

Type	Value
Delimiter	-
Primary Scheme Format	Numeric
Secondary Scheme Format	Numeric
Tertiary Scheme Format	Alphabetic
	Default ASME Y14.35M

8. At any point, you can see an example of the changes in the Preview tab.

Revision primary sequence values:

1
2
3
4
5
6
7
8

Example Revision Formats

Delimiter Character:	-
Primary:	1
Secondary:	1-A
Tertiary:	1-A-1

9. To create a new scheme format to use in this scheme or any other schemes select the Scheme Format tab and select New.

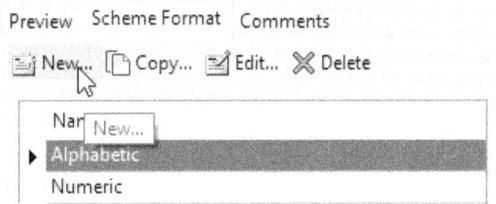

Preview   Scheme Format   Comments

New...   Copy...   Edit...   Delete

Nar New...
▶ Alphabetic
Numeric

10. In the List Scheme Format dialog box, you can either enter and arrange the values manually or select the button next to the Scheme Format Name field to import a list of values from a plain text (.TXT) file. Select OK when done to add the new format to the list.

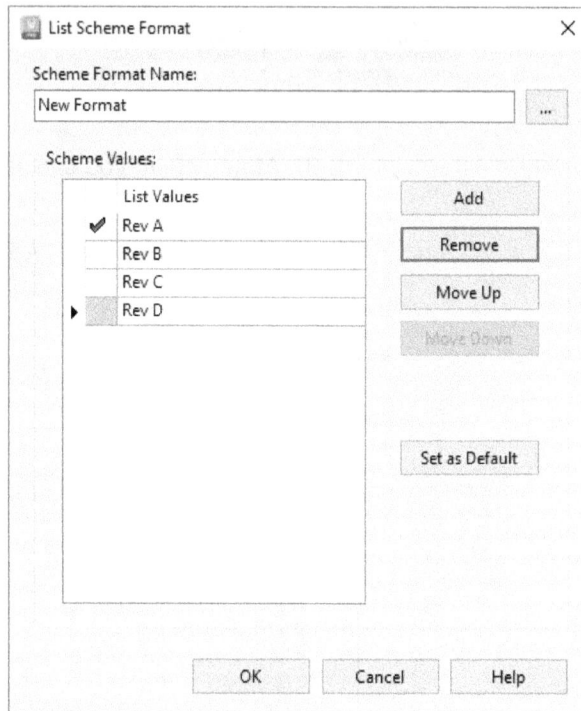

11. In the Comments tab, you can create one or more comments that will display in the Revise dialog box.

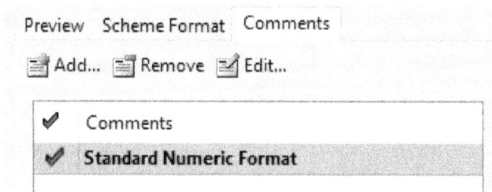

12. Select Add to add a new Comment in the Comment for dialog box. Select OK to dismiss this dialog box and add the new entry to the list.

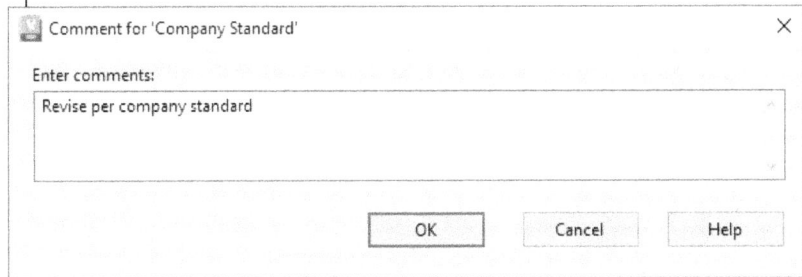

13. Select any unwanted comments by first selecting the comment and then selecting Remove.

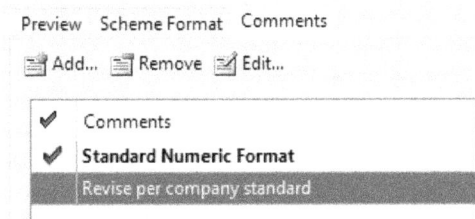

14. Now when the file is revised the Revision Definition displays in the list of revised files and the comment displays in the Enter comments text box.
15. Select OK to dismiss the Revision Scheme Definition dialog box for this revision scheme.
16. Select Close to dismiss the master Revision Scheme dialog box and return to the Vault Settings dialog box.

Practice 3a | Create a Revision Scheme

In this practice, you will create a new revision sequence. The primary revision scheme will be imported from a file. The secondary and tertiary formats along with the delimiter will be configured from the supplied formats. The method used will be a variation on the one shown in the procedure.

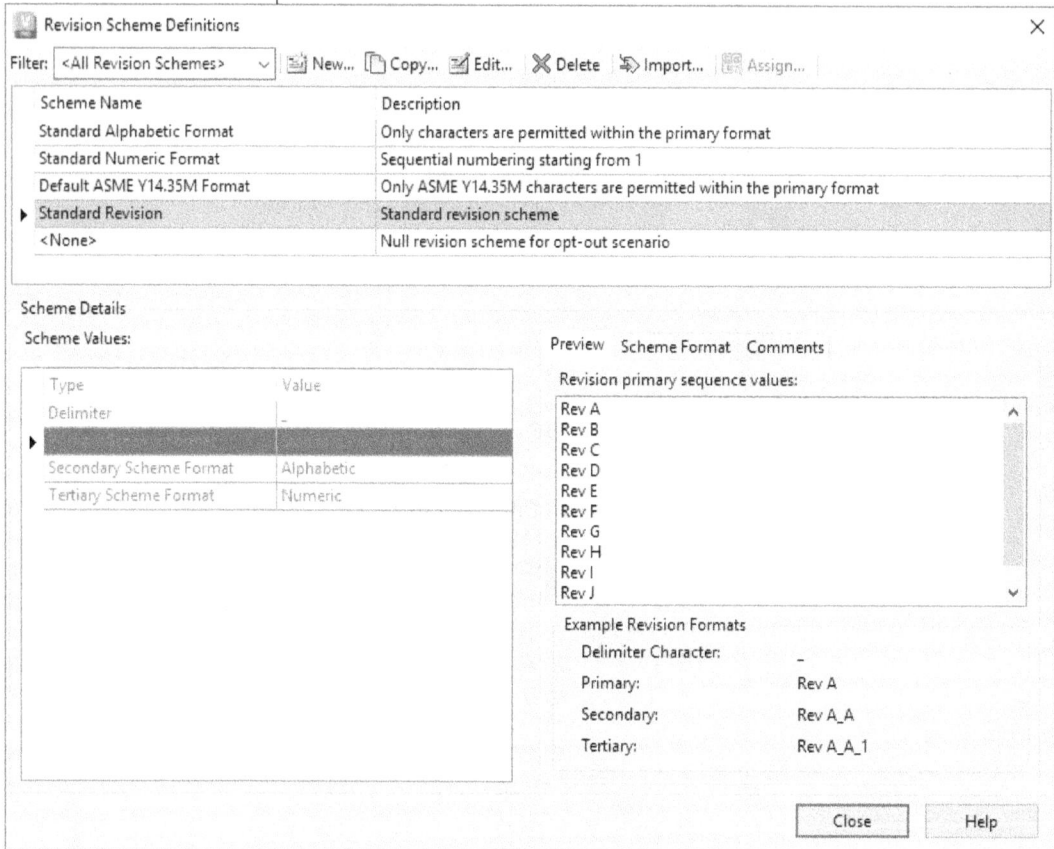

Revision Scheme Definitions ✕

Filter: <All Revision Schemes> ⌄ | New... Copy... Edit... Delete Import... Assign...

Scheme Name	Description
Standard Alphabetic Format	Only characters are permitted within the primary format
Standard Numeric Format	Sequential numbering starting from 1
Default ASME Y14.35M Format	Only ASME Y14.35M characters are permitted within the primary format
▶ Standard Revision	Standard revision scheme
<None>	Null revision scheme for opt-out scenario

Scheme Details

Scheme Values:

Type	Value
Delimiter	_
▶	
Secondary Scheme Format	Alphabetic
Tertiary Scheme Format	Numeric

Preview Scheme Format Comments

Revision primary sequence values:

Rev A
Rev B
Rev C
Rev D
Rev E
Rev F
Rev G
Rev H
Rev I
Rev J

Example Revision Formats

Delimiter Character:	_
Primary:	Rev A
Secondary:	Rev A_A
Tertiary:	Rev A_A_1

Close   Help

Task 1 - Create the file.

1. Start Microsoft Notepad to create an empty text file.

2. Enter **Rev A** in the first line.

3. Enter 9 more lines, each time incrementing the letter. For example, the second line should read Rev B.

4. Save the file on your desktop with the name Revision File.txt.

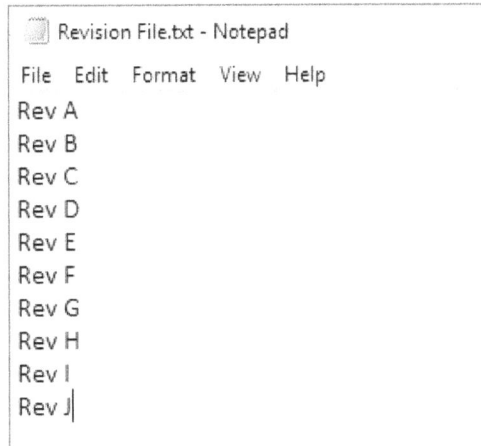

```
Revision File.txt - Notepad

File  Edit  Format  View  Help
Rev A
Rev B
Rev C
Rev D
Rev E
Rev F
Rev G
Rev H
Rev I
Rev J
```

Task 2 - Create the revision scheme.

1. Log in to Autodesk Vault Workgroup using the following information:

   - For User name enter **Administrator**.
   - Leave the password blank.
   - Select AOTCVault from the list of Vaults.

2. In the Tools menu, select Administration>Vault Settings.

3. In the Behaviors tab, select Revisions to display the Revisions Schemes Definitions dialog box. Click New.

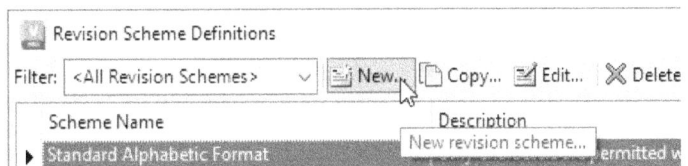

```
Revision Scheme Definitions

Filter: <All Revision Schemes>   ∨    New...   Copy...   Edit...   Delete

Scheme Name                        Description
▶ Standard Alphabetic Format        New revision scheme...    ermitted w
```

4. Do the following:

- For the Definition Name, enter **Standard Revision**.
- For the Description, enter **Standard revision scheme**.
- Leave the Category drop-down as None selected.

5. In the Scheme Details section, select the Delimiter line and then select the Value field to display the drop-down list. At the bottom of the list select the underscore (_).

6. Select the Primary Scheme Format line.

7. In the tab section, select the Scheme Format tab.

8. Select New to display the List Scheme Format dialog box.

9. Select the button next to the Scheme Format Name to display an Open dialog box. Browse to the file you created at the beginning of the practice and select Open to return to the List Scheme Format dialog box.

10. Click Add to add a new line to the list.

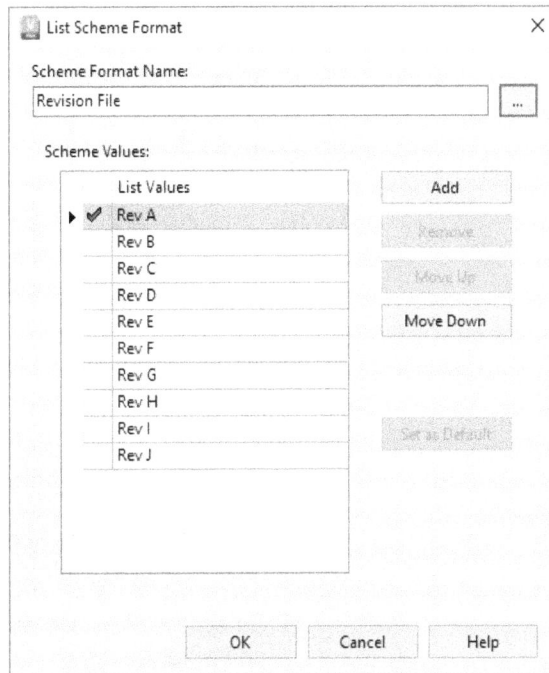

11. Enter **Rev K**. Move it to the bottom of the list.

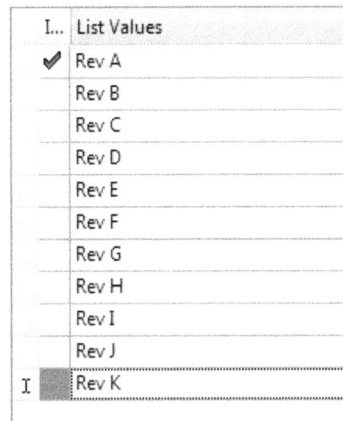

12. In the Scheme Format Name, edit the name populated by opening the file with Standard Primary Format.

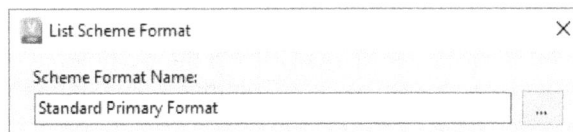

13. Select OK to dismiss this dialog box and return to the Revision Scheme Definition dialog box.

14. Select the Value field for the Primary Scheme Format and select the new format.

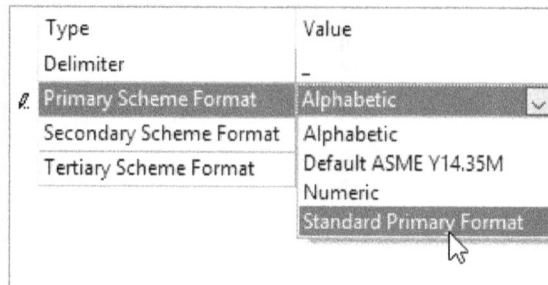

Type	Value
Delimiter	_
✎ Primary Scheme Format	Alphabetic ⌄
Secondary Scheme Format	Alphabetic
Tertiary Scheme Format	Default ASME Y14.35M
	Numeric
	Standard Primary Format

15. Select the Secondary Scheme Format Value field to display the drop-down list. Select Alphabetic.

16. Select the Tertiary Scheme Format Value field to display the drop-down list. Select Numeric.

17. Select the Preview tab to preview a sample revision character display.

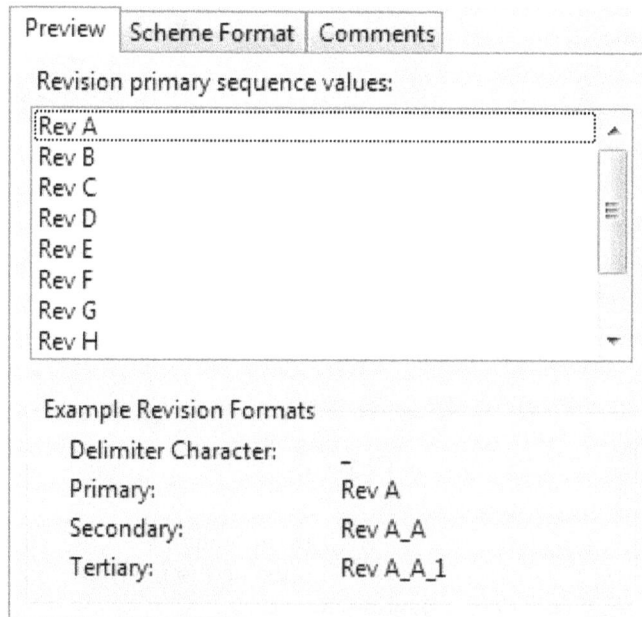

Preview	Scheme Format	Comments

Revision primary sequence values:

```
Rev A
Rev B
Rev C
Rev D
Rev E
Rev F
Rev G
Rev H
```

Example Revision Formats

Delimiter Character:	_
Primary:	Rev A
Secondary:	Rev A_A
Tertiary:	Rev A_A_1

18. Select the Comments tab and then click Add to display the Comments for 'Standard Revision' dialog box.

19. Enter the text **New Revision**.

> ![Comment for 'Standard Revision']
>
> Comment for 'Standard Revision'
>
> Enter comments:
>
> New Revision|

20. Select OK to dismiss the dialog box and return to the Revision Scheme Definition dialog box.

21. Select OK to dismiss this dialog box and return to the Revision Scheme Definitions dialog box that shows all of the schemes.

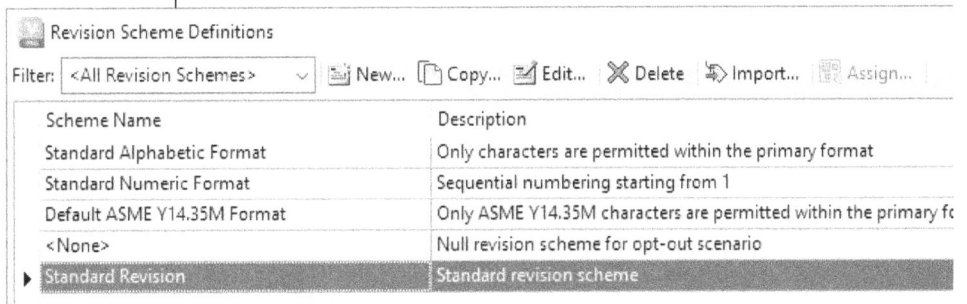

Revision Scheme Definitions

Filter: <All Revision Schemes> ∨ | 🗋 New... 📋 Copy... ✑ Edit... ✖ Delete ➥ Import... 🔲 Assign...

Scheme Name	Description
Standard Alphabetic Format	Only characters are permitted within the primary format
Standard Numeric Format	Sequential numbering starting from 1
Default ASME Y14.35M Format	Only ASME Y14.35M characters are permitted within the primary fc
<None>	Null revision scheme for opt-out scenario
▸ Standard Revision	Standard revision scheme

22. Select Close to dismiss this dialog box and return to the Vault Settings dialog box.

3.3 Revising Files

Overview

The document revision management system in Autodesk Vault Workgroup software is very flexible. There are several ways in which a file or item can be revised.

Revisions enable you to label a significant milestone or change to a file or item and all related files. The collection of files affected in a revision are considered a revision level, stored as part of the revision label you assign. A revision level can be stored and retrieved, ensuring that a document, item, and related files associated with that particular revision are preserved.

Objectives

After completing this lesson, you will be able to:

- Describe the different ways a file or item can be revised.

- Explain the concepts of revision controlled documents and describe what released biased means.

- Understand how the concept of released biased revisions gives the designer increased flexibility in the design process.

- Use the Change Revision command to manually revise a file or item.

Revision Controlled Documents

When using documents that are related to each other, such as an assembly and its referenced components, a relationship is created between the specific revisions of those documents. When an assembly is checked into a vault, the revision of each of its components is recorded so that when that revision is recalled, each related document is retrieved using the recorded revision.

Editing a referenced file without creating a new revision

If a document references other files and those files are edited without bumping the revision, the referencing document will consume the edits. For example:

1. Revision A of an assembly references revision B of a part.

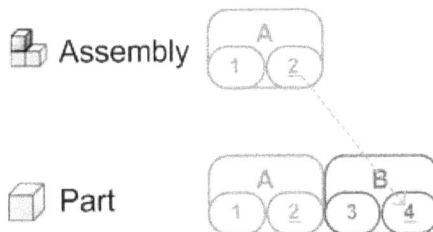

2. Changes are made to revision B of the part after revision A of the assembly has been checked in.

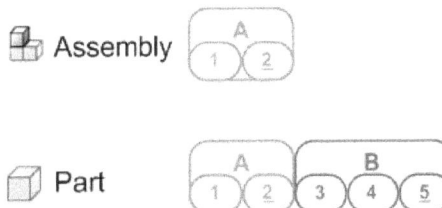

3. The changes to revision B of the part will show in revision A of the assembly when it is next checked out or opened.

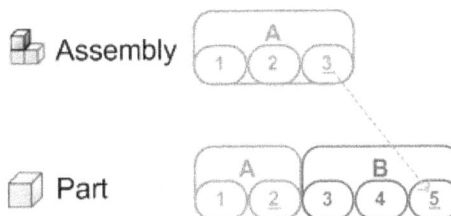

Editing a referenced file after creating a new revision

If a document references other files and a new revision is created for one of those files, the referencing document still maintains a relationship with the original revision. For example:

1. Revision A of an assembly references revision B of a part.

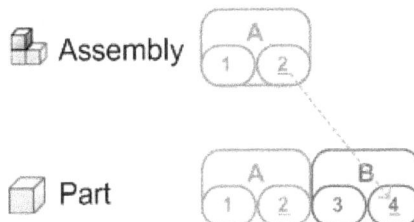

2. A new revision of the part is created and labeled C.

3. Edits are made to revision C of the part.

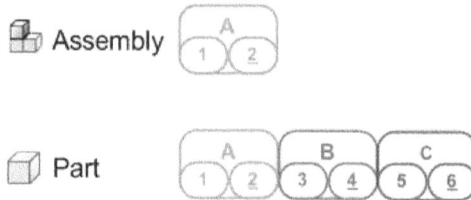

4. The changes to revision C of the part will show in revision A of the assembly if the Revision in the Get/Check Out dialog box for the Assembly is set to Latest.

Revisions and Lifecycles

Using revisions and lifecycles together provides significantly more flexibility than revisions alone can provide. For example, a given revision of a component can be edited and released out of context of any referencing assemblies, and the released changes will be used when the assembly is opened.

What does it mean when a revision is marked as released?

When a version in a revision is marked as released, it is given priority over newer versions and will represent the revision. This prioritization is known as a released bias and is an option that can be toggled off in several of the dialogs.

Note: Versions marked as released can never be purged from the system and can only be deleted by an administrator.

What does Released Biased mean?

Released biased is an option in several of the dialogs indicating that released data should take priority over non-released data. This will help to ensure that new, non-released revisions of parts are not consumed unintentionally. This option can be toggled off.

Note: Released bias is enabled by default.

Example 1: Released Biased Options in Vault Workgroup

In the following illustration, Assembly1.iam is in a Release state at Revision A. It uses two parts. Part1.ipt is in a Work In Progress state at Revision C. Part2.ipt is in a Released State at Revision A.

		File Name	Revision	Version	State	Comment
		Assembly1.iam	A	3	Released	Released at Rev A
		Part1.ipt	C	8	Work in Progress	edited at C
		Part2.ipt	A	3	Released	Released at Rev A

Uses tab of Assembly1.aim is shown in the next illustration.

	File Name	Revision		State	Comment	
	Assembly1.iam	A	3	Released	Released at Rev A	
	Part1.ipt	B	6	Released	Released at rev B	
	Part2.ipt	A	3	Released	Released at Rev A	

Released Biased
Use released data for related files when available.

By default the view is Released Biased. The Released revision of Part1.ipt is shown. In the next illustration the Released Biased option is toggled off.

	File Name	Revision		State	Comment	
	Assembly1.iam	A	3	Released	Released at Rev A	
	Part1.ipt	C	8	Work in Progress	edited at C	
	Part2.ipt	A	3	Released	Released at Rev A	

Non-Released Biased
Use newer edits for related files.

In this case, the Uses tab shows that the assembly uses the Work In Progress Revision C of Part1.ipt.

Example 2: Released Biased Option in Inventor

Using the parts shown in the previous example, a new Assembly2.iam file is created in Autodesk Inventor software. The Place From Vault command is used to place an instance of Part1.ipt in the new Assembly.

The default in Autodesk Inventor is to use Non-Released Biased revisions. If the part were placed and the assembly checked in the results in the Uses tab of Assembly2.iam is shown in the illustration below.

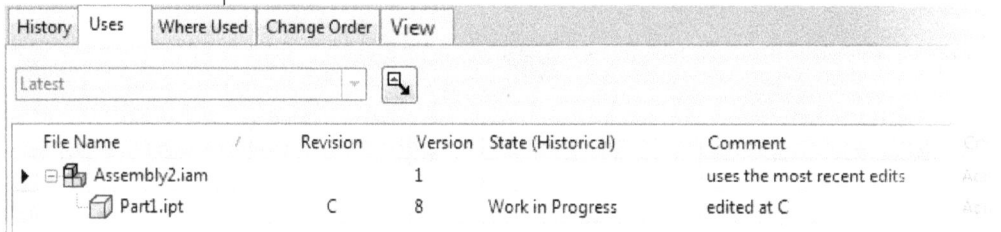

Another Assembly3.iam file is created. The Place From Vault command opens the Select From Vault dialog box. This time the user specifies to use the Released version of Part1.ipt. Note the Released Bias indicator now shows that the released data will be used.

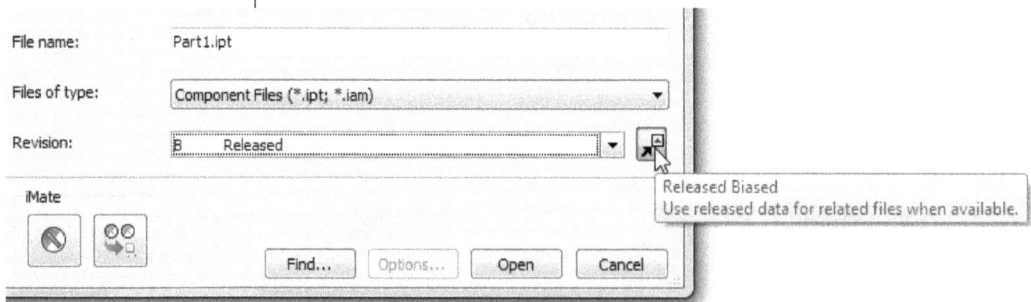

When this new assembly is checked in, the Uses tab shows that the Released revision of Part1.ipt is used.

What does leading mean when referring to a version or revision?

The leading version is always the latest version of a file, even if Released Bias is enabled.

The leading revision is always the latest version of the latest revision of a file, even if Released Bias is enabled.

Change Revision Command

You can also change the revision in the Autodesk Inventor software by selecting Revise in the Vault tab>Control panel or in the shortcut menu in the Autodesk Vault Browser.

The Change Revision command is used to manually create a new revision of a file or item.

The Change Revision command is available in the following location:

*   In the Actions menu

Procedure: Revise a File or Item

To create a file revision using the Change Revision command, do the following:

1. Select the file or group of files from the main pane that are to be changed. If you need to change a set of related files you can use the options in the dialog box to select these for you. If the files are not related use <Shift> + select or <Ctrl> + Select option to select the files from the list.

2. Select Change Revision in the Actions menu.
3. The Change Revision dialog box displays with the selected file(s).

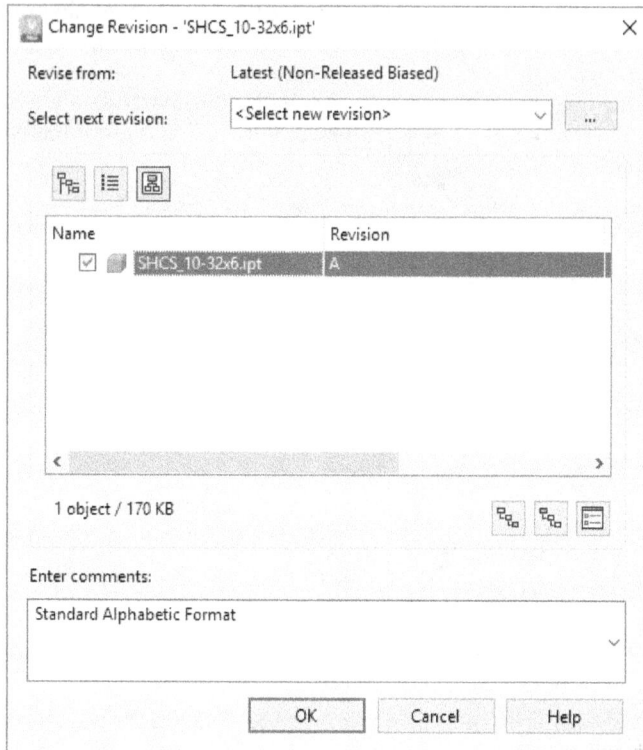

You can also specify that the value of a user defined property can be used to create the next revision. In a later lesson you will learn how you can map a file property value to a user defined value. This is especially useful when the authoring application controls the revision. For example, you might want to use the Autodesk Inventor Rev Number file property to control the revision.

4. The dialog box indicates that the latest non-released biased revision will be copied to the new revision. In the Select next revision drop-down list, indicate which revision scheme format type (primary, secondary, or tertiary) will be used to determine the next revision.

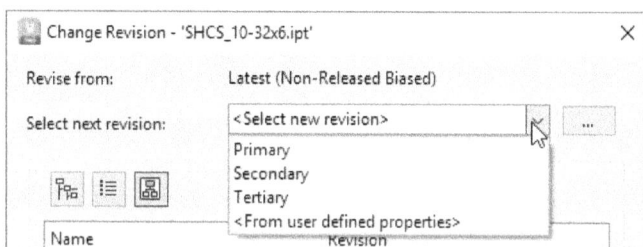

5. To change the revision scheme definition to use to generate the next revision, select the button next to the drop-down list to display the Change Revision Definition dialog box. Select the new revision scheme definition from the list. Select OK to dismiss the dialog box and return to the Change Revision dialog box.

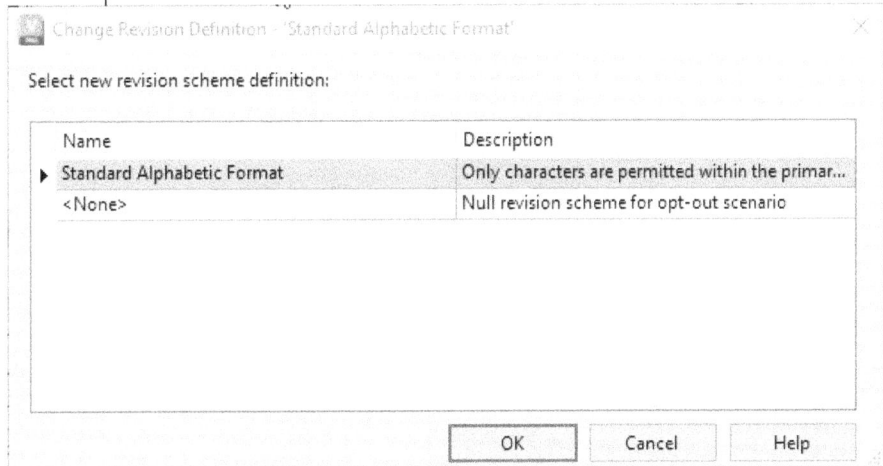

Change Revision Definition - 'Standard Alphabetic Format'

Select new revision scheme definition:

Name	Description
▶ Standard Alphabetic Format	Only characters are permitted within the primar...
<None>	Null revision scheme for opt-out scenario

OK   Cancel   Help

6. Use the View buttons to change the view to help understand file relationships.

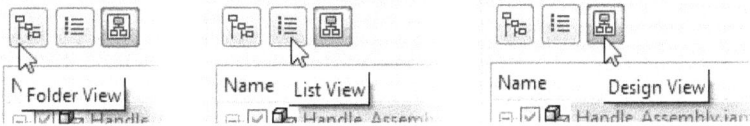

Folder View   List View   Design View

7. Use the Parent / Child selection buttons to modify the selection.

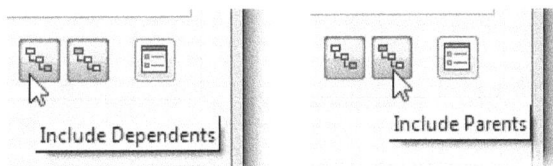

Include Dependents   Include Parents

8. Select Settings to display the Setting dialog box. Here you can refine the selection of related files.

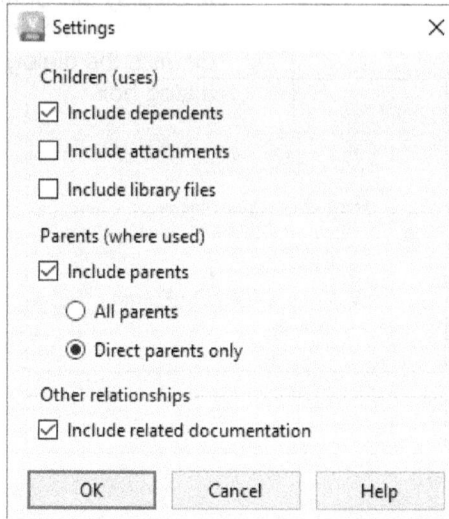

9. Select a comment from the drop-down list (if configured) or enter a custom comment.

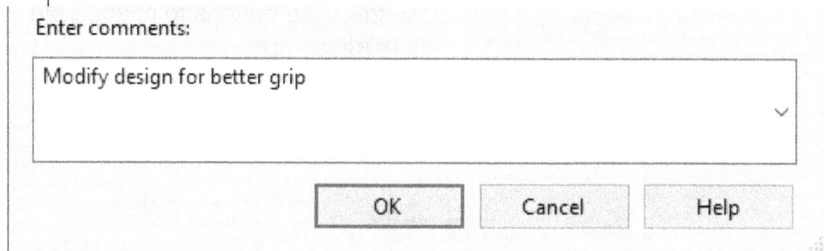

10. Select OK to complete the procedure.

Practice 3b | Revise a File

In this practice, you will release the Clamp Handle Assembly to Manufacturing. Based on feedback from the users, Handle is not long enough to generate the required clamping force. So you will then create two design variations of a new handle, assigning a revision for both variants. The first revision will be created by changing the lifecycle state and the second revision will be created manually. Finally, you will then design a new handle assembly using both the released and non-released revisions of the handle.

The completed practice

Task 1 - Release assembly.

1. Log in to Autodesk Vault Workgroup using the following information:

   - For the user name, enter **userb**.
   - For the password, enter **vault**.
   - Select AOTCVault from the list of Vaults.

2. In the Navigation pane, go to Project Explorer ($), expand the directory and select Designs, expand the directory and then select Clamp.

3. In the Main pane, select the file Handle_Assembly.iam.

4. Select Change State from the Behaviors toolbar.

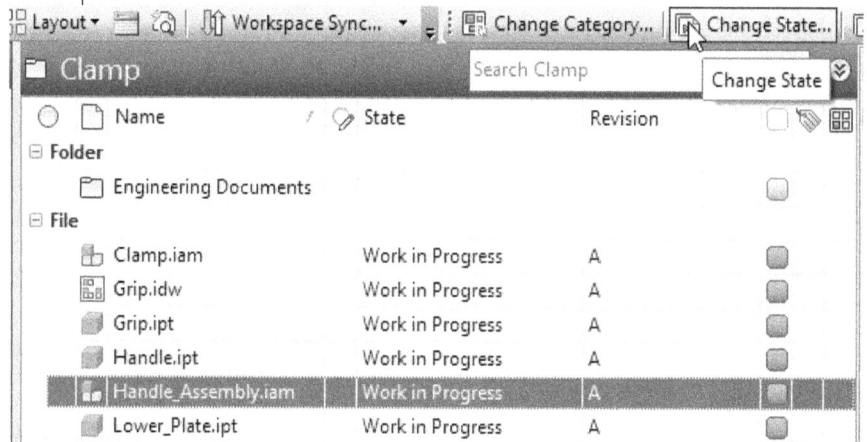

5. In the Change State – 'Handle_Assembly.iam' dialog box, do the following:

- In the right side drop-down list, select Released.
- Select the Folder View from the display option buttons above the file list.
- Select Include Dependents from the options buttons below the file list.
- Select all of the files in the files list.
- In the Enter Comments text box, enter **Release to manufacturing**.
- Select OK to complete the state change.

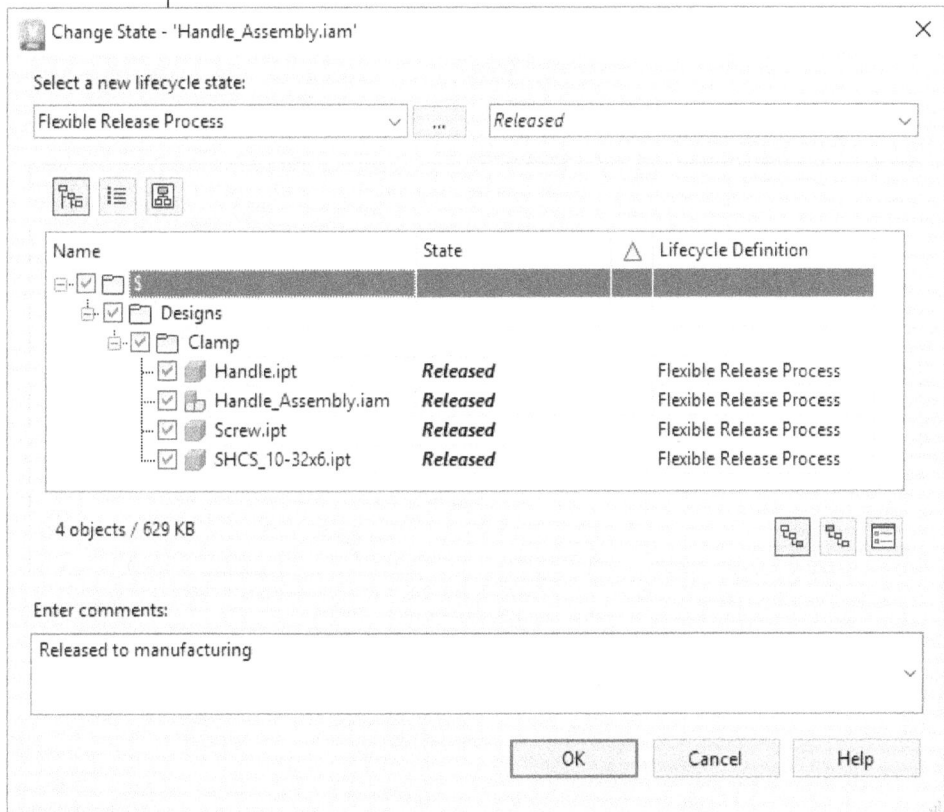

6. Review the results.

The handle assembly and its constituent parts are in the Released State at Revision A. The constituent part files are locked and cannot be edited.

Clamp		Search Clamp			
○ ▯ Name / ◇	State	Revision		▢ 🏷 ▦
⊟ Folder				
⊡ Engineering Documents				▢
⊟ File				
🔧 Clamp.iam	Work in Progress	A		▢
📑 Grip.idw	Work in Progress	A		▢
⬦ Grip.ipt	Work in Progress	A		▢
🔒 ⬦ Handle.ipt	Released	A		▢
🔒 🔧 Handle_Assembly.iam	Released	A		▢
⬦ Lower_Plate.ipt	Work in Progress	A		▢
⬦ Pin_A.ipt	Work in Progress	A		▢
⬦ Pin_B.ipt	Work in Progress	A		▢
⬦ Pivot_Lower.ipt	Work in Progress	A		▢
⬦ Pivot_Threaded.ipt	Work in Progress	A		▢
🔒 ⬦ Screw.ipt	Released	A		▢
🔒 ⬦ SHCS_10-32x6.ipt	Released	A		▢
⬦ Upper_Plate.ipt	Work in Progress	A		▢

Task 2 - Create new revision using lifecycle state change.

The first step will be to change the lifecycle state of the handle part to Work In Progress using the Change State command. Because the lifecycle state transition from Released to Work In Progress specifies a new Revision to be made (Bump Primary Revision) the file.

▦ Transition		✕
From State:		To State:
Released	➡	Work in Progress

Criteria Actions Custom Job Types Security

Filter:

All	⌄
☑ Bump primary revision	⌄
☐ Synchronize properties using Job Server	⌄

1. Select the file Handle.ipt in the file list. Right-click and select Change State.

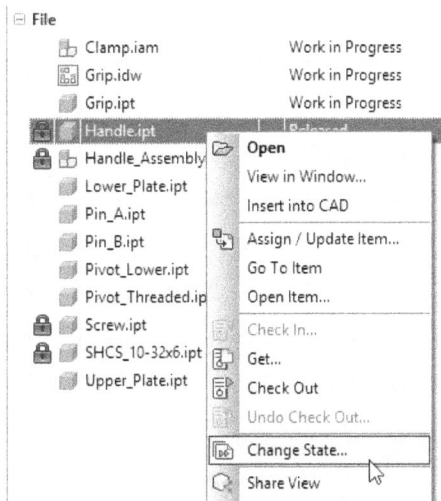

2. In the Change State dialog box, do the following:

   - In the right side of Select a new lifecycle state section drop-down list, select Work In Progress.
   - In the file list, ensure that the only file selected is Handle.ipt
   - In the Enter Comments text box, enter **Create design variations**.
   - Select OK to complete the state change operation.

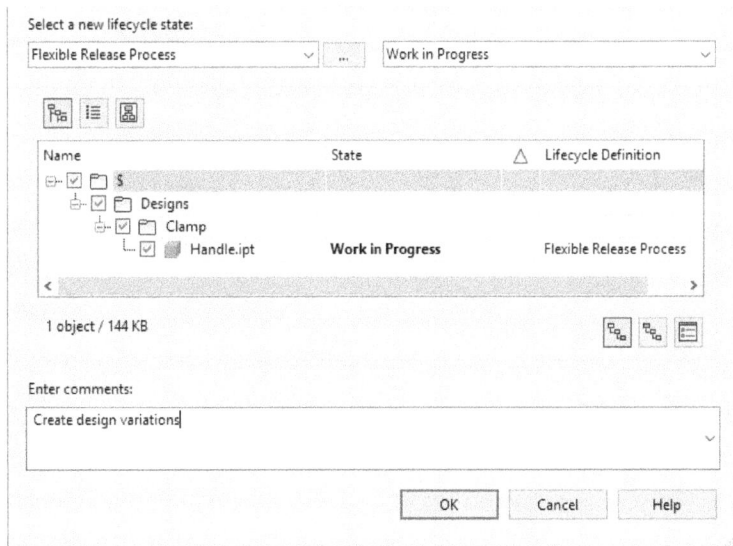

3. Review the results.

File				
Clamp.iam	Work in Progress	A		⬤
Grip.idw	Work in Progress	A		⬤
Grip.ipt	Work in Progress	A		⬤
Handle.ipt	Work in Progress	B		⬤
Handle_Assembly.iam	Released	A		⬤
Lower_Plate.ipt	Work in Progress	A		⬤

Changing the lifecycle state of the file bumped the primary version to 'B'. The file is no longer locked and can be edited.

4. Double-click on the file Handle.ipt to open it in Autodesk Inventor. When the Open file dialog box displays prompting you to check out the file, click Yes.

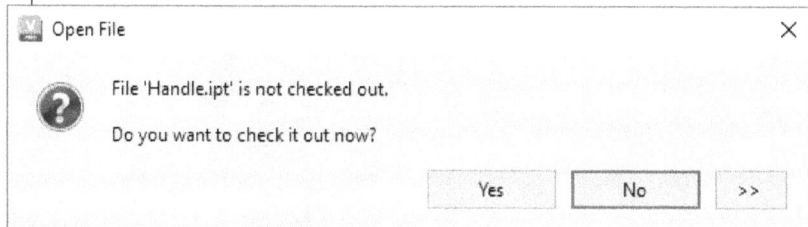

Open File   ✕

?   File 'Handle.ipt' is not checked out.

Do you want to check it out now?

[Yes]   [No]   [>>]

5. In Autodesk Inventor software, right-click on Extrusion1 in the Model Browser and select Edit Feature.

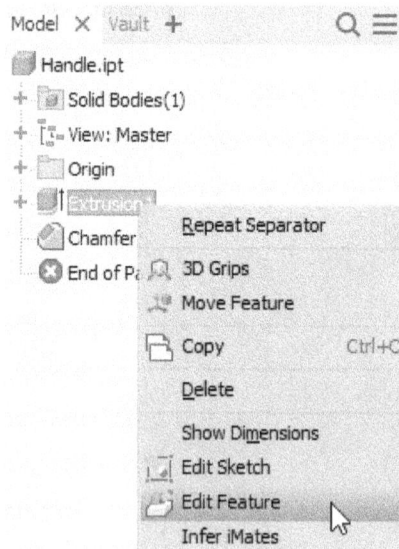

Model ✕ Vault +   🔍 ≡

Handle.ipt
+ Solid Bodies(1)
+ View: Master
+ Origin
+ Extrusion
Chamfer   Repeat Separator
End of Pa   3D Grips
              Move Feature
              Copy   Ctrl+C
              Delete
              Show Dimensions
              Edit Sketch
              Edit Feature
              Infer iMates

6. In the Properties dialog box, enter **4** in the Distance A field. Click OK to dismiss the dialog box and change the length of the shaft.

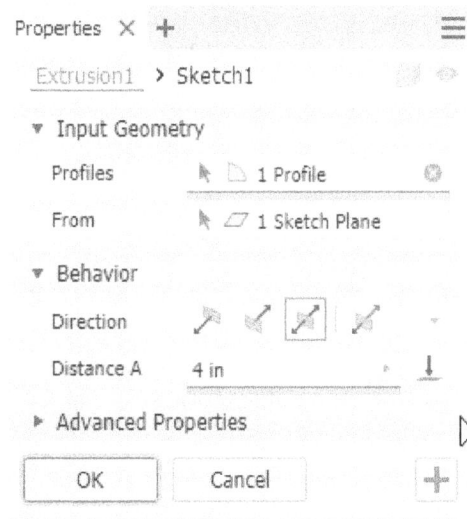

7. In the Vault tab, in the File Status group, click Check In.

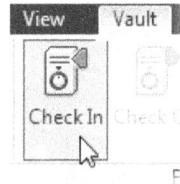

8. In the Vault dialog box, click Yes when prompted to save the file.

9. When the Check In 'Handle.ipt' dialog box displays, enter the comment **Changed length to 4'** and select OK to check the file in.

10. View the results. A new Version is created. The Revision is still 'B'.

Task 3 - Create new revision.

A design variation will be created using the secondary revision scheme format.

1. In Vault Workgroup, select the file Handle.ipt and then select Actions>Change Revision.

2. The Change Revision – 'Handle.ipt' dialog box displays.

3. In the dialog box, do the following:

   - In the Select next revision drop-down list, select Secondary.
   - Enter the comment **Create design variation** in the Enter comments dialog box.

4. View the result.

🔧 Clamp.iam	Work in Progress	A
📄 Grip.idw	Work in Progress	A
📄 Grip.ipt	Work in Progress	A
⚠ 📄 Handle.ipt	Work in Progress	B.1

   The Revision is now 'B.1'. A new version was created by copying the version from the leading version in Revision B.

5. Double-click on the file to open it in Autodesk Inventor. Following the steps above to create a new design variation do the following:

   - When the Open file dialog box displays asking if you want to check out the file, select Yes.
   - In Autodesk Inventor, double-click on Extrusion1 from the Model Browser.
   - In the Properties dialog box, enter **5** in the Distance A field.
   - Select OK to dismiss the dialog box and change the length of the shaft.
   - In the Vault tab, in the File Status group, select Check In.
   - In the Vault dialog box, click Yes when prompted to save the file.
   - The Check In 'Handle.ipt' dialog box displays. Enter the comment **Changed length to 5** and select OK to check the file in.

6. View the results. The Revision remains at 'B.1' and a new Version is created with the design change.

7. Select the file 'Handle_Assembly.iam' and then select the Uses tab. Review the results:

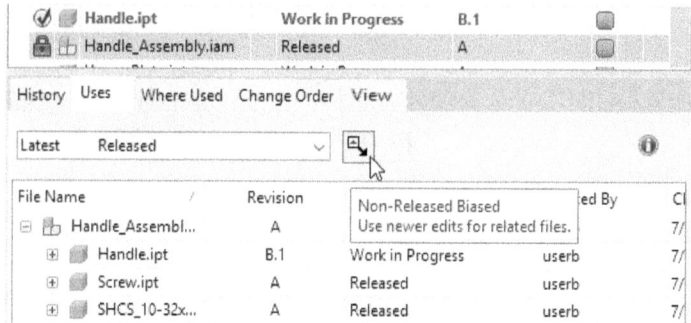

The default display shows the Non-released Biased configuration. The Handle Assembly shows the Work In Progress B.1 Version of the Handle as a child.

8. Select Non-Released Biased in the Uses tab to change it to Released Biased. Review the results:

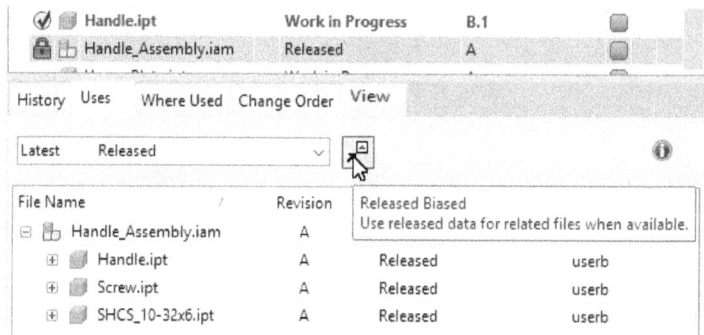

With the Released Biased option, the Handle Assembly shows the Released A Version of the handle as a child.

Task 4 - Create new assembly.

1. Open Autodesk Inventor software. Close any open files and Select New Assembly from the Quick Access toolbar to create a new assembly file.

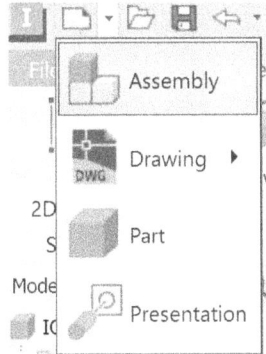

2. In the Vault tab, select Place.

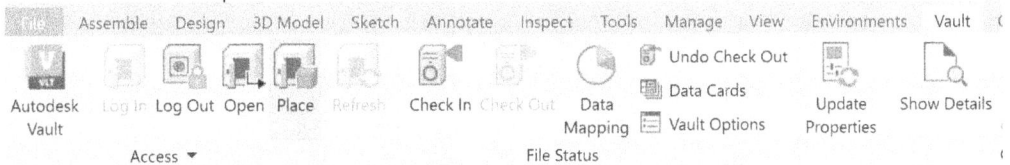

3. The Select File From Vault dialog box displays. Navigate to
    Designs\Clamp and highlight Handle.ipt. Next to the Revision
    drop-down list, note that Non Released Biased displays. In
    the drop- down field, Latest Work in Progress revision is
    shown.

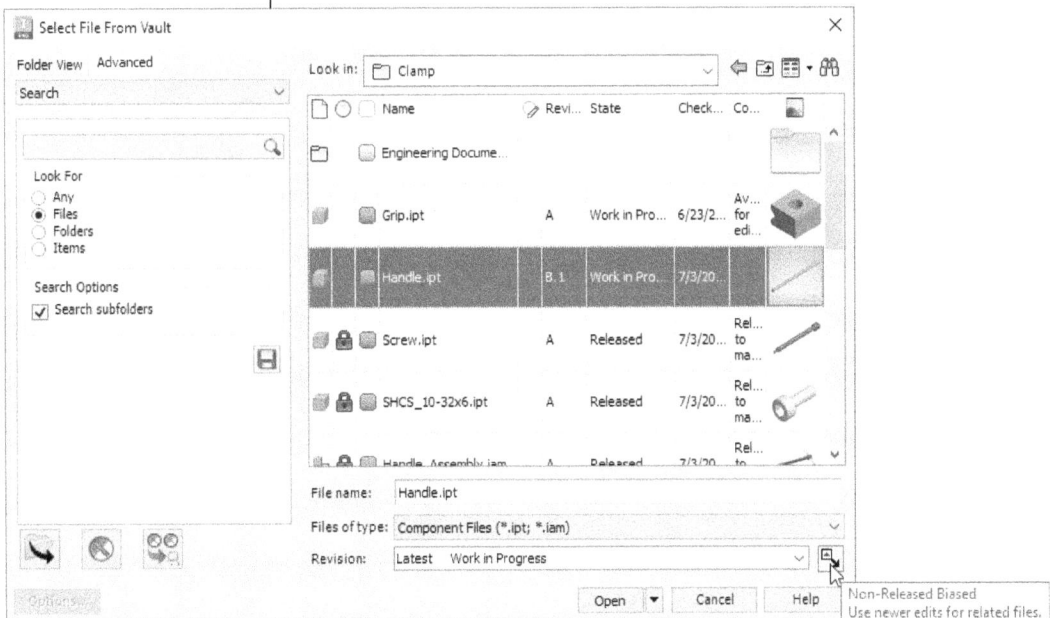

4. In the Revision drop-down list, select the Released Version A file.

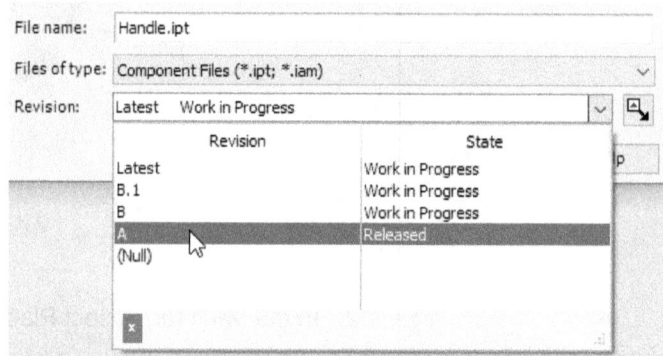

5. The button changes to Released Biased to show this is the released revision of the file.

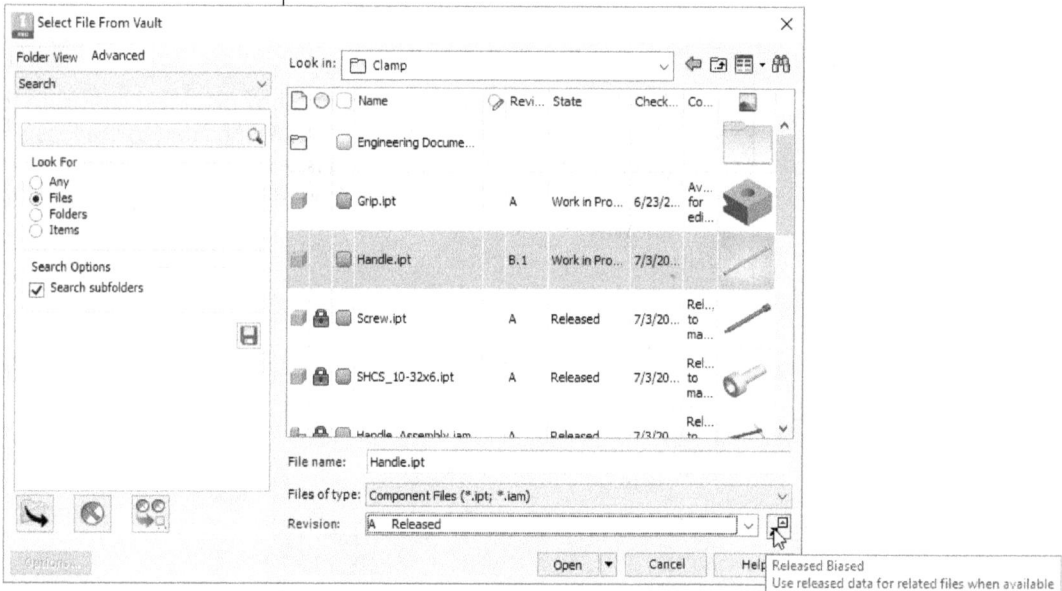

6. Cancel the operation. Close Autodesk Inventor software without saving the assembly file.

Roll Back the Lifecycle State of a File

Return a file or files to a previous lifecycle state with the Roll Back Lifecycle State Change command.

When a file is rolled back, it:

- returns to the file version associated with the rolled-back state.

- returns to the security, lifecycle definition, and revisions scheme associated with the rolled-back state.

- retains any property definitions associated with the current version.

The current version of the file is deleted when the file is rolled back to a previous state.

Rules for Rolling Back a File Lifecycle State

The lifecycle of a file can be rolled back if:

- the file is currently checked in.

- no parent versions consume the current child version that you want to roll back.

- the previous lifecycle state has not been deleted.

- the file is not in <null> definition.

- there is no label on the current version of the file.

- the administrator has not enabled the Restrict File and Item Lifecycle State Changes to Change Orders option.

Roll Back a File's Lifecycle State

You must be a Document Manager Level 2 or Administrator to roll back a file's lifecycle state.

1. Select one or more files in the main view and select Actions>Roll Back Lifecycle State Change.

   A dialog box displays describing to which state the file will be rolled back.

2. Click Continue to complete the lifecycle state rollback.

3.4 Chapter Summary

Revision management is a fundamental part of the product lifecycle management process. There is industry standards used to mark a file with a single or set of characters to denote its revision level. Revisions can be automatically incremented and assigned during lifecycle management processes or manually created to denote a significant event in the evolution of a product and the files associated with it. When used in conjunction with lifecycle states, Autodesk Vault Workgroup enables you significant flexibility in managing the revisions of related documents.

Having completed this chapter, you can:

- Describe the difference between a Revision and a Version and why both are important.

- Explain what Revision Schemes and Revision Scheme Formats are.

- Know the details of the Default Revision Schemes and Revision Scheme Formats supplied with Vault Workgroup.

- Know how to modify an existing Revision Scheme

- Create a new Revision Scheme.

- Describe the different ways a file or item can be revised.

- Explain the concepts of revision controlled documents and describe what released biased means.

- Understand how the concept of released biased revisions gives the designer increased flexibility in the design process.

- Use the Change State command to automatically revise a group of files or items.

- Use the Change Revision command to manually revise a file or item.

Categories in Autodesk Vault Workgroup

Categories enable the grouping of documents by predetermined labels. This labeling can be set up to happen automatically during check in based on rules or a user can manually change a category.

Learning Objectives in This Chapter

- Change a file or folder category.
- Create and edit categories.
- Assign rules to categories.

4.1 Categories and Rules

Overview

Categories in Autodesk® Vault Workgroup software are a powerful method of not only classifying different types of files or folders but automatically assigning other behaviors. Combined with Rules, as users add new files to the vault or migrate from Autodesk Vault, lifecycle definitions and states, revision schemes and revision levels and specific properties can be automatically assigned to the files. This ensures a very high level of both consistency and completeness to the data.

If you have Autodesk® Vault Professional software, you can also configure categories to items and custom objects.

Objectives

After completing this lesson, you will be able to:

- Understand the predefined categories.

- Change the category of a file or folder.

- Understand the basic category rules.

Categories

On one level, Categories are a very simple way of grouping different files or folders based on how your company creates, uses and manages those files or folders. A very common example is that of files created by CAD applications and those created by word processing and graphics applications. Historically and functionally, the process for creating and releasing a set of models and drawings that represent a product or component has been very different than supporting documentation such as specifications and graphics used by marketing and sales. The CAD-generated files often go through a more formal, multi-step review and change process where as the supporting documentation can be managed in a simpler 'Work In Progress' or 'Released' fashion.

Categories give you the flexibility to categorize the files or folders in a way that best suits your organization. With categories you can:

- Visually identify different types of file groupings or purposes.

- Assign one or more lifecycle states based on the category and specify the default lifecycle definition and state for a new or migrated file.

- Assign one or more revisions based on the category and specify the default revision scheme and initial revision for a new or migrated file.

- Assign a set of existing properties or metadata to the file based on the category.

Predefined File Categories

There are four preconfigured file Categories shipped with Autodesk Vault Workgroup. The details are listed in the table.

Name	Glyph	Description
Base		Default category for migrated data and new files if no other rules are setup.
Engineering		Data created for design purposes. Use this for the management of CAD-based files, such as Inventor, if you are going to use multiple file categories and have more formal lifecycle management needs.
Office		General data created by word processors, spreadsheet and image files. Use this for the management of office-type files if you are going to use multiple categories.
Standard		Standard design data created by any application. Use this for the management of any file formats if you are going to only use a single category and have simpler lifecycle management needs.

The predefined categories use the following lifecycle definitions, revision schemes and property sets.

Name	Lifecycle Definitions	Revision Schemes	Property Set
Base	None (opt-out scheme)	None (opt out scheme)	Biased towards Inventor file property mapped user defined properties.
Engineering	Flexible Release Process Long Lead Time Release Process None (opt out scheme)	Standard Alphabetic Format None (opt out scheme)	Biased towards Inventor file property mapped user defined properties.
Office	Simple Release Process None (opt out scheme)	Standard Numeric Format None (opt out scheme)	Biased toward standard file property mapped user defined properties.
Standard	Basic Release Process Simple Release Process None (opt out scheme)	Standard Alphabetic Format None (opt out scheme)	Biased towards Inventor file property mapped user defined properties.

Assigning Categories

When a file is added to the vault or a user migrates from Autodesk Vault Basic to Autodesk Vault Workgroup, files are automatically assigned the default category. For the default configuration this is the Base Category. This can be changed by the Administrator.

Predefined Folder Categories

There is one preconfigured folder Category shipped with Autodesk Vault Workgroup. The details are listed in the table.

Name	Glyph	Description
Folder		Default category for migrated data and new folders if no other rules are setup.

Change Category

The Change Category command enables the authorized user to change the current category to a new one. The file must not be a state which locks the file and the user must have the permission to change the category. For example, a file which is in a Released state cannot change category.

Changing the Category of a file will apply the default Lifecycle State Definition and State and the default Revision Scheme and Revision if they have not been previously assigned. If they are, changing the category will not change the current State or Revision. If the file was assigned a Lifecycle Definition and Revision Scheme in the current category, changing the category will not change the Lifecycle Definition or Revision Scheme. They must be manually changed after the category change.

Procedure: Change Category

To change the category of a file, use the following steps.

1. Before you attempt to revise a file you should determine whether you have permission to do so. You must be at least a Document Manager (Level 1) to revise a file. If you attempt to change the category and do not have permission to do so, you will not be informed until after you dismiss the Change Category dialog box (e.g. there is no precheck). You can have this permission as a user or by being a member of a group that has this permission. It is always best to manage permission at the Group level if possible.
2. The file must not be locked. Changing the category will create a new file version and new file versions cannot be created if the file is locked. Ensure that the file is not in a 'Released' state it has a lifecycle definition and state associated with it.
3. Select the file or group of files from the main pane that are to be changed. If you need to change a set of related files you can use the options in the dialog box to select these for you. If the files are not related use <Shift> + select or <Ctrl> + Select option to select the files from the list.

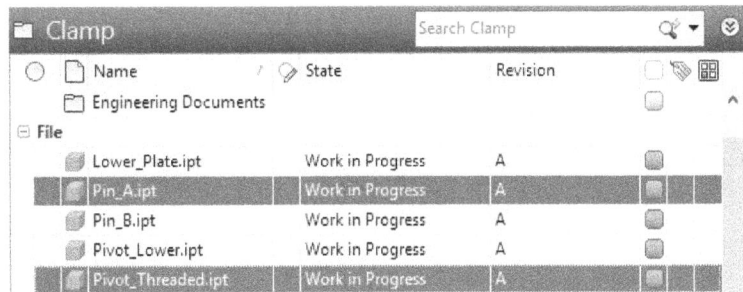

4. Select the Change Category from the Actions menu.

You can also change categories in Autodesk Inventor by selecting Change Category from either the Vault tab>Control panel or from the shortcut menu in the Autodesk Vault Browser.

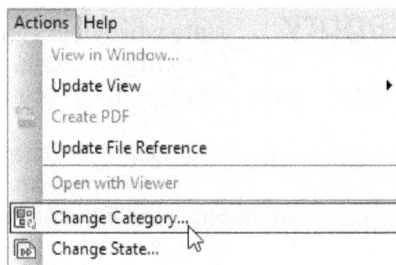

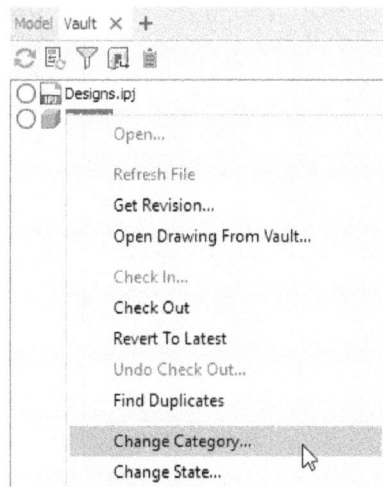

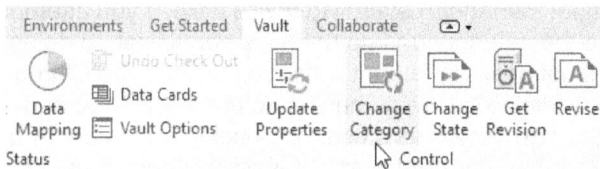

5. The Change Category dialog box displays.

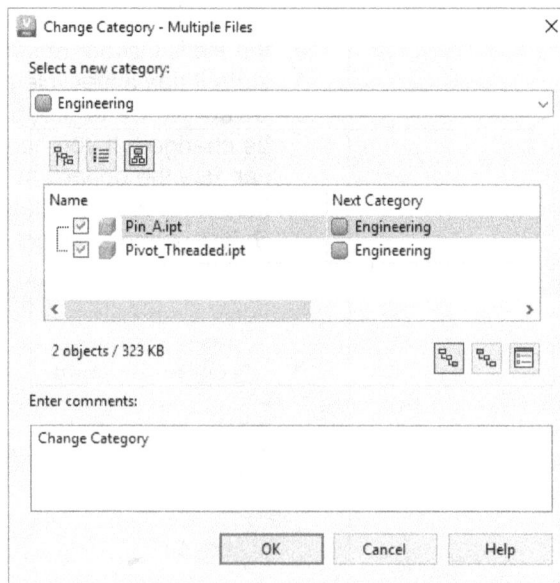

6. In the Select a new category section, select a new Category from the drop-down list. Alternatively, you can change the category in the New Category column for each individual file.

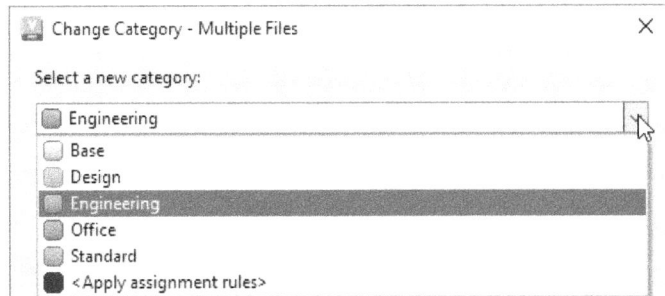

7. Use the View buttons to change the view to help understand file relationships.

8. Use the Parent / Child selection buttons to modify the selection.

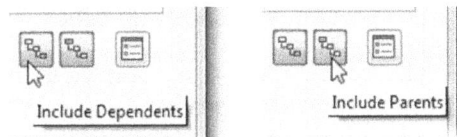

9. Select Settings to display the Setting dialog box. Here you can refine the selection of related files.

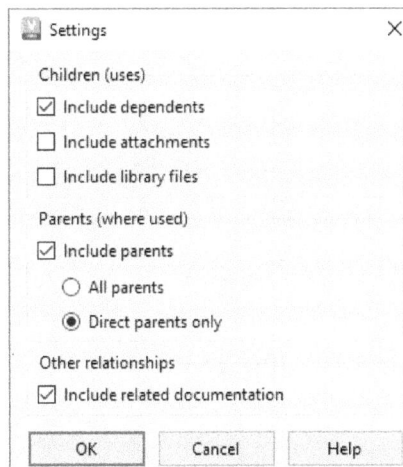

10. Accept the default comment, select a comment from the drop-down list (if configured), or enter a custom comment.

Enter comments:

Change Category

| OK | Cancel | Help |

11. Select OK to complete the procedure.

Rules

Rules enable you to automatically categorize a file based on one or more file property values. This gives you the ability to assign a category to a file when it is added to the vault using Autodesk Vault explorer or the CAD add-ins.

Rules works like the Advanced Find workflow in that you can specify a list of conditions to be met based on the system, user defined property values or filename values of the file being added. For example:

- Assign the file to the Engineering category if the filename ends with either 'IPT', 'IAM' or 'DWG'.

- Assign the file to the Office category if the user defined property Category contains 'document'.

- Assign the file to the Standard category if the user defined property Title contains 'Specification'.

Practice 4a | Changing Categories

In this practice, you will open the Autodesk® Inventor tutorial file Arbor_Press.iam and check it into Autodesk Vault. Ensure that Arbor_Press.exe has been extracted from the training dataset into *C:\AOTCVaultPro\VaultWorkingFolder\Designs* before beginning this practice.

1. Open Arbor_Press.iam in Autodesk Inventor and check in the file.

2. In Autodesk Vault, select the file Arbor_Frame.ipt under the Components folder.

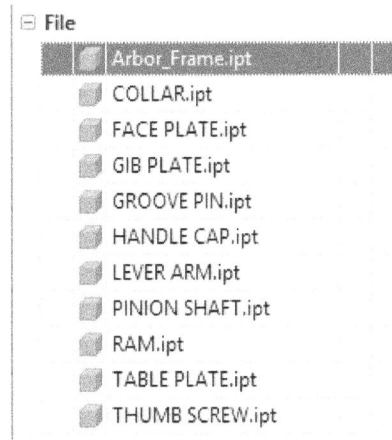

3. From the Actions menu, select Change Category.

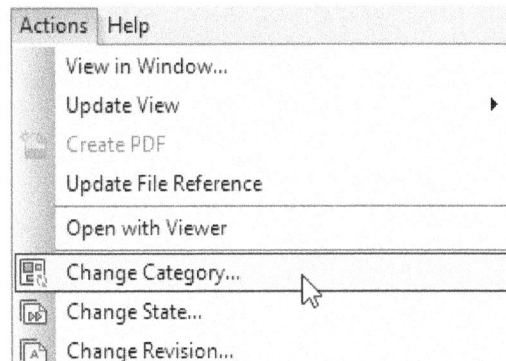

4. In the drop-down list in the Change Category dialog box, select Engineering and fill in the comment field with a sample comment.

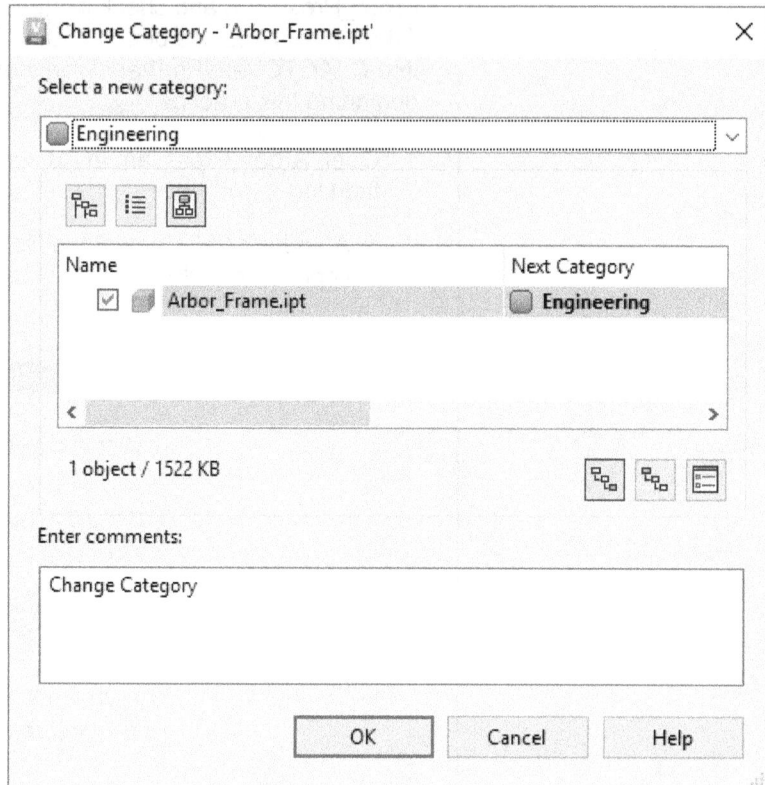

5. Click OK.

4.2 Managing Categories and Rules

Overview

The Administrator can create and configure Categories to specify the category glyph, Lifecycle Definitions, Revision Schemes, and Property sets that will be assigned when a file is assigned a Category. The Administrator can also create and manage a set of rules to automatically assign a file to a Category when it is added to the system.

Objectives

After completing this lesson, you will be able to:

- Edit a category.
- Add a custom category.
- Delete a category.
- Apply rules to a category.

Managing Categories

The Administrator can manage the set of Categories using the Configure Categories dialog box.

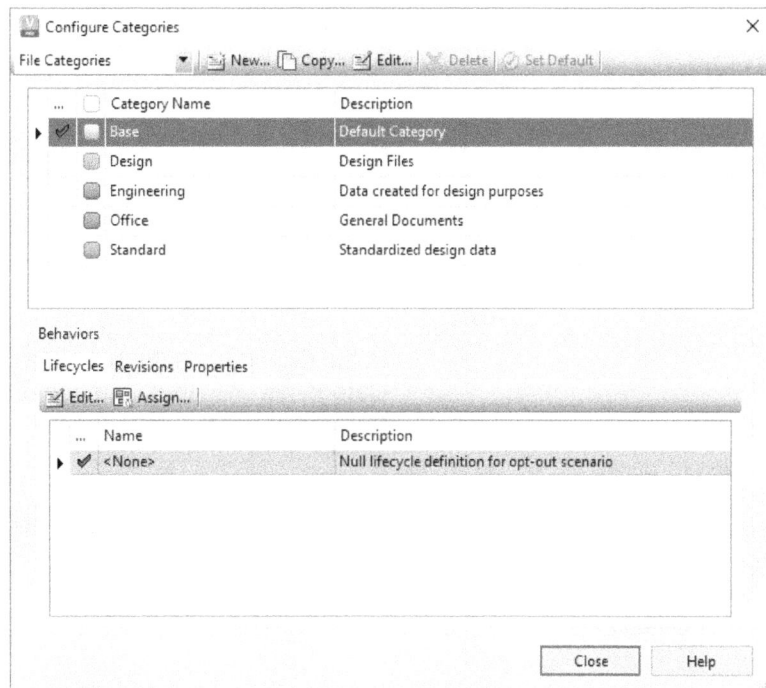

New Categories can be created and existing Categories can be edited. Categories that are not required and have not been used can be deleted. The category assigned to new files during migration or in the absence of any rule can be changed.

Procedure: Create Category

If the categories provided do not meet your requirements you can create a new one by doing the following.

1. From the Tools menu, select Administration>Vault Settings.

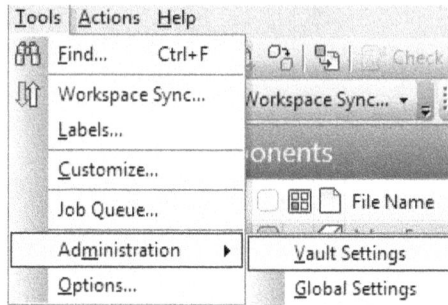

2. Select the Behaviors tab and click Categories....

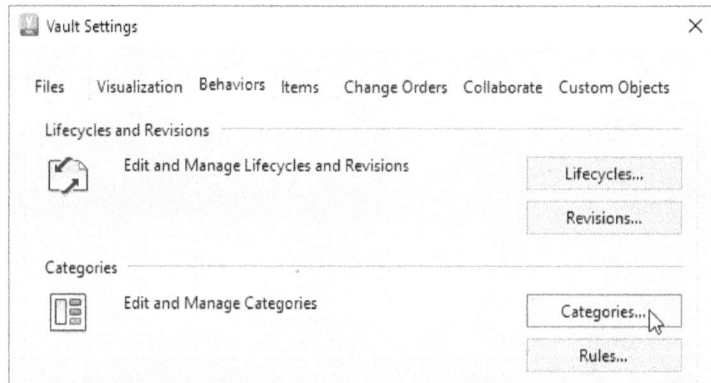

3. In the Configure Categories dialog box, select either File Categories or Folder Categories from the drop-down list and then select New.

If you are using Autodesk Vault Professional software, you can also create Item Categories and Custom Object Categories.

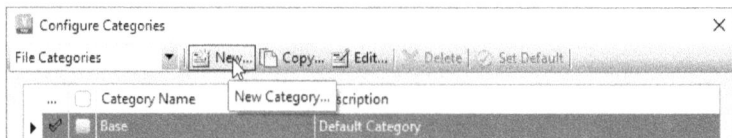

4. In the Category Edit dialog box, enter a Name and Description for your new category. Select a color for the new category and click OK.

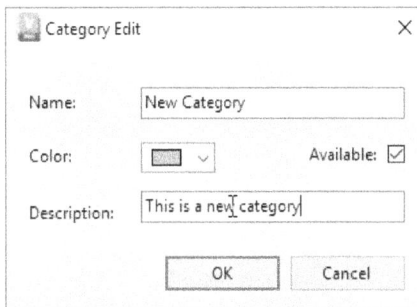

Procedure: Editing Category

Once you have a base category defined, or for any of the existing categories, do the following to edit:

1. In the Tools menu, select Administration>Vault Settings.

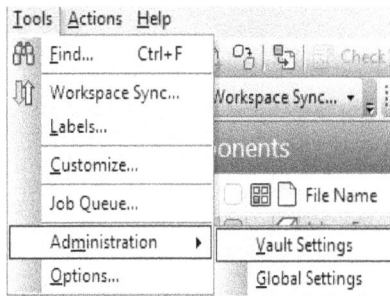

2. Select the Behaviors tab and click Categories.

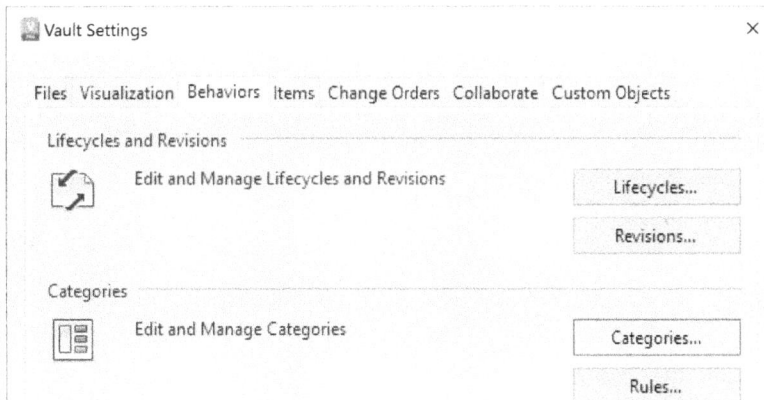

3. In the Configure Categories dialog box, select either File Categories or Folder Categories from the drop-down list and then select the Category you want to edit. Select Edit.

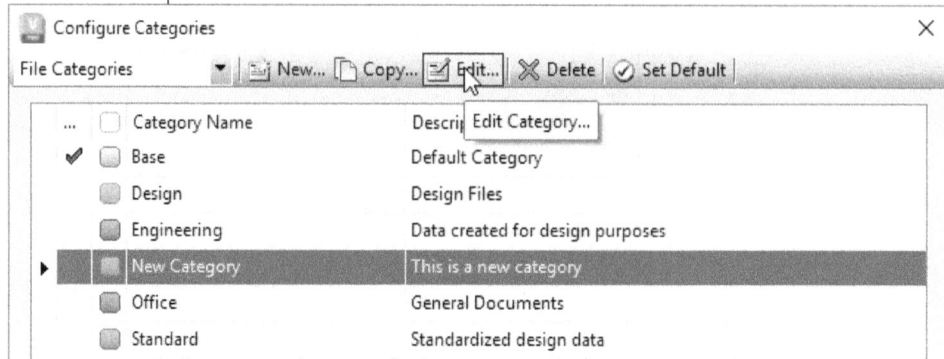

4. Make any changes to the category and click OK.

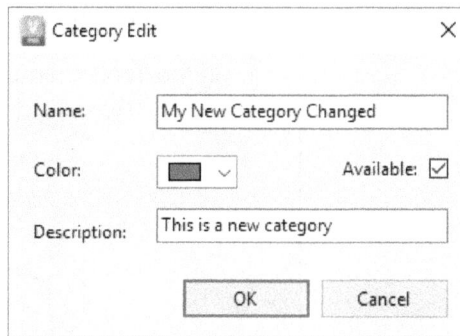

Procedure: Apply Rules for Categories

Once you have a new category defined, or for any of the existing categories, do the following to edit

1. From the Tools menu, select Administration>Vault Settings.

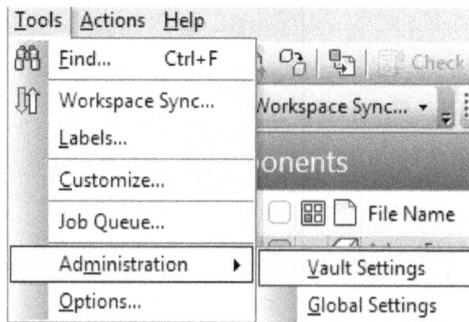

2. Select the Behaviors tab and click Rules.

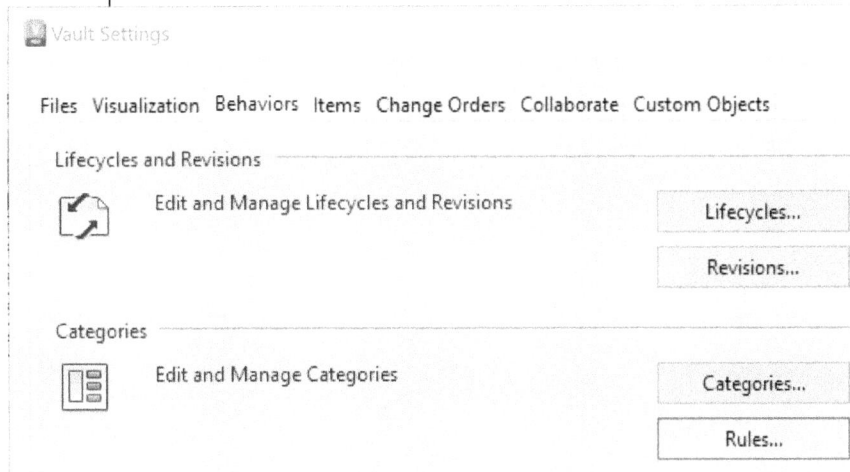

Vault Settings ✕

Files Visualization Behaviors Items Change Orders Collaborate Custom Objects

Lifecycles and Revisions

Edit and Manage Lifecycles and Revisions

Lifecycles...

Revisions...

Categories

Edit and Manage Categories

Categories...

Rules...

3. In the Assign Rules dialog box, select New.

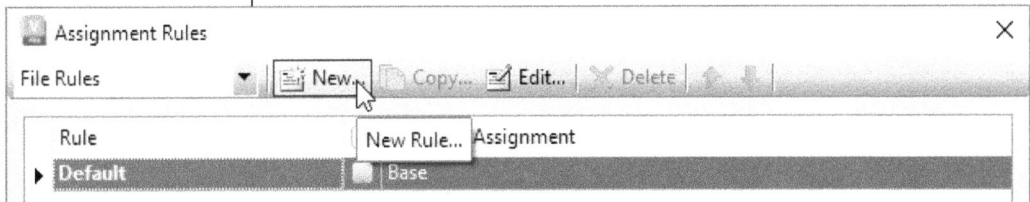

Assignment Rules ✕

File Rules ▼ | New. | Copy... | Edit... | Delete | ⬆ ⬇

Rule		Assignment
Default	New Rule...	Base

4. You will make a rule to apply the Engineering Category to all Autodesk Inventor part files. Name the rule Inventor Parts and select the Engineering category.

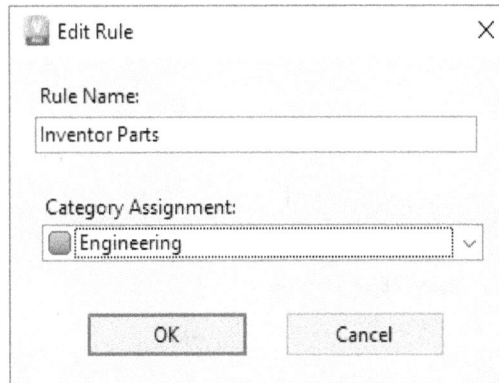

Edit Rule ✕

Rule Name:

Inventor Parts

Category Assignment:

Engineering ⌄

OK   Cancel

5. Once you click OK, the new rule is added to the list and you can select it to add the criteria. Select the Property Name to be File Name, select ends with in the Condition drop-down list, and set the Value as .ipt.

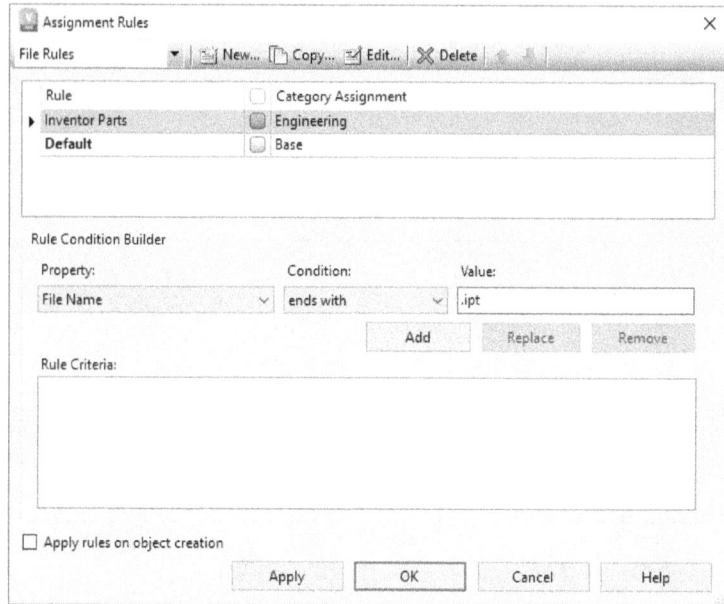

6. Click Add and the criteria is added automatically in the Rule Criteria section. Check the Apply rules on file creation option. Checking this box will place all new Autodesk Inventor parts in the Engineering category when they are checked in. Once this is complete click OK.

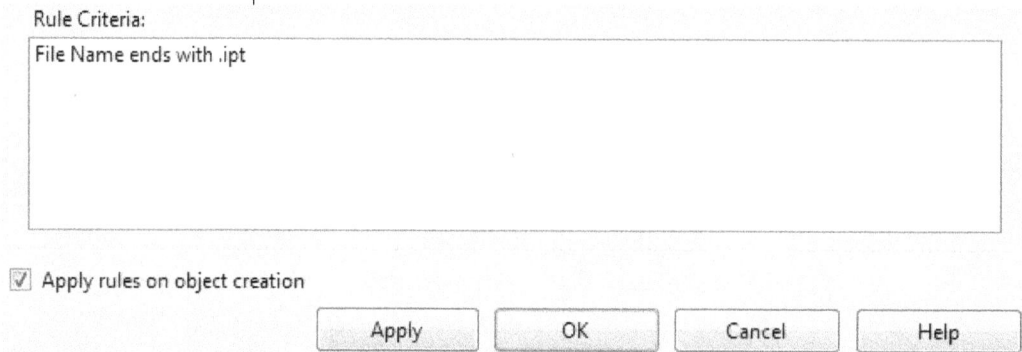

Practice 4b

Managing Categories

Use the procedures in this section to create your own category and at least one rule to apply this new category to files you can check in.

Task 1 - Create categories and apply rule.

---

1. Log in to Autodesk Vault Workgroup using the following information:

   - For User name enter **Administrator**.
   - Leave the password blank.
   - Select AOTCVault from the list of Vaults.

2. In the Tools menu, select Administration>Vault Settings.

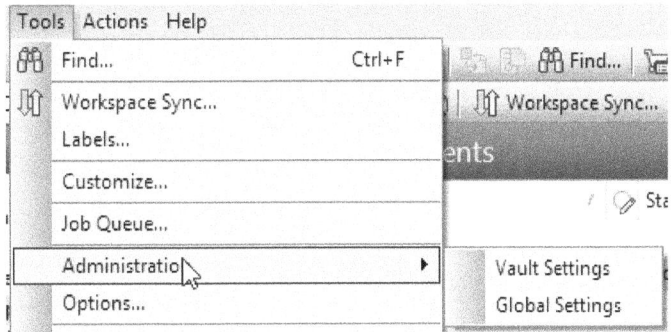

3. In the Behaviors tab, click Categories.

4. In the top left of the window, select File Categories.

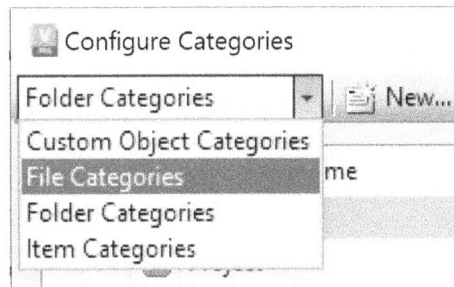

5. Click New….

- For the name, enter **Survey**.
- For color, select Green.
- In the Description field, enter **Survey Drawings.**

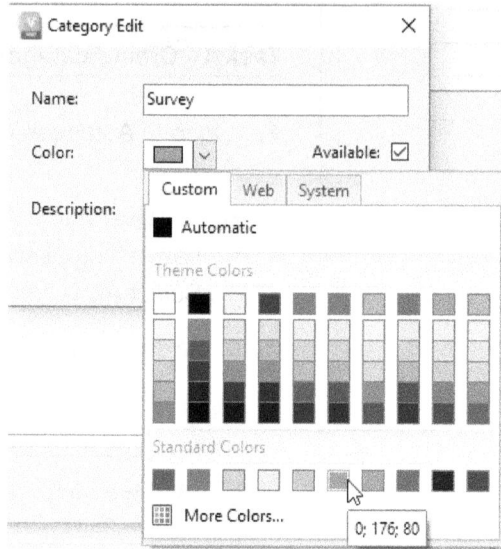

6. Repeat Step 5 for the following:

- For the name, enter **Civil**.
- For color, select Blue.
- In the Description field, enter **Civil Drawings**.

7. Repeat Step 5 for the following:

- For the name, enter **Architectural**.
- For color, select purple.
- In the Description field, enter **Architectural Drawings**.

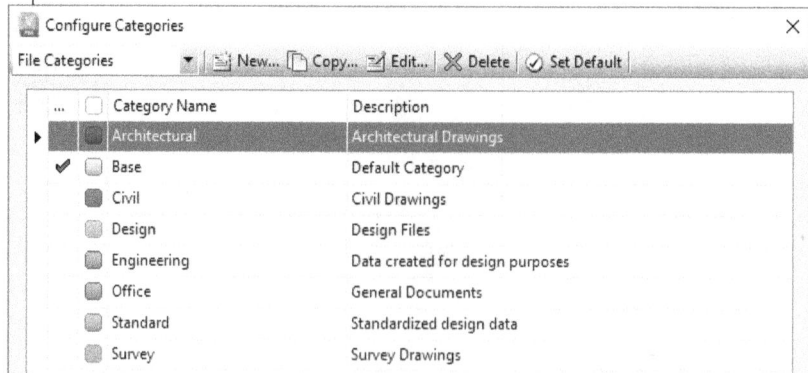

8. Close the Configure Categories dialog box.

9. In the Behaviors tab of the Vault Settings, click Rules.

10. Click in the top left window, select File Rules.

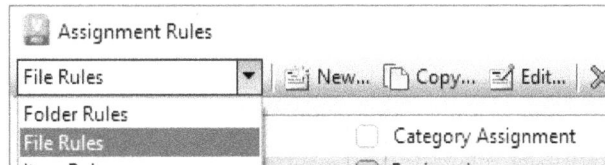

11. Click New... to create the following rules using the File Name property:

- Rule Name: Survey, Category Assignment: Survey, Condition: Starts with, and for the Value, enter **V-**.
- Rule Name: Architectural, Category Assignment: Architectural, Condition: Starts with, and for the Value, enter **A-**.
- Rule Name: Civil, Category Assignment: Civil, Condition: Starts with, and for the Value, enter **C-**.

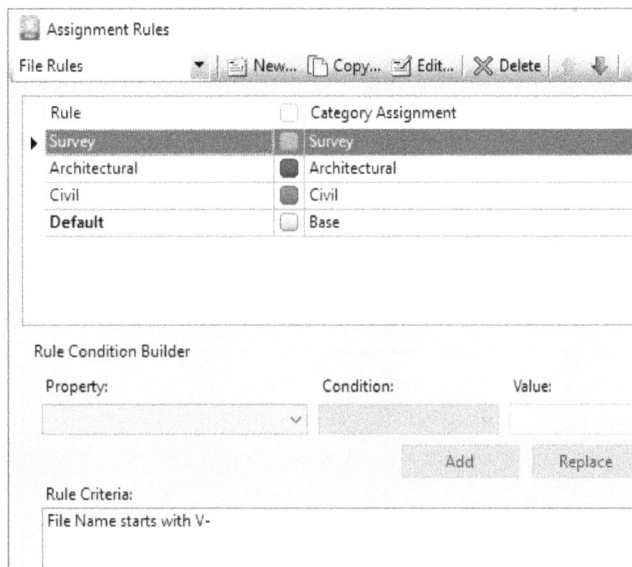

12. Select Apply rules on object creation and click Apply.

13. Click OK and close all dialog boxes and exit Autodesk Vault Workgroup.

4.3 Chapter Summary

Category management provides a way to group properties logically. Grouping by category provides a means for assigning a defined set of behaviors and rules to one or more files or items. A category labels the file or item and also sets the defined behaviors that can be used on the file or item.

Having completed this chapter, you can:

- Change a file or folder category.

- Create and edit categories.

- Assign rules to categories.

Managing Properties

Streamline your vault environment by managing property values for easier indexing and searching. Use the mapping feature to automatically update property values based on other file input, establishing property constraints to ensure that values meet your specifications.

Learning Objectives in This Chapter

- Understand the difference between system-defined properties and user-defined properties.
- Manage user-defined properties (Create new, Edit, Add or Remove Properties).
- Work with the Properties Grid in Autodesk Vault and Edit property values.
- Configure property constraints.
- Map Properties.

5.1 System-Defined Properties vs. User-Defined Properties

Overview

Properties are attributes associated with a file. Autodesk® Vault recognizes two types of property definitions: system-defined properties and user-defined properties (UDPs). System-defined properties are those properties that are derived from the vault. Autodesk Vault has a global set of properties that are applied to files in the vault. User-defined properties are created by using the administrative tools.

Objectives

After completing this lesson, you will be able to:

- Differentiate between System-Defined Properties and User-Defined Properties.

- Create, Delete, and Edit User-Defined Properties.

- Administrate System-Defined Properties in Vault Property Administration.

Learn About Terms, Data Types, and Attributes

Before working with properties, it is important to become familiar with the terms, data types, and attributes associated with the Autodesk Vault properties system.

The following table contains terms commonly used with properties.

Term	Definition
Associations	Attribute that determines whether the property is associated with a file, folder, item, or change order.
Compliant	The status of a property that meets all property policies and equivalence evaluations.
Data Type	The type of data accepted for the property value. This type can be text, number, Boolean, or date.
Database Property	Any property in the database, either user-defined or system.
Entity	An entity is the system class with which a file can be associated. Entities are files, items, or change orders.
Equivalent	The status of a mapped property when its value matches the source value.

File Property	A property associated with a file.
Mapped Property	A property from which the propriety being defined gets its value. For example, a UDP can get its value from several different file properties. A file property can get its value from a system property.
Mapping	A set of relationships between the property being defined and a property from which it receives its value. There can be multiple mappings for a given property definition.
Master	The property from which a mapped property gets its value. The master property writes its value to the subordinate property.
Non-compliant	The status of a property when it has failed to meet one or more property policies or its equivalence evaluation.
Non-equivalent	The status of a mapped property when its value does not match the source value.
Property Definition	All attributes and constraints about the property including its name, data type, initial value, mapping, minimum and maximum values, case values, in-use value, and basic search value. The name used in the GUI (graphical user interface) to identify the property.
Property Name	The name used in the GUI (graphical user interface) to identify the property.
Property Policy	Depending on the data type, the property policy specifies certain constraints that must be met. The constraints can include a value range, a value type, or a value format must be met. For example, a property policy can be described as follows: the property must have a value and that value must be in the range of 1 to 10. When a property fails to meet its property policies, it is considered non-compliant.
Property Value	The literal content of a property attribute for a specific file version.
Override	Determines whether the property value is overridden by the policy defined by its category.
Subordinate	The mapped property that receives its value from the master property.
System-Defined Property	A property in the database created by the system, which is then assigned to a file.
User-Defined Property (UDP)	A property in the database created by an administrator. The property can be applied to a file when it is added to a vault.

Every property value has a data type that determines how that value is read and processed.

Data Type Name	Description
Boolean	True or False.
Date Type	Can be a specific date or date range expressed by a beginning and end date.
Number	Numbers only.
Text	Letters, numbers, and punctuation.

Properties have attributes that determine how the property is described and the constraints for its value.

Attribute Name	Description
Basic Search	A constraint that determines whether or not the property should be included in basic searches.
Case Sensitivity	A constraint that applies to text data types. This constraint can be set to none, UPPER CASE, lower case, Name Case, or Sentence case.
Enforce List of Values	A constraint that determines whether the property must have a value from a list.
Initial Value	An attribute that specifies the initial property value when one is not specified.
	Note the initial values are best used with write mappings. If an initial value is set on a regular read mapping, that read mapping has higher priority and will overwrite the initial value. The only case in which an initial value will not be overwritten by a read mapping is if the value it maps to is blank.
List Values	Displays the List Type dialog box from which you can enter and order values for a list. At least one item must display in the list.
Minimum Length	The minimum number of characters a property value can have.
Maximum Length	The maximum number of characters a property value can have.
Requires Value	A constraint which determines whether the property must have a value to be compliant.

State	The state of a property definition specifies whether it is enabled or disabled in the vault. A disabled property is not displayed or searched and cannot be used to store a value for a given file.
Usage	Indicates the number of files currently using the property. Use this information to determine which properties are used more than others, to help decide which properties can be removed from the vault.

The main view in the vault client has a Property Compliance column that lists various status icons. The Icons in this column indicate whether a property associated with the file is compliant, non-compliant, pending, or has failed the equivalence evaluation.

Icon	Value	Definition
No icon	Compliant	All properties meet policy requirements and equivalence.
	Non-compliant	One or more properties do not meet property policy requirements or equivalence. Hover the cursor over the icon to learn more about why one or more properties failed compliance.
	Not calculated	There has been a change to one or more properties but equivalence and policy have not been verified yet.
	Pending	Properties are currently being evaluated for equivalence.
	Evaluation failed.	The equivalence evaluation failed. This is a rare situation and can result when the processor enters an evaluation loop. **Note:** In the Find dialog box, an evaluation failed value is added. This enables you to search for any files for which the evaluation failed.

Introduction to the Property Definitions Dialog Box

When files are checked into the Vault, only the properties that are set enabled are automatically extracted and indexed by default. All the extracted properties being tracked by the vault can be managed using the Property Definitions dialog box. The Property Definitions dialog box lists:

Property Name	The name of the property as it displays in the interface. The display name can be edited by the vault administrator.
Data Type	The type of data represented by the property. The data types are: text, number, date, and Boolean.
Usage	Indicates the number of files currently using the property. Use this information to determine which properties are used more than others, to help decide which properties can be removed from the vault.
State	Indicates whether or not the property is enabled for indexing and visible to the user. **Enabled** If a property is set to Enabled, the property is indexed and extracted from files when they are added or checked into the vault. **Disabled** If a property is set to Disabled, it is not indexed and it is not extracted from files when they are added or checked in to the vault. Administrators can clean up unwanted properties by marking them Disabled.
Associations	Lists the entity class that can use the property. Classes are files, folders, items, change orders, and custom objects.
Folder Categories	If the property is associated with a folder category, the category name displays. Category values will override property values if the property Override attribute is enabled.
File Categories	If the property is associated with a file category, the category name displays. Category values will override property values if the property Override attribute is enabled.
Item Categories	If the property is associated with an item category, the category name displays. Category values will override property values if the property Override attribute is enabled.
Basic Search	Indicates if a string property is searched when using the basic search feature. The possible values are: Searched: the property is included in the basic search. Not Searched: the property is excluded from the basic search. Not Allowed: the property is not a string value and therefore cannot be included in the basic search.

Important: When a new user-defined property is created, it does not have to be associated with any categories. However, even if the property is associated with an entity (e.g., file, folder, change order, item, or custom object), if it is not associated with any categories, it will not display in the properties grid for that entity.

When migrating an existing vault database, all existing properties set to Enabled are migrated. However, any new properties default to Disabled. To improve indexing performance, all properties without mappings are not created unless specified by the administrator.

Procedure: Renaming the Property

The display name of a property can be edited to make it more meaningful. Both system-defined and user-defined names can be changed by selecting Edit in the Property Definitions dialog box.

1. Select Tools>Administration>Vault Settings.
2. In the Vault Settings dialog box, select the Behaviors tab.
3. In the Properties section, click Properties. The Property Definition dialog box opens. Here you can rename the selected Property by using the command Edit.

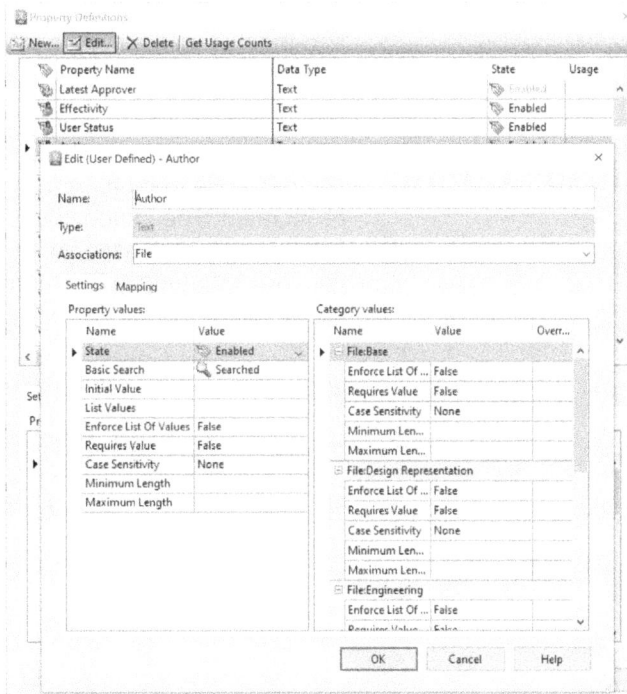

Change the State

The state of a property determines whether or not the property is included in the vault index.

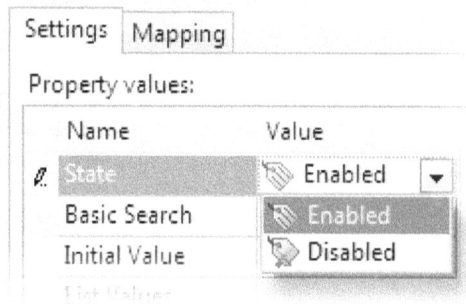

You specify which properties to include in the vault by setting the state to Enabled. Marking properties as Disabled lets administrators remove unused properties from view.

When a property is not in use, it is no longer associated with any files and it is removed from the index. This makes searching more efficient overall because there are fewer properties. You cannot search on a property that is not in use. You cannot display an unused property as a column in a grid. You cannot map properties to unused file properties. Unused properties can be re-associated with files by changing the state back to Enabled and then using the server console to re-index the properties.

Examining Usage Count

The usage count of a property tells you how prevalent the property is throughout the vault. The number in the Usage column is the number of files with which the property is associated. The usage count of a property tells you how many files have a value associated with them for this property. You will find the command in the menu pane of Property Definitions dialog box.

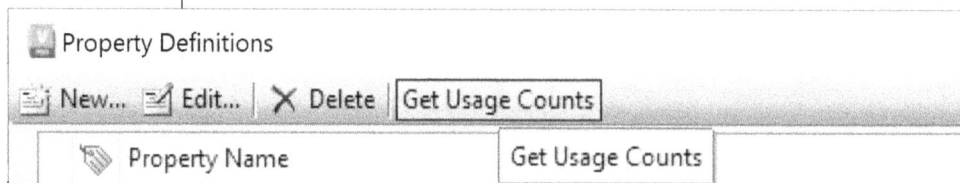

Specifying Searchable Properties

The Basic Search setting for a property determines whether or not that file property is available for searching when a basic search is performed. The Basic Search setting applies only to the basic search and not to searches using the query builder or the Find dialog box. Only string type file properties can be set to Searched.

String type file properties that are set to Searched are available for the basic search. Properties set to Not Searched are not currently available for the basic search. By setting unused file properties to Not Searched, you can increase search performance. Properties set to Not Allowed are not string type properties and are not available for the basic search. A property set to Not Allowed cannot be changed to any other setting.

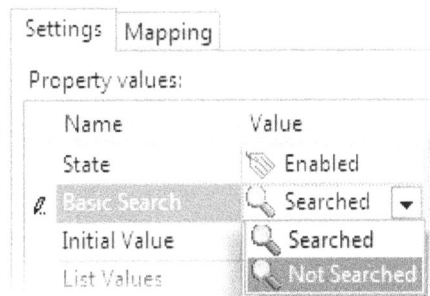

When the state of a property is set to Disabled, the basic search setting is automatically set to Not Searched. If that property is later set to Enabled, the basic search setting remains Not Searched. In order for the property to be available for searching, the administrator must manually set the property to Searched.

Initial Value

The Initial Value is applied once when the property is initially associated with an object. The initial value is only applied in the absence of a user-supplied or a mapped value.

The initial association occurs in three circumstances: 1) object is created (ex: adding a file or creating an item) 2) assignment to a category that automatically attaches the property, and 3) manual property attachment.

There are two types of Initial Value: static and mapped. The static value is a fixed value and can be any value that is valid for the selected data type. An initial mapped value copies the value from a file or BOM property.

Initial Values should NOT be used on properties where all regular mappings read the value from a file or BOM. A blank value in the mapped file or BOM field takes precedence over the initial value. This can appear as if the initial value is not applied when in fact the mapped value of 'blank' takes precedence.

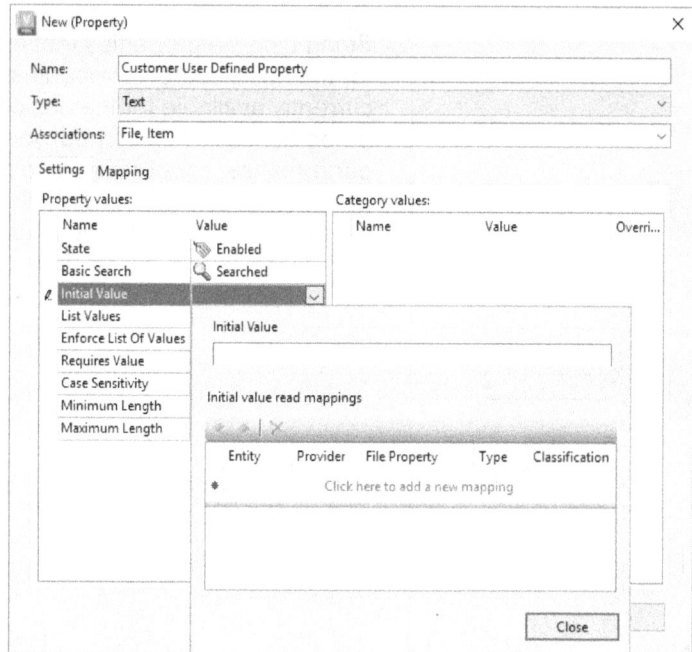

List Values

Properties of type Text and Number can provide a list of values for user selection and searching. The administrator can add or remove values from the list at any time. Removal of a value from the list does not remove the value from any property where that value has been applied. When specifying the value for this property, the user can choose from the list of values. Entering values that are not on the list is permitted. If this property is mapped to read a value from a file or BOM, the imported value is not required to be on the list.

Enforce List Values

When enabled, the Enforce List Values option provides a warning symbol adjacent to this property if the value is not on the list. When a value is in violation of this policy, the default configuration for lifecycle transitions will not permit for a file or item to be released.

Add or Remove a User-Defined Property

A user defined property (UDP) can be added to a file or removed from a file. When a new version of the file is created, the change to the property assignment is shown. You must have administrative access to perform these tasks. To use the Add & Remove Properties command, you cannot have the file checked out for edit.

Procedure: Add or Remove a Property

1. From the main file list, select one or more files.
2. Select Actions>Add or Remove Property.
3. In the Add or Remove Property dialog box, select the property from the Property list.
4. From the Action value of the property select Add or Remove from the drop-down list.

   - Add: The property is added to the selected file or files using the default value. If the property is already assigned to a selected file, no action is taken for that file.

   - Remove: The property is removed from the selected file or files. If the property is not assigned to a selected file, no action is taken for that file.

If a property is assigned by means of a category, it cannot be removed from a file.

If any restrictions occur with a selected file, the property is neither added nor removed and an error message displays.

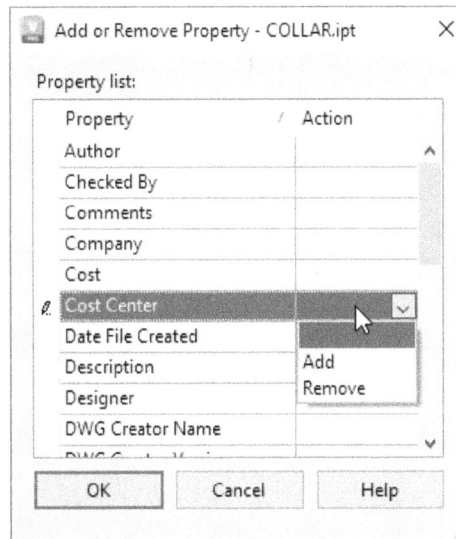

5. Click OK.

Practice 5a

Create a New User-Defined Property

In this practice, you will create a new User-Defined Property (UDP). After the new property is created, you will edit some settings and finally add this property to a selection of files.

Task 1 - Create a new UDP.

1. Click Tools>Administration>Vault Settings.

2. In the Vault Settings dialog box, Behaviors tab, click Properties.

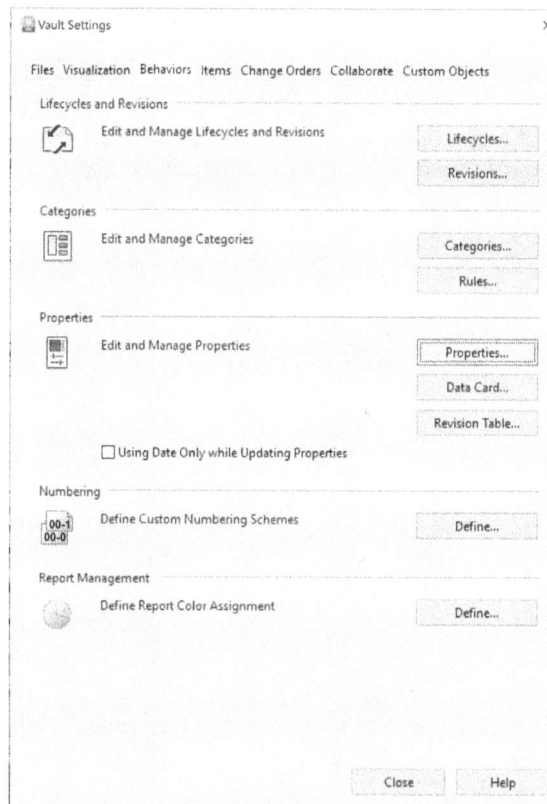

3. In the Property Definitions dialog box, click New.

4. In the New Property dialog box, enter a name.

5. In the Type list, select the property type.

6. Assign the UDP to one or more categories by selecting the category checkboxes in the Associations drop-down list. Categories can be preselected in this list based on the filter previously selected in the Property Definitions dialog box. You can select or clear categories as required.

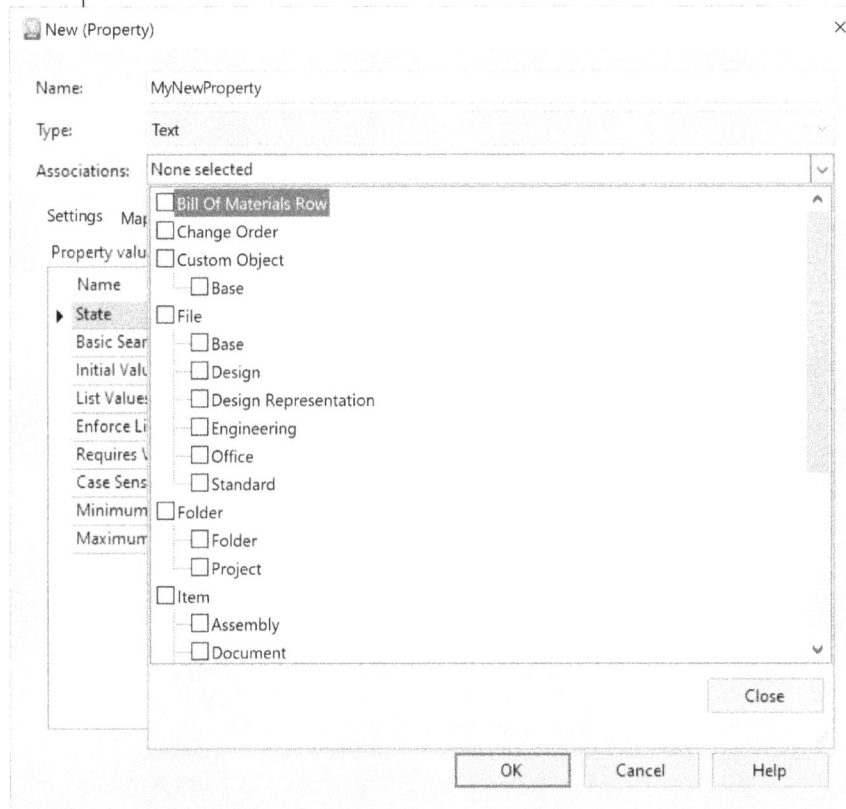

New (Property) ✕

Name:	MyNewProperty
Type:	Text
Associations:	None selected

Settings   Map

Property valu

- ☐ Bill Of Materials Row
- ☐ Change Order
- ☐ Custom Object
  - ☐ Base
- ☐ File
  - ☐ Base
  - ☐ Design
  - ☐ Design Representation
  - ☐ Engineering
  - ☐ Office
  - ☐ Standard
- ☐ Folder
  - ☐ Folder
  - ☐ Project
- ☐ Item
  - ☐ Assembly
  - ☐ Document

Name
▸ State
Basic Sear
Initial Valu
List Values
Enforce Li
Requires \
Case Sens
Minimum
Maximum

Close

OK   Cancel   Help

Task 2 - Edit the new property.

---

1. Click Tools>Administration>Vault Settings.

2. In the Vault Settings dialog box, Behaviors tab, click Properties.

3. In the Properties Definitions dialog box, select Property then select Edit.

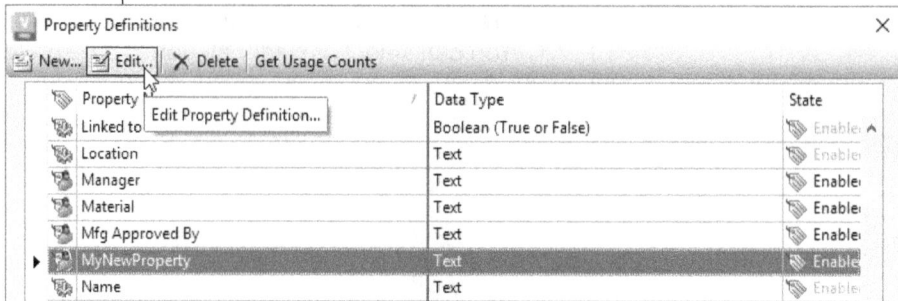

4. Rename your new Property (e.g. change from MyNewProperty to MyEditedProperty).

5. Modify some other settings like State or Basic Search, Category options, etc.

6. Set the Initial Value.

7. Set Requires Value to True.

8. Click OK to save the changes.

Task 3 - Add/remove properties to files.

---

1. Select one or more files you want to get added the new property.

2. Click Actions>Add or Remove Property.

3. In the Add or Remove Property dialog box, search for the new property named MyEditedProperty.

4. In the Action column, you can select Add or Remove to add and remove properties.

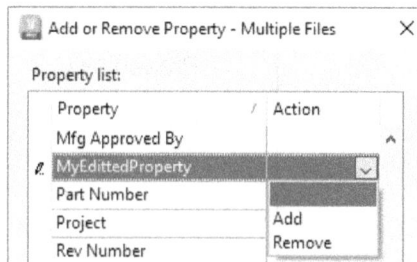

5. Click OK to confirm and save these settings.

5.2 The Properties Grid

Overview

You can customize the files in the vault by creating, adding, and removing properties, and modifying property values. The Properties grid lists all properties for a selected file. The tab for the Properties grid displays at the bottom of the right pane when a file is selected from the file list.

Properties are separated based on whether they are system-defined or user-defined. Collapse or expand each group to review the properties for those definitions.

The Properties grid displays the name and value of each property associated with the selected file. You can configure the properties grid to show only certain properties

System-defined Property values cannot be modified. You can only modify values of user-defined properties.

Properties	⊓ ✕
FACE PLATE.ipt	▼ ✚ ✏ ▾
⊟ **System**	⌃
Category Name	Base
Category Name (Historical)	Base
Change Order State	
Checked In	7/3/2020 4:49 PM
Checked Out	
Checked Out By	
Checked Out Local Spec	
Checked Out Machine	
Classification	None
Comment	
Controlled By Change Or...	False
⊟ **User Defined**	
Author	Autodesk, Inc.
Comments	
Company	
Cost	
Description	
Designer	Autodesk, Inc.
Engineer	
Engr Approved By	
Keywords	
Manager	
Material	Steel, Mild
Mfg Approved By	
Part Number	FACE PLATE
Project	
Stock Number	
Subject	
Title	⌄

Hide/Restore Properties

To hide and restore Properties from the grid there are two buttons in the upper right place in grid.

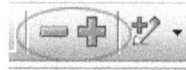

1. Select a Property that should disappear from the grid list. By clicking on the "minus"-symbol (Hide Properties) the Property is hidden and can be restored by clicking the "plus"-symbol (Restore Properties).
2. A Property Filter dialog box opens. Select the Property you want to restore and select Restore Selected Properties.
3. All selected Properties are restored and available in the grid.

   You can make selections on one or more properties and hide/restore them by one click, conform to the windows shortcut standards (press <Shift> or <Ctrl> for selection).

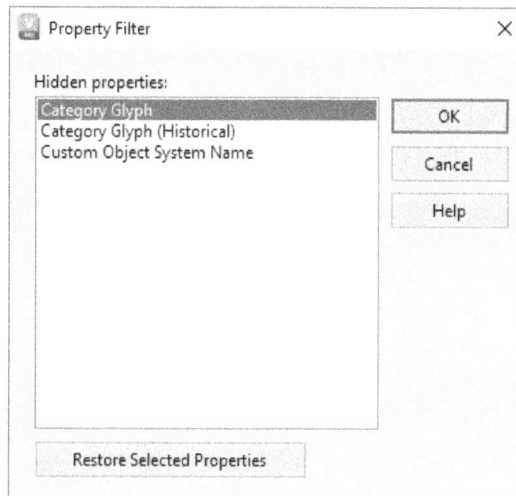

Edit Properties from the Grid

User-defined properties in a vault can be edited using the Property Editing Wizard. The wizard enables you to select any number of files, regardless of type, and edit their properties. The selected files are checked out, the properties are updated, and then the files are checked back in to the vault.

You must be assigned the role of either Editor or Administrator to perform this action. Contact your vault administrator to verify your role. The files must also be checked in and unlocked.

Files can be selected from the main pane, the Properties grid, or while in the property editor, to have properties edited. You can select multiple files at once to edit properties. For example, you can select an Inventor assembly and all of its children from the Uses tab and then use the Property Editing Wizard to edit all the properties for the entire design.

For Autodesk® Inventor® files, including Inventor .DWG files, and Microsoft Office documents, all user-defined properties are available for editing. If a property is missing a value, you can fill it in and it will be added to the file. If the file does not contain the property as a predefined object, then a custom property can be created containing the value.

If using Autodesk® Vault Professional, items and Change Orders can also be selected along with other files for editing their properties in a heterogeneous view.

1. Select multiple files (e.g., Autodesk Inventor .IPT files) and open the Properties Grid.
2. Select the property (or multiple properties) you want to edit.
3. By selecting the command Edit Selected Properties, the Property Edit dialog box opens enabling you to edit the selected properties of the selected files.

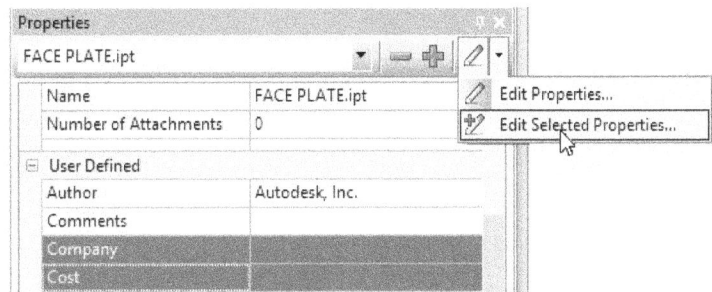

4. You can edit the properties and confirm the changes by clicking OK.

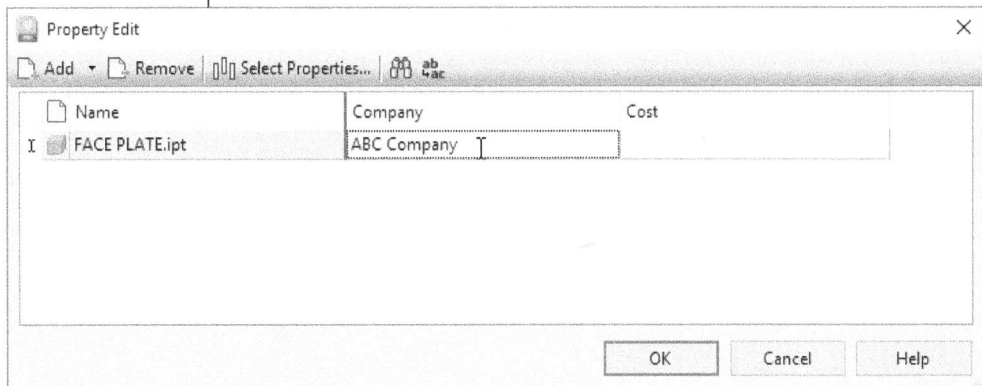

5. The property values are saved and you will get a confirmation dialog box with the results.

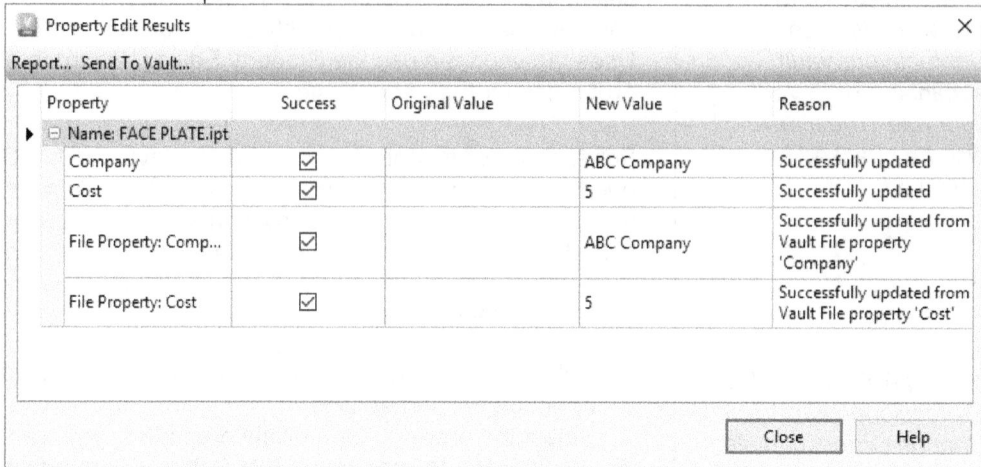

Property	Success	Original Value	New Value	Reason
▸ ⊟ Name: FACE PLATE.ipt				
Company	☑		ABC Company	Successfully updated
Cost	☑		5	Successfully updated
File Property: Comp...	☑		ABC Company	Successfully updated from Vault File property 'Company'
File Property: Cost	☑		5	Successfully updated from Vault File property 'Cost'

Property Edit Results ✕

Report... Send To Vault...

Close   Help

Practice 5b	# Working with the Properties Grid

In this practice, you will set up your own working environment with system-defined properties and user-defined properties in the Properties Grid by hiding and restoring properties in the view. Finally you will modify the property values of single and multiple selections of files and properties.

Task 1 - Set up your working environment with the Properties Grid.

---

1. Select a file and open the Properties Grid.

2. Collapse the system-defined Properties in the Grid.

3. Expand the user-defined Properties when collapsed and select one or more properties you want to hide from the Grid as they seem unnecessary for your work.

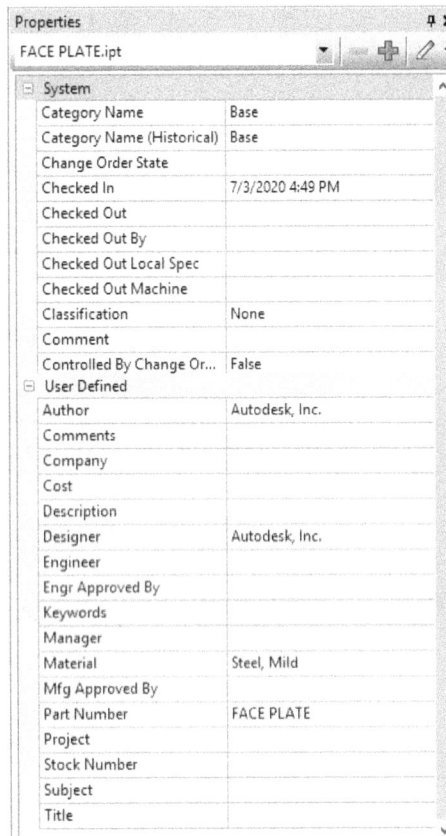

Properties	🔒 ✕
FACE PLATE.ipt	▾ ┃ ➖ ➕ ✏ ▾

⊟ System		⌃
Category Name	Base	
Category Name (Historical)	Base	
Change Order State		
Checked In	7/3/2020 4:49 PM	
Checked Out		
Checked Out By		
Checked Out Local Spec		
Checked Out Machine		
Classification	None	
Comment		
Controlled By Change Or...	False	
⊟ User Defined		
Author	Autodesk, Inc.	
Comments		
Company		
Cost		
Description		
Designer	Autodesk, Inc.	
Engineer		
Engr Approved By		
Keywords		
Manager		
Material	Steel, Mild	
Mfg Approved By		
Part Number	FACE PLATE	
Project		
Stock Number		
Subject		
Title		⌄

4. Click the "minus-symbol" (Hide Properties) from the menu on top of the Properties Grid.

5. The selected properties should be gone from the Grid. To restore them click the "plus-symbol" (Restore Properties) from the menu, right next to the Hide Properties command.

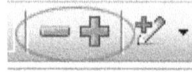

6. Select the Properties you have hidden in the step before and restore them by clicking Restore Selected Properties.

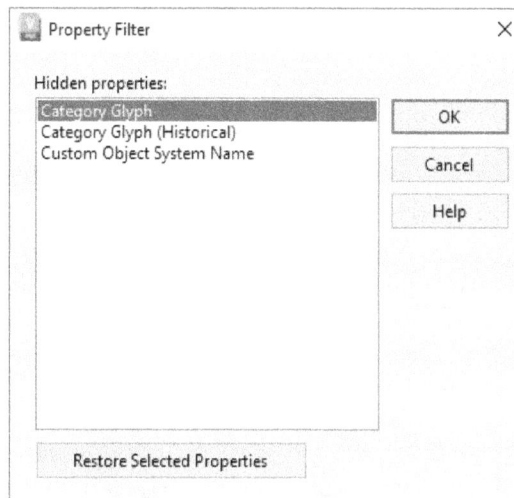

7. Check your Properties Grid whether the selected properties were restored.

Task 2 - Modify the property value directly in the Grid.

1. Expand the user-defined properties section in the Properties Grid.

2. Select the one or more properties in the grid.

3. Click the Edit Selected Properties command from the menu on top of the Grid.

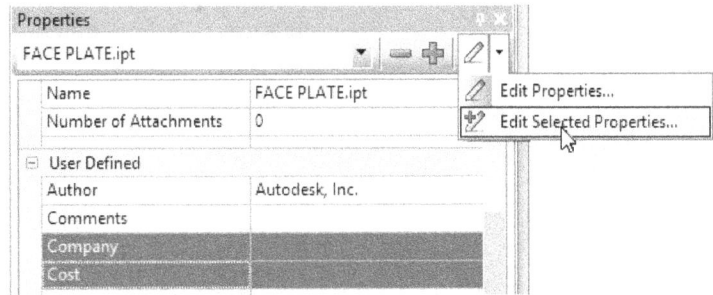

If you only want to customize the order of the fields (columns), drag the column headers to rearrange them in the list.

4. The Property Edit dialog box opens. Modify your property values and confirm the settings with OK.

5. The changes are saved and the Property Edit Results dialog box opens.

6. Check whether your Changes were saved successfully.

5.3 Map Properties

Overview

Powerful tools and options make it easy for administrators to map their file and item UDPs properties in a flexible and user friendly way.

Objectives

After completing this lesson, you will be able to:

- Map Properties

- Set Mapping Priorities

Mapping Priority

Mapping priority determines the order in which properties are written to a file. If more than one property writes to a particular file, the highest ranking property takes precedence.

You can map properties to a user-defined property (UDP) so that values from the master file, such as a file property, are written to the subordinate UDP.

Importing and exporting values between Vault and file properties

There are two ways in which a file property value is added to the vault:

- Certain file property definitions come with the client and are already included in the vault.

- Adding a file to the vault only captures the values based on the existing mappings. In the case of a mapping that writes to the file, it will only write if the file property field exists, or if the write setting is set to 'create' for a custom property. Otherwise, only property definitions already defined in the vault will be created for the file to reduce extraneous property definitions or duplicates.

Mapping

To create a property mapping, the administrator must first choose which object group is to be mapped. In the image below, this is specified under the first column titled Entity. The available choices are based on the value of the Associations field. Several Content Providers are included but in most cases it is best to leave the selection on All Files (*.*). Vault will automatically select the most appropriate Content Provider based on the file format. Next, select a file that contains the property or BOM field to be mapped. The image below shows the file properties available for mapping in the file manifold_block.ipt.

The Type column shows the data type of the source property. Mapping can be done across data types. However, there are special considerations that are detailed in the next section. The mapping direction by default will choose bi-directional unless the file or BOM property does not support the input of values. When this occurs the mapping option will be limited to Read only. Read only mappings should be used sparingly because any UDP that contains only 'Read only' mappings cannot be modified in Vault.

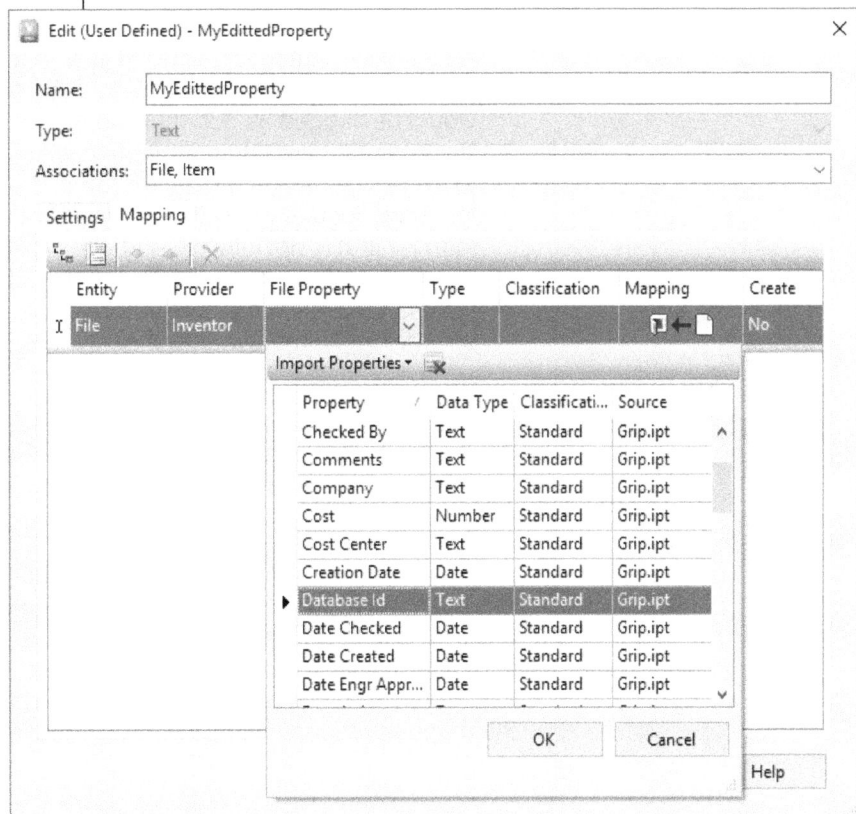

Mapping Across Data Types

There are four property types: Text, Number, Boolean & Date. The following matrix defines valid property mappings.

		Source Property (File or BOM)			
		Text	Number	Boolean	Date
UDP	Text	Yes	Yes(2)	Yes(1)	Yes(2)
	Number	Yes(2)	Yes	Yes	No
	Boolean	Yes(1)	Yes	Yes	No
	Date	Yes(2)	No	No	Yes

Whenever a mapping is created between two different property types there is the possibility of incompatibility. The onus is on the user to input valid values. If an invalid value is entered in most cases, the equivalence will flag the property as non-equivalent. The exceptions are listed below.

1. Mapping Boolean with Text: The supported valid text values are: Yes/No, True/False and 1/0. These values are localized. A string like 'Autodesk' entered in a Text property cannot be transferred to a Boolean property. This property mapping would be flagged as not equivalent.
2. Mapping Text with Number or Text with Date: Works well when all clients and the server are in the same language-locale. With mixed locales, values can convert in a manner that is not intuitive and can produce an undesirable result. Therefore, mapping Text with Number or Text with Date is only recommended when the server and all clients are working in the same locale.

Create Option

The Create option applies to write mappings. If the file property does not exist when a value is pushed to the file, the administrator can choose whether the file property is created or not.

The Create option has another function that is not obvious. When enabled, the equivalence calculation will consider the absence of the property definition in the file as a blank value and compare it against the value of the UDP in Vault. When the Create option is disabled, equivalence will be set to 'Good' when the mapped property definition does not exist in the file.

Example: I have two departments in my organization that both create .DWG files but they use different file properties to represent the same information. The R&D department uses the file property DwgNum. The Tooling department uses the file property DrwNo. I want to manage all drawings from both groups in a single Vault and with one UDP 'Drawing Number'. The correct configuration is to create bidirectional mappings and set the Create option to Off for both mappings. The result is that a modification of the UDP Drawing Number will write its value back to whichever property exists and it will not create an extra property.

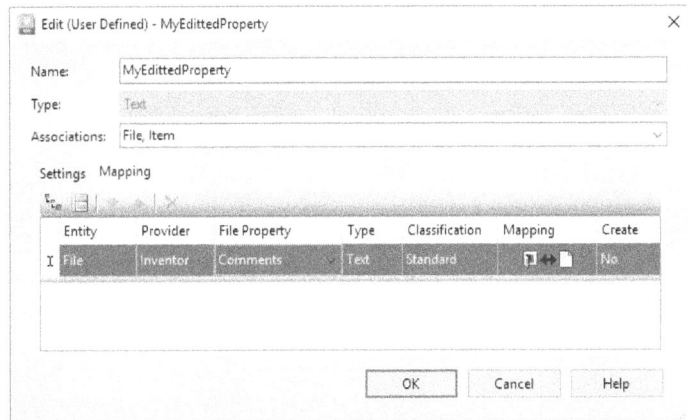

Mapping AutoCAD Block Attributes

Autodesk® AutoCAD® block attribute mapping requires configuration on the ADMS. Select Index Block Attributes from the Tools menu in Autodesk Data Management Server Console. Enter the AutoCAD block names from which to extract attributes. Note that the block names are case sensitive. After this is done, it is possible to map a UDP to an attribute using the mapping process described above. Configured mappings enable the system to read and/or write values between the UDP and the attribute.

Usage of attribute mapping is intended for single instances of a block or when all block instances have the same attribute values. It is not possible for multiple block instances to be mapped to separate UDPs. Many companies have one instance of a title block in a given .DWG files. Occasionally, there are companies that use multiple instances of a title block in a single file. In these cases, the attributes often share the same values. An example is a drawing file that contains three borders of different size. Each border uses the same title block with attributes.

The attributes for Customer Name, Engineer, Project Number, etc. will share the same value for all instances. Such attributes that share the same value can be mapped to a UDP. Attributes like Border Size will have a unique value for each block instance. Therefore, Border Size should not be mapped to a UDP in Vault.

AutoCAD Mechanical

Autodesk® AutoCAD® Mechanical software (ACM) supports three distinct sets of properties, all of which can be mapped to Vault UDPs. The three ACM property sets are: file, assembly and component. See the ACM documentation for details about the intended use and differences between these properties.

Vault file properties can map to ACM file properties and Vault item properties can map to ACM assembly and component properties.

It should also be noted that ACM assembly and file properties having the same name, should not be mapped to the same Vault UDP.

AutoCAD Electrical

Autodesk® AutoCAD® Electrical software (ACE) supports both file and BOM properties. ACE BOM properties can be mapped to Item properties. ACE uses properties located in .DWGs, .WDPs, and associated databases. ACE properties are exposed to Vault in four ways:

First: Ordinary DWG™ file properties and block attributes can be mapped to Vault File objects. The majority of these mappings support bi-directional mapping. Creation of these mappings is described in the Mapping section of this document.

Second: WDP properties support mapping to Item properties. They also support bi-directional mapping. Creating a mapping with WDP properties requires the AutoCAD Electrical Content Source Provider. The provider is specified in the second column of the image at the right. This provider is automatically set when a file of type .WDP is selected under the File Property column. If an associated .WDL file has been created both the line number and the alternate property name will automatically display in the list for selection. You can select the line number or the alternate display name to create the mapping. All WDL properties will display in the list of selectable properties; it does not matter if a value is present.

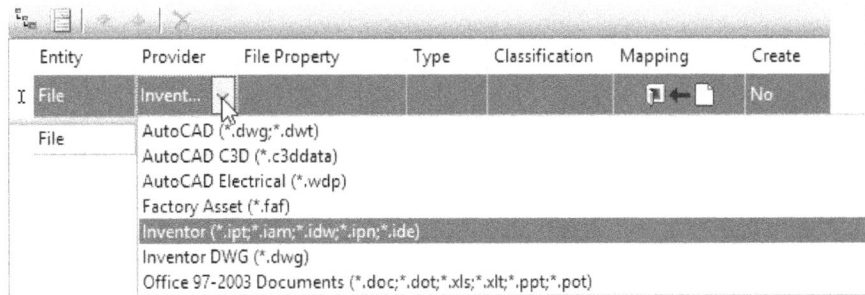

Third: Component BOM properties can be mapped to Item properties. This includes properties such as: Catalog Number, Component Name, Component Type, Electrical Type, Equivalence Value & Manufacturer and more...

To create a mapping to a component BOM property, create a new UDP and associate it to Items. Then, in the Mapping tab, create a new mapping, ensuring that the first column Entity is set to Item. Under the File Property column, browse and select any file that contains the property to which you will create the mapping. Some properties require that a value exist or the property is not available for selection in the list.

Reminder: When creating new properties it is best to associate them to a category which will automatically associate them to the files and/or items where the property should display. If this is not done, the property will have to be manually associated to the file or item.

Fourth: Reference Designator properties, when mapped will display in Vault as optional data on an Item BOM. There are eighteen Reference Designator properties available:

INST, LOC, TAG, DESC1...3, RATING1...12

These properties can be mapped to an Item BOM using the DWG content source provider.

To create a mapping to a Reference Designator, create a new UDP and associate it to Reference Designator. Then, in the Mapping tab, create a new mapping, ensure that the first column Entity is set to Reference Designator. Under the File Property column select the DWG containing the Reference Designator to which the mapping needs to be created. All Reference Designators are available for selection in the list without requiring a value.

Practice 5c | # Map Properties

In this practice, you will learn how to map your newly created user-defined property.

Task 1 - Create a user-defined property and map it with a file property.

---

1. Click Tools>Administration>Vault Settings.

2. In the Vault Settings dialog box, Behaviors tab, click Properties.

3. As the customer is working with SAP, the File Property Part Number should be mapped with a new User-Defined Property called SAP-ID. Therefore create a new UDP with name SAP-ID.

4. Ensure that your Type is set to Number.

Name:	SAP-ID
Type:	Number
Associations:	File

5. Now select the Mapping tab.

6. Click in the * Click here to add a new mapping field.

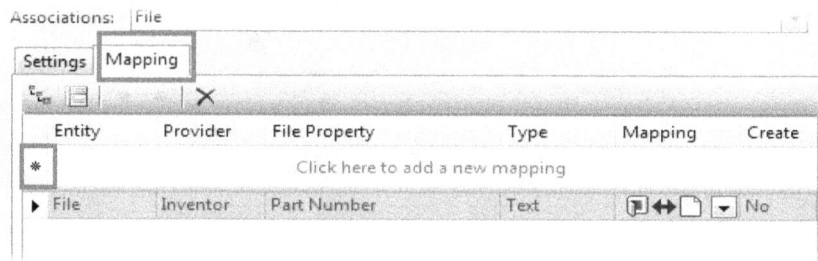

7. Select the entity type for this property mapping.

8. Click in the blank field under Provider and select the content provider for the file to which you want to map.

---

9. Click in the field under File Property and then click Import Properties.

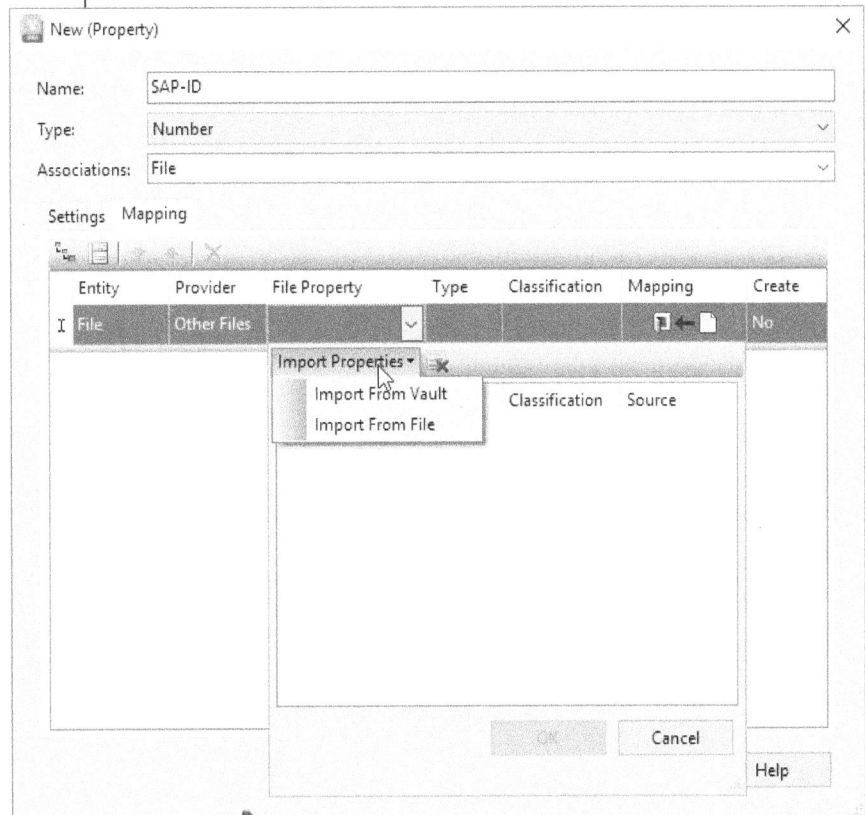

10. Select whether you want to import properties from a file in the vault or from a source file.

11. In the Select File dialog box, locate the file from which you want to import. Click Open.

12. The Import Properties list is updated with the properties available for import from the specified source.

13. Click OK to save the imported property list and create the mapping.

14. Click the Clear Properties list icon ❌ at any time to remove all imported properties.

15. In the Mappings tab, click OK to commit all changes and return to the Edit Property dialog box.

Task 2 - Edit mapping priorities.

Properties at the top of the list take precedence over those lower on the list. You can reorganize the list using the Move Up and Move Down arrow icons in the Mapping tab.

1. In the Mapping tab, select the property that you want to prioritize, and click the Move Up or Move Down arrow icons as required to change mapping priority.

A subordinate property is a property that receives its values from other properties that are mapped to it. The mapped properties (the master properties) write values to the subordinate property.

2. Click OK to commit all changes and return to the Property Definitions dialog box.

5.4 Chapter Summary

You can streamline your vault environment by creating and managing properties associated with files. Establish constraints to ensure that properties conform to certain policies, and map property values so that they are automatically updated based on changes made to other files.

Having completed this chapter, you can:

- Understand the difference between system-defined properties and user-defined properties

- Manage user-defined properties (Create new, Edit, Add or Remove Properties)

- Work with the Properties Grid in Vault and Edit property values

- Configure property constraints

- Map Properties

Automatic File Naming in Autodesk Vault Workgroup

The Automatic File Naming feature lets you configure how files and items are named when they are added to the vault. You can select from two existing schemes, Mapped and Sequential, or you can create custom numbering schemes using one or more parameters. In this chapter, you will learn how to use and configure Automatic File Numbering schemes.

Learning Objective in This Chapter

*   Create, edit and delete custom numbering schemes that automatically create a filename or number on save.

6.1 Create Custom Numbering Schemes

Overview

In Autodesk® Vault Workgroup or Autodesk® Vault Professional software, it is possible to assign a numbering scheme which gives the ability to apply an automatic file naming or numbering on save from a new file created from a template inside of Autodesk® Inventor® or AutoCAD®.

Objectives

After completing this lesson, you will be able to:

- Define several different numbering schemes in the Administration panel.

- Set a default numbering scheme.

- Understand the different Field Types for Numbering Schemes.

- Delete an existing numbering scheme.

- Create a file from Inventor or AutoCAD and automatically save it with the defined numbering scheme/file naming.

Define Numbering Schemes

You can select from several existing schemes, Mapped, Sequential, ECO or you can create custom numbering schemes using one or more parameters.

Mapped	Numbers are generated based on the user-defined properties mapped to the file or item in the Map Properties dialog box.
Sequential	Numbers are generated sequentially. This is the default number scheme and cannot be edited or deleted.
ECO (if using Autodesk Vault Professional)	Change Order names are generated based on a defined fixed text, a delimiter, and an auto-generated number.
Custom	Numbers are generated based on a custom design. This feature provides the flexibility to create a numbering scheme where the number carries information about the file.

Where to Define the Numbering Schemes for Auto File Naming

1. Select Tools>Administration>Vault Settings.
2. In the Vault Settings dialog box, click the Behaviors tab.
3. In the Numbering section, click Define.

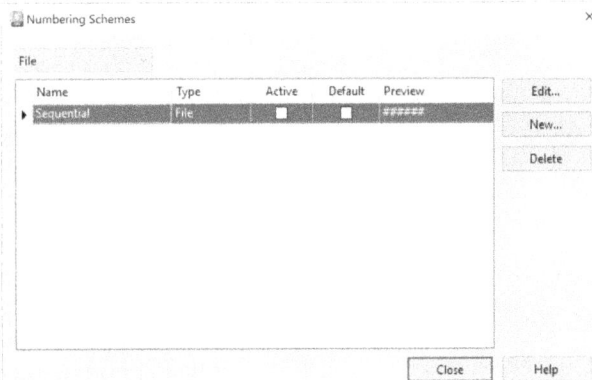

Numbering Field Essentials

Each separate part in a file number is called a field. There are six basic fields:

	Example	Description
Autogenerated	1001, 1002, 1003	Creates a sequential file number automatically each time a file is created. No user input is required.
Delimiter	-	A single character, such as a dash that separates each field.
FixedText	2004	Use this for a value you do not want changed and want to have in each file number.
FreeText	prototype	Creates a free form field so users can enter additional information.

PredefinedList	blue, yellow, green	Provides a list of choices to the user each time a file is created.
Workgroup Label	WG1	The workgroup ID for the workgroup in which the number is generated.

Numbering Generator

There are three types of number generators:

Simple Number Generator	It produces numbers based on the other information provided in the numbering scheme.
Centralized Number Generator	It avoids duplicated generated number at the same time in a replicated environment.
Custom Generator	User specified numbering generators configured on the Vault server.

General numbering scheme rules:

- Only one auto-generated field per numbering scheme sequence is allowed.

- A user-defined numbering scheme can only be edited or deleted when it is not in use. That is, the user defined numbering scheme has not been used or all the objects using it have been deleted.

- The sequential numbering scheme cannot be edited or deleted.

Defining File Fields

The field type selected in the Add Field dialog box determines the available field settings. The default choice is Auto-generated sequence.

Auto-generated Field Settings

- Use the Name text box to give a name to the auto generated field.

- The Length determines the number of characters of the Range field, and must be a positive value.

- The Range specifies the beginning and end of the auto generated number.

  Note: The lower limit must be less than the upper limit.

- StepSize controls how the auto generated number is incremented.

Delimiter

- The value **must be a character**. The delimiter is used to separate fields.

Fixed Text

- Use the Name text box to give a name to the fixed text field.

- The value entered in the Fixed Text field always displays in the file number and cannot be modified by the user.

Free Text

- Use the Name text box to give a name to the free text field.

- Max Length controls the maximum number of characters permitted for this field.

- Max Length required forces user to enter the number of characters specified in the Max Length field. The number length cannot be over 50.

Predefined List

- Use the Name text box to give a name to the predefined list field.

- Specify a list of values in the Code field. You can optionally enter a description for each of the values.

- Use Move up and Move down to change the order of the values.

- Use Delete to remove a value.

Workgroup Label

- Selecting this option automatically assigns the workgroup label as a fixed value in the numbering scheme.

Preview and Edit Numbering Schemes

The New Numbering scheme dialog box and the Edit Numbering Scheme dialog box enable you to review and edit a numbering scheme.

- The name displays in the Name field. The name of the numbering scheme cannot be modified.

- The Preview field displays all fields defined. A field requiring user input displays as a question mark (?). Auto-generated fields display as a pound sign (#).

- The Number of Digits field shows the maximum possible file number length.

- The Append workgroup label checkbox lets you add the workgroup label to the file or item name. This label is useful in differentiating files between workgroups.

- Use Move up and Move down to change the order of the values.

- Use Edit, Delete and Add to perform their respective operations.

- Force letters to uppers case by selecting To Upper-case checkbox.

Delete an Existing Numbering Scheme in Vault

1. Open the Numbering Scheme dialog box using Tools>Vault Settings>Behaviors Tab>Numbering section>Define.
2. Now you can view all defined numbering schemes in Vault. To delete, select the numbering scheme you want to delete permanently from the system and click Delete.

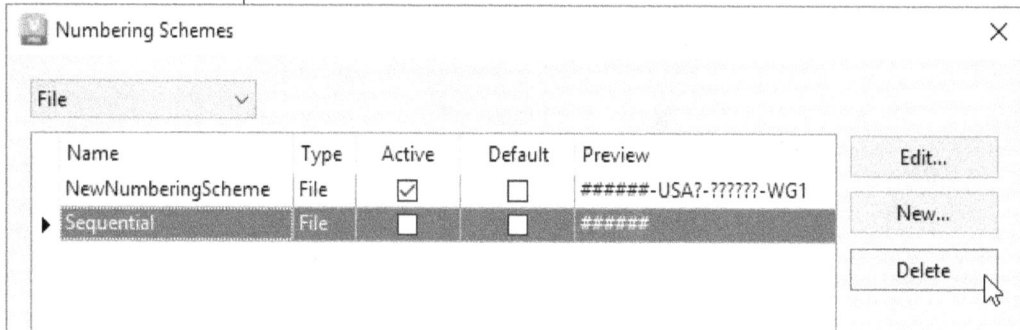

3. A dialog box opens to confirm the deletion.
   • Click **OK** to delete it permanently.

Hint: General Numbering Scheme Rules

• Only one auto generated field per numbering scheme sequence is permitted.

• A user defined numbering scheme can only be edited or deleted when it is not in use. That is, the user defined numbering scheme has not been used or all the files using it have been deleted.

• The sequential numbering scheme cannot be edited or deleted.

Practice 6a

Define a Custom Numbering Scheme

In this practice, you will learn how to use numbering schemes. You will manage existing numbering schemes, create and edit new ones and finally delete the created scheme.

Task 1 - Manage numbering schemes.

1. Select Tools>Administration>Vault Settings.

2. In the Vault Settings dialog box, select the Behaviors tab.

3. In the Numbering section, click Define.

4. The Numbering Schemes dialog box lists the available numbering schemes. The default numbering scheme is indicated with a checkmark. You can also create new schemes, edit existing schemes, and set the default scheme.

5. Select whether you want to view File, Item, Change Order, or All numbering schemes, from the Filter drop-down list.

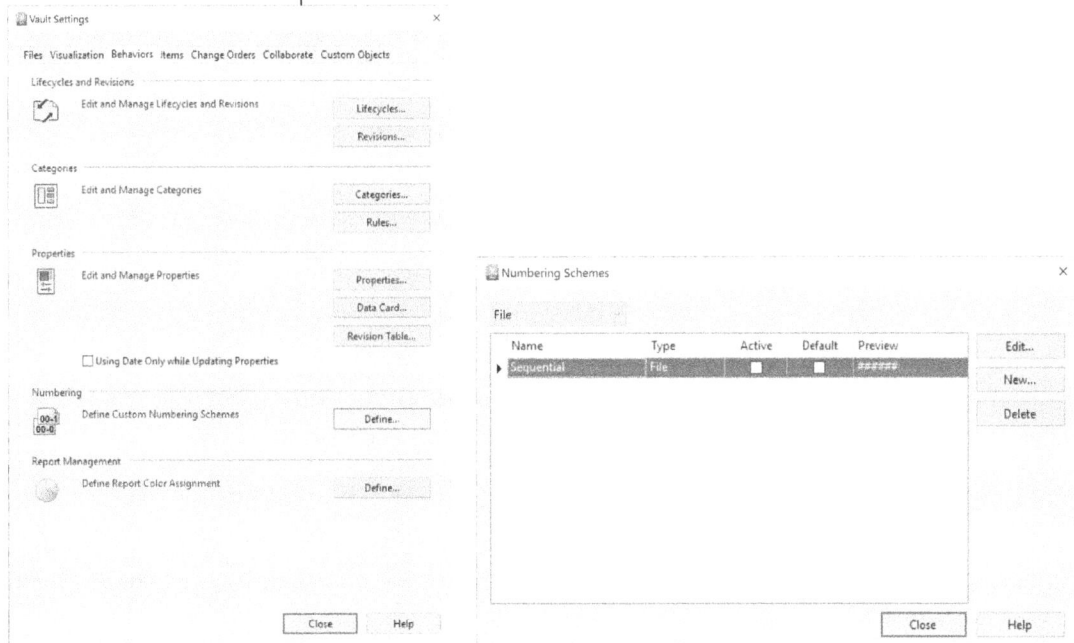

Task 2 - Create a new numbering scheme.

1. Click New.

2. In the New Numbering scheme dialog box, enter the scheme name.

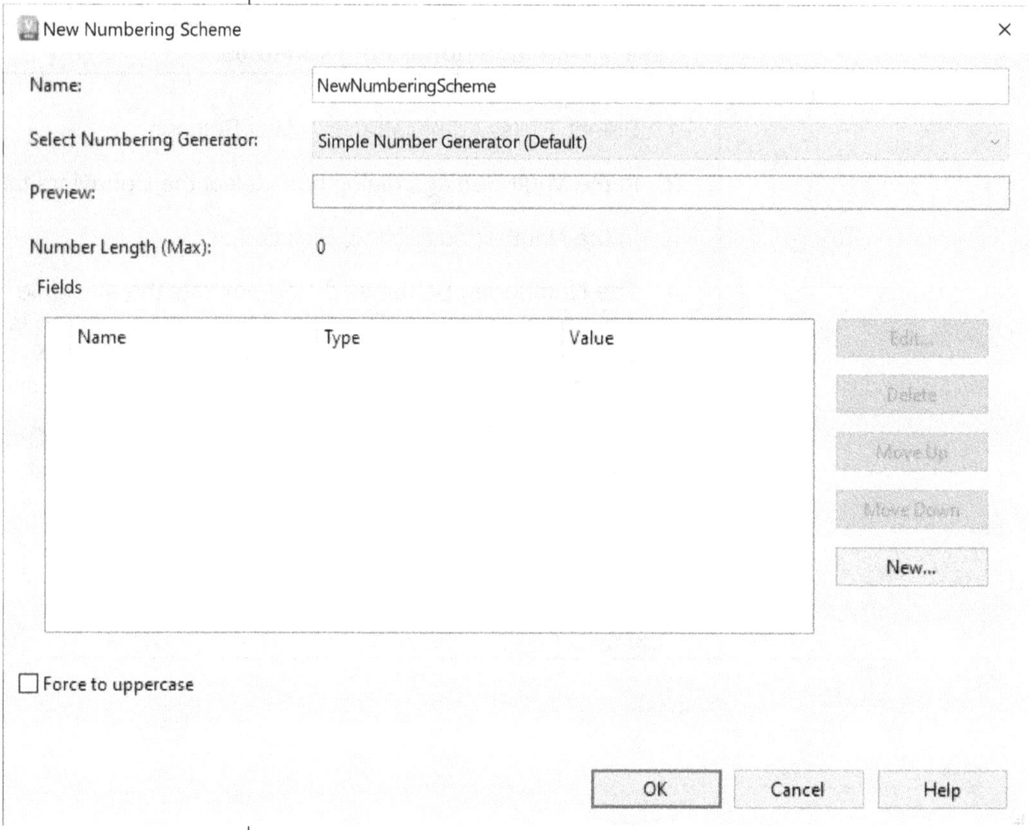

New Numbering Scheme   ✕

| Name: | NewNumberingScheme |

Select Numbering Generator: Simple Number Generator (Default)

Preview:

Number Length (Max): 0

Fields

Name	Type	Value

Edit...
Delete
Move Up
Move Down
New...

☐ Force to uppercase

OK   Cancel   Help

---

3. Click New to add fields for the numbering scheme.

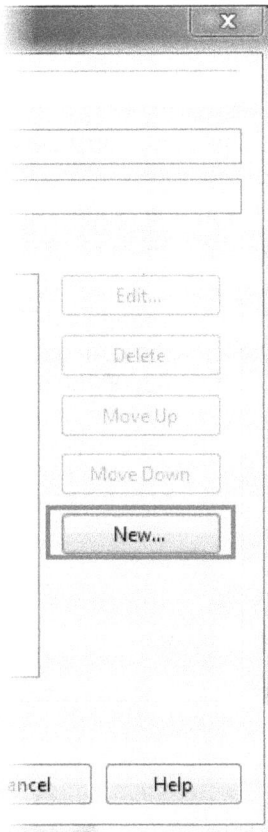

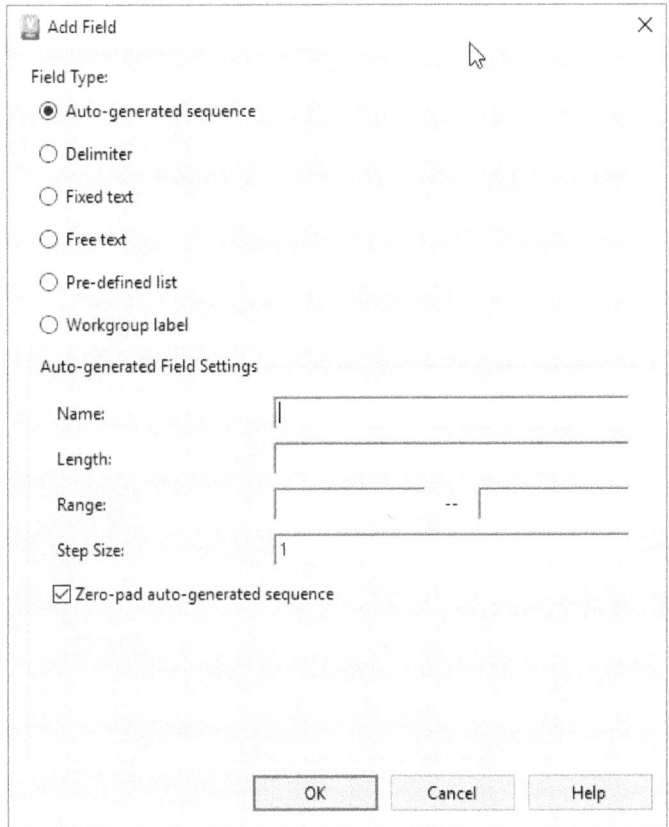

4. In the Add Field dialog box, select one of the following field types:

Auto-generated sequence

- Enter a name for the auto-generated field.
- Specify the length for the range. The length must be a positive number.
- Enter the starting and ending value for the range.
- Enter the StepSize. The StepSize value must be at least 1.
- The auto-generated sequence is zero-padded by default. To remove zero-padding, clear the checkbox. An example of zero-padded numbers: 000001, 000002, 000003.

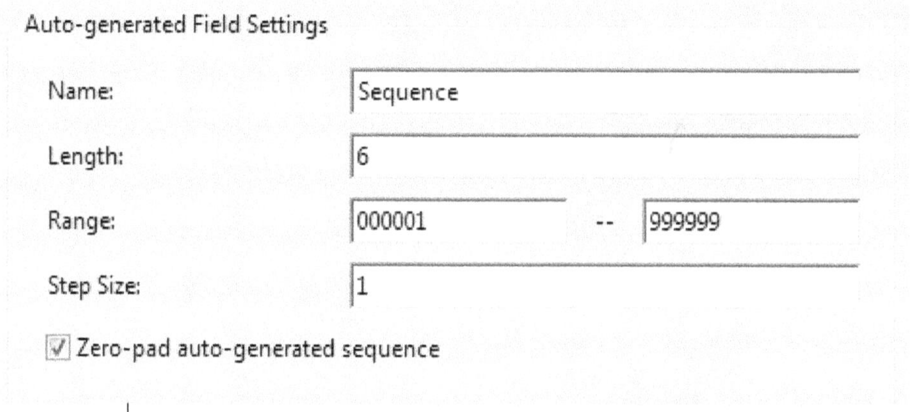

Auto-generated Field Settings

Name:	Sequence
Length:	6
Range:	000001 -- 999999
Step Size:	1

☑ Zero-pad auto-generated sequence

Delimiter

- Enter the delimiter value. It must be a character, such as a dash (-), used to separate fields.

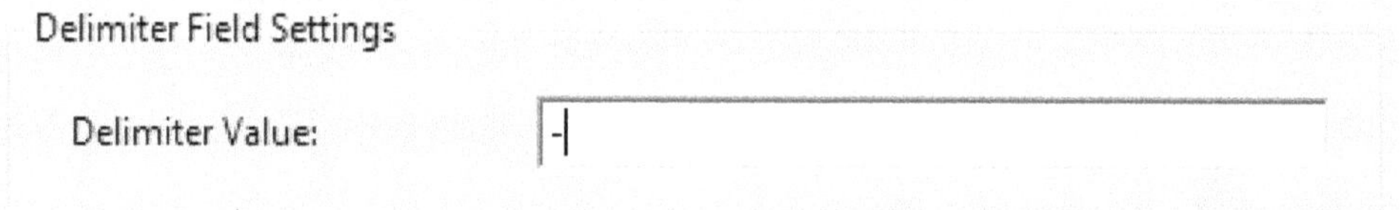

Delimiter Field Settings

Delimiter Value:	-

Fixed text

- Enter a name for the fixed text field.
- The value entered in the Fixed text field is a constant and cannot be edited. The value cannot exceed 50 characters.

Fixed Text Field Settings

Name: Location

Fixed Text: USA

Free text

- Enter a name for the free text field.
- Enter the maximum length of the field.
- Select the Max length required checkbox to fix the length of the field to the value specified in the Max length field.

Free Text Field Settings

Name: My free text

Default Value: ADSK

Max Length: 4

☑ Max length required

Predefined list

- Enter a name for the free predefined list field.
- Enter a value in the Code field. You can optionally enter a description for each of the values.
- To change the order of the entries, highlight a value, and then click Move up or Move down.
- To delete an entry, highlight a value, and then click Delete.

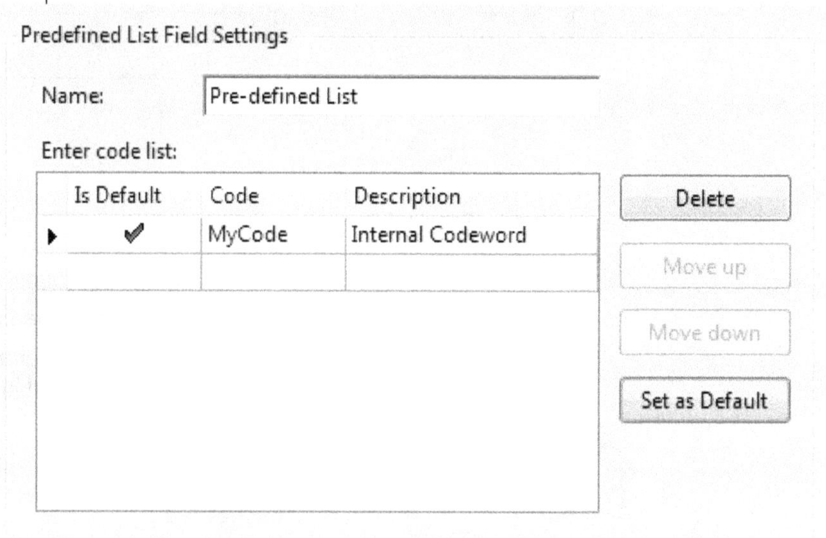

Predefined List Field Settings

Name: Pre-defined List

Enter code list:

Is Default	Code	Description	
✔	MyCode	Internal Codeword	Delete
			Move up
			Move down
			Set as Default

Workgroup label

- This option automatically assigns the workgroup ID to the number. The workgroup ID is based on the workgroup in which the number is generated.

◉ Workgroup label

Workgroup label Settings

Workgroup label: WG1

The new Numbering Scheme dialog box should now look similar to following picture (here you can see, that two more delimiter were created, to separate the values). You can use Move up and Move Down to change the order.

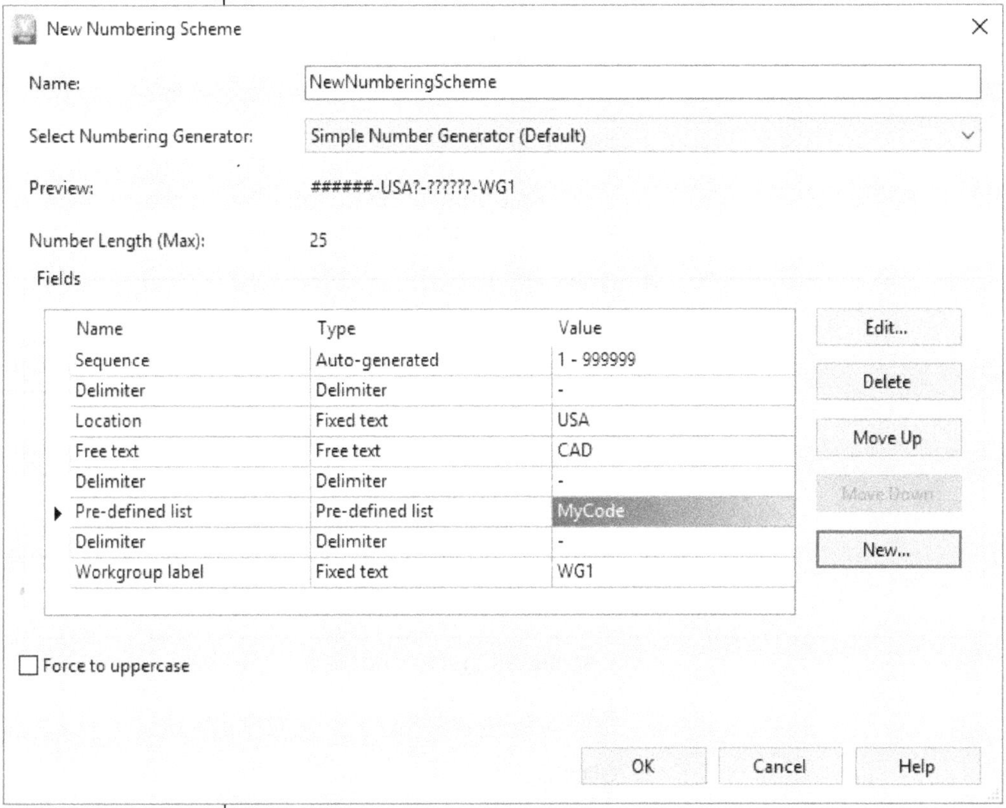

New Numbering Scheme			✕

Name: NewNumberingScheme

Select Numbering Generator: Simple Number Generator (Default) ⌄

Preview: ######-USA?-??????-WG1

Number Length (Max): 25

Fields

Name	Type	Value	
Sequence	Auto-generated	1 - 999999	Edit...
Delimiter	Delimiter	-	Delete
Location	Fixed text	USA	
Free text	Free text	CAD	Move Up
Delimiter	Delimiter	-	
▶ Pre-defined list	Pre-defined list	MyCode	Move Down
Delimiter	Delimiter	-	New...
Workgroup label	Fixed text	WG1	

☐ Force to uppercase

OK	Cancel	Help

5. Click OK.

    The New Numbering Scheme dialog box displays a preview of the settings defined in the Add/Edit dialog box.

6. To change the settings, click Edit. To delete, click Delete. To add another numbering scheme, click New.

7. To display text in all capital letters, select the Force to uppercase checkbox.

8. Click OK.

Task 3 - Edit an existing numbering scheme.

Only numbering schemes that have not been used by a file can be edited, with the exception that in-use schemes can have their ranges increased.

1. Select a numbering scheme from the list.

2. Click Edit.

3. In the Edit Numbering Scheme dialog box, change the values for the selected numbering scheme.

4. Click OK.

Task 4 - Set the default numbering scheme.

1. Select a numbering scheme from the list.

2. Click Default checkbox.

Task 5 - Delete a numbering scheme.

Only schemes that are not in use can be deleted.

1. Select a numbering scheme from the list.

2. Click Delete.

Note: You cannot delete a default scheme. Select another scheme to be the default before deleting it.

Practice 6b

Create a New Autodesk Inventor File Numbering Scheme

In this practice, you will create a new Autodesk® Inventor® part and save it from within the Autodesk Inventor software to the Autodesk Vault software. The new part will be created with the new Numbering Scheme you create.

Task 1 - Create your own number scheme.

1. Go through the steps explained in Practice 6a.

2. Create your own Numbering Scheme which works for you.

3. After you are done, ensure that your new Numbering Scheme is set to active and default.

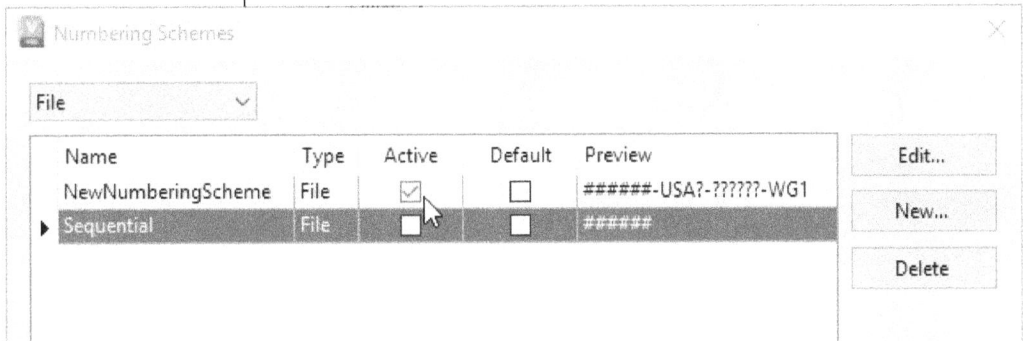

Task 2 - Create an Inventor component and save it to Vault.

1. Open Autodesk Inventor and create a new simple component (e.g. plate).

2. After you have finished your work on the component, ensure that you are connected to the right Vault. Select the Vault tab and log in to the AOTCVault Vault as administrator.

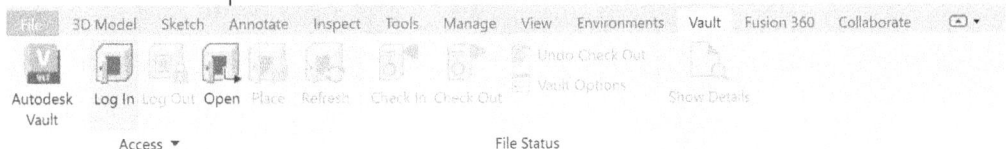

3. Then save your component. Clicking Save in Inventor, the Generate File Numbering dialog box opens automatically and asks you to confirm the new numbering scheme.

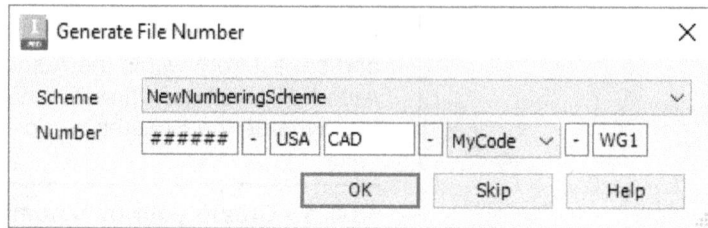

4. Click OK to confirm the Numbering Scheme.

5. The component is saved to your folder structure.

6. Now open the Vault Browser in Autodesk Inventor and select the component you just created.

7. Right-click to open the context menu and click Check in to check the component into Vault. You can edit the comment in the confirmation dialog before you click OK to finish this task.

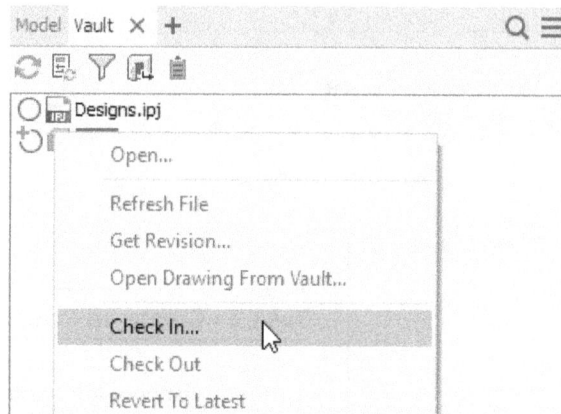

8. Your newly created component is saved to Autodesk Vault with the new Numbering Scheme.

⊟ File

   000001-USACAD-MyCode-WG1.ipt

Creating Reports

Autodesk® Vault Workgroup and Autodesk® Vault Professional software provide the ability to generate formatted reports representing data contained in a vault. You can generate reports for files and organize the report based on specific properties. For example, a report can display files grouped by a category or show the distribution of lifecycle states across a model. Reports can display the data in a variety of ways, including charts, tables, and data sheets. You can also format data using dozens of predefined operators.

In this chapter, you learn how to create and modify report templates so that you can customize Vault reports that contain information relevant to your business, in a format that suits your needs.

Learning Objectives in This Chapter

- Create reports from an advanced search and configure how the data displays.
- Identify the different out-of-the box report templates and the information they are formatted to display.
- Create new report templates using the Autodesk Template Utility (for advanced users).

7.1 Creating Reports

Overview

In this lesson, you learn how to create a report from an advanced search and configure how the report data displays.

Use search reports to illustrate details about files stored in the vault by using charts, tables, and data sheets.

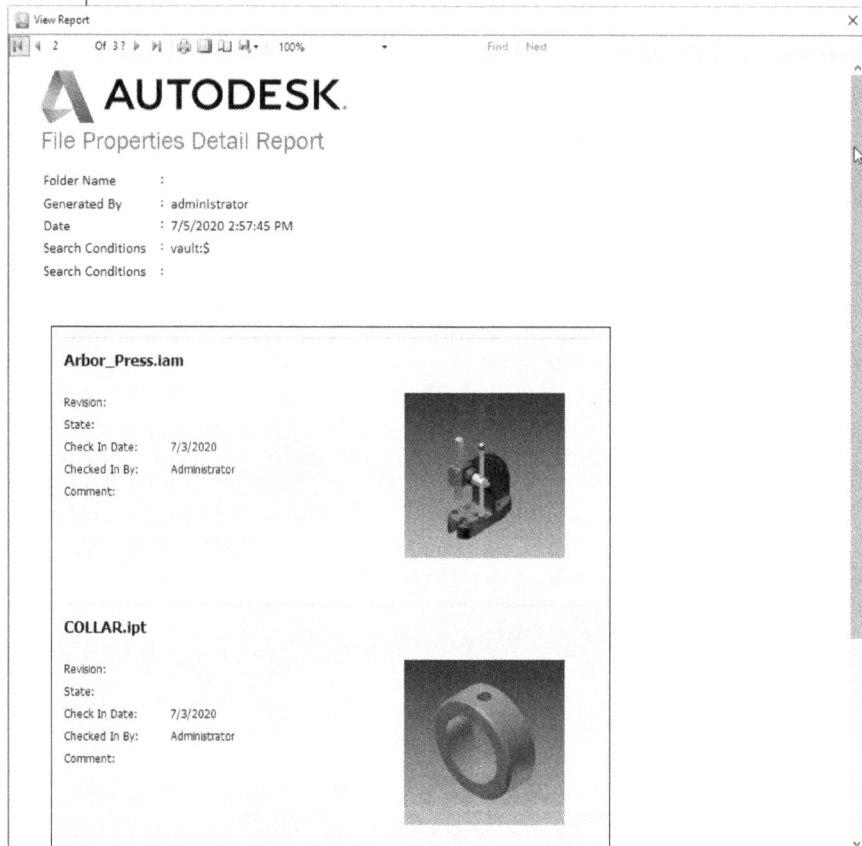

Objectives

After completing this lesson, you will be able to:

- Create reports from an advanced search.

- Understand how to use each of the out-of-the box templates included with Autodesk Vault Workgroup.

- Configure how the report data displays

About Reports

Working with reports is a way of illustrating file details for those who do not have direct access to the vault. Reports can be organized to suit the needs of your business and to illustrate certain file details.

Search options specified in the Advanced Find dialog box determine which vault objects display in a report. The properties displayed in the report and the report layout are specified in a report template file that is selected during the report generation. Through the report template, you have complete control of the report content, layout, and format.

You generate reports by creating an advanced search with specified parameters and then clicking Report. After selecting a template for the report, the information displays in a window for viewing.

Example of Creating a Report

A report must be generated to determine which files in a vault have been released for manufacturing. You create an advanced search with the condition that the search return files only with the lifecycle state of released. Once the search is complete, you generate a report and choose the template that shows the details of each file listed. Once the file is generated, you save a copy to the vault and email a copy to the project manager for review.

Report Templates

Report descriptions for Autodesk Vault reports are contained in RDLC files stored on the Vault client machine. These report description files are referred to as report templates. Autodesk Vault report templates are fully RDLC compliant, but Autodesk Vault requires certain naming conventions in the <DataSet> section of the template for integrating Vault data into the report.

A report template authoring utility is installed with the vault client to help you create simple client report definition files (.RDLC) for storing search data. This utility provides only a raw template structure for categorization purposes. A more sophisticated template authoring tool is required for custom visual layouts.

Pre-existing Report Templates

When the Autodesk Vault Client is installed, several pre-existing report templates are provided. The following table describes some of these templates, some of which are applicable to the Autodesk Vault Professional software.

Template Name	Description
ECO Average Close Rate	Displays the average number of days it takes to close an ECO.
ECO By State	Displays the ECOs in groups based on ECO state.
ECO Detail	Displays the ECO Number, Change Order Properties, State, Due Date, and submission information without table formatting.
ECO Status Created on Month	Displays the number of ECOs per State.
ECO Table	Displays the ECO Number, Change Order Properties, State, Due Date, and submission information in table format.
File by Category	Displays the filename, revision, state, comments, and check-in information in a pie-chart organized by category.
File Detail	Displays the filename, revision, state, check-in information, and comments without table formatting.
File Table	Displays the filename, revision, state, check-in information, and comments in a table format.
File Transmittal	Displays the filename, revision, state, vault folder location, and date the version was created for each file.
File by Lifecycle State	Displays the filename, revision, state, comments, and check-in information in a graph by lifecycle state.
File Checked Out By	Displays checked out information in a graph.
Item By State	Displays the item information in groups based on state.
Item Detail	Displays the item name, revision, state, type, units, modification information, compliance status, and description without table formatting.
Item Table	Displays the item name, revision, state, type, units, modification information, compliance status, and description in a table.
Project Dashboard	Displays project data in graphical format, including graphs for Lifecycle State Distribution by Category, Category Distribution, Lifecycle State Distribution, and Checked-Out Files Distribution by Users.

Vault Professional In-CAD	Displays check out information, lifecycle state, category, designer, and other In-CAD data displayed in pie-charts.
BOM - First-Level	Displays the BOM First Level details.
BOM - Multi-Level	Displays the BOM Multi-Level details.
BOM - Parts-Only	Displays the BOM Parts Only details.

Microsoft Report Viewer

Autodesk Vault uses the Microsoft Report Viewer to generate and display reports. Microsoft Report Viewer contains a full-featured, highly customizable reporting engine to display reports for SQL Server Reporting Services. However, the report viewer can also be run in "local mode" - enabling applications like Vault to provide data for report rendering without requiring the overhead of SQL Server Reporting Services. Autodesk Vault runs the report viewer in local mode. Report descriptions for Vault reports are contained in RDLC files stored on the Vault client machine.

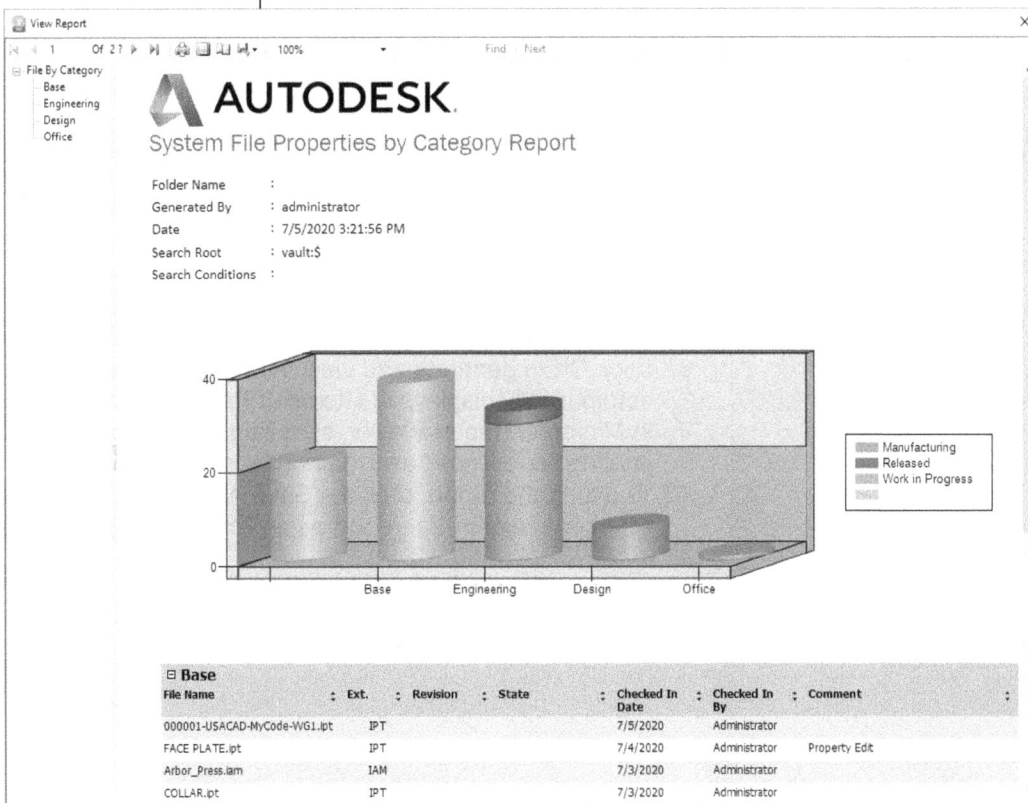

Creating Search Reports

To create a search report, you must be familiar with how to generate searches with conditions. Familiarize yourself with the template you intend to use before creating the search. Once you understand which file properties will be displayed, you can specify search conditions to return the required vault objects for the report.

Report templates can be stored in a local folder or in a vault. During installation, the pre-existing report templates are placed in a local folder at C:\Program Files\Autodesk\Vault *<edition> <year>*\ Explorer\Report Templates.

Procedure: Creating a New Report

The following steps describe how to create a new search report.

1. Click Find. The Find dialog box displays.
2. Click the Basic tab or the Advanced tab depending on the type of criteria for which you want to search.
3. Specify the search criteria for this report.
4. Click Report. The Select Report Template dialog box displays.
5. Enter the path of a template that you would like to use or click Browse to navigate to the required template. The last selected report template displays by default.
6. Click OK to generate a report. If none of the search criteria is set to ask me later, the report is created and displayed automatically.
7. If any of the criteria has a value set to ask me later, the Specify Search Values dialog box displays. Specify the search values for the listed properties, and then click OK. The Select Report Template displays.
8. Click OK to generate and view the report. The report automatically displays in Microsoft Report Viewer.
9. In Microsoft Report Viewer, click Page Setup to configure printing preferences and to print the report.
10. To export the report, click the Save As command and select whether to export the report as an Excel file or a PDF file.

Practice 7a | Create a Search Report

In this practice, you create a search report using a pre-existing template and save the report to Autodesk Vault.

◣ AUTODESK.

System File Properties Table Report

Folder Name	:
Generated By	: administrator
Date	: 7/27/2020 8:57:40 AM
Search Root	: vault:$
Search Conditions	: State contains Work in Progress

File Name	Extension	Category	Revision	State	Checked In Date	Comment
Handle_Assembly.iam	IAM	Engineering	B	Work in Progress	7/5/2020	
Handle.ipt	IPT	Engineering	B.1	Work in Progress	7/5/2020	
Screw.ipt	IPT	Engineering	B	Work in Progress	7/5/2020	
SHCS_10-32x6.ipt	IPT	Engineering	B	Work in Progress	7/5/2020	
Grip.ipt	IPT	Engineering	B	Work in Progress		
Grip.idw	IDW	Engineering	B	Work in Progress	7/5/2020	Available for editing
Arbor_Frame.ipt	IPT	Engineering	A	Work in Progress	7/3/2020	Change Category
Engineering Document.doc	DOC	Office	1	Work in Progress	6/2/2020	Set Office Category
Upper_Plate.ipt	IPT	Engineering	A	Work in Progress	6/1/2020	Set Engineering category
Pivot_Threaded.ipt	IPT	Engineering	A	Work in Progress	6/1/2020	Set Engineering category
Pivot_Lower.ipt	IPT	Engineering	A	Work in Progress	6/1/2020	Set Engineering category
Pin_B.ipt	IPT	Engineering	A	Work in Progress	6/1/2020	Set Engineering category
Pin_A.ipt	IPT	Engineering	A	Work in Progress	6/1/2020	Set Engineering category
Lower_Plate.ipt	IPT	Engineering	A	Work in Progress	6/1/2020	Set Engineering category
Clamp.iam	IAM	Engineering	A	Work in Progress	6/1/2020	Set Engineering category

The completed practice

Task 1 - Create a search report.

1. Start Autodesk Vault Workgroup software. Log in using the following information:

   - User Name: **usera**
   - Password: **vault**
   - Vault: AOTCVault

2. In the Navigation pane, click Project Explorer ($).

3. Click Find in the toolbar.

4. In the Find dialog box, click the Advanced tab.

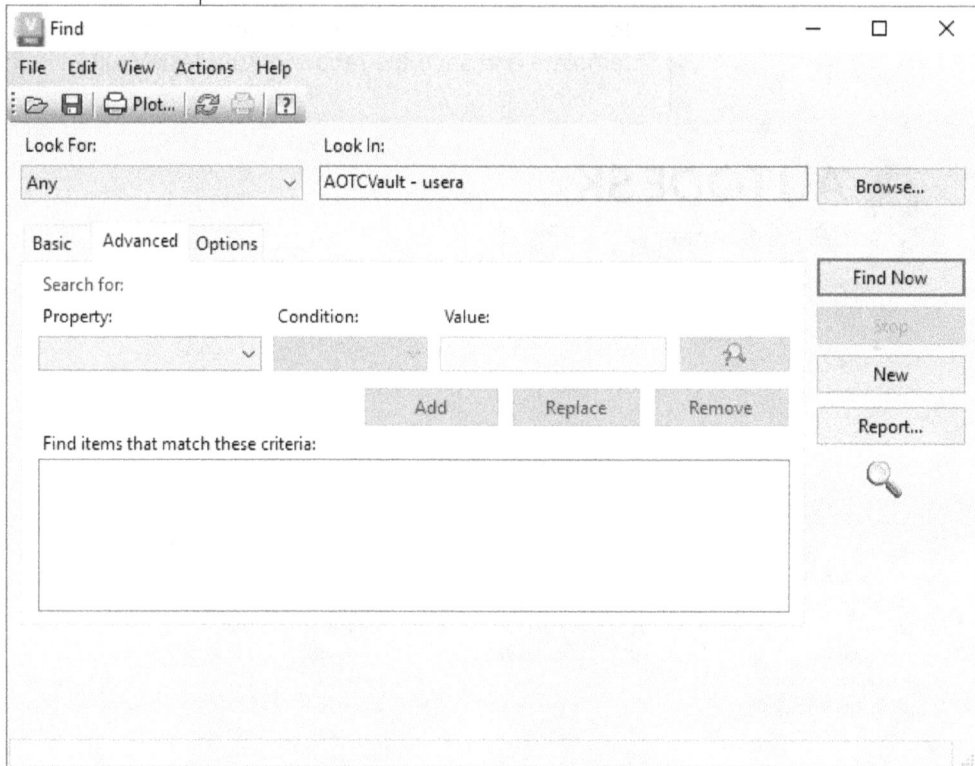

5. In the Advanced tab, do the following:

- Select State from the Property drop-down list.
- Select contains from the Condition drop-down list.
- Enter **Work in Progress** in the Value field.
- Click Add.

6. Click Find Now. All of the files in a Work in Progress state are listed.

	Name	Revision	State	
▶	Pivot_Lower.ipt	A	Work in Progress	^
	Pin_B.ipt	A	Work in Progress	
	Arbor_Frame.ipt	A	Work in Progress	
	ICU Valve Main Assembly.iam	A	Work in Progress	
	ICUVALVEASSY.iam	A	Work in Progress	
	ICUVALVE.ipt	A	Work in Progress	
	ICUSPRNG.ipt	A	Work in Progress	∨

7. Click Report.

8. In the Select Report Template dialog box, do the following:

   • Click the ellipses (…) button.
   • Select File Table.rdlc.
   • Click Open.

9. Click OK in the Select Report template dialog box. The report is generated and immediately launched in Microsoft Report Viewer.

7.2 Creating Custom Report Templates

Overview

The Autodesk Template Authoring Utility is intended for advanced users who are familiar with XML and RDLC authoring applications. You must have Microsoft Visual Studio installed to complete this lesson.

In this lesson, you learn how to create and modify custom report templates using the Autodesk Template Authoring Utility and Microsoft Visual Studio.

Use custom report templates to illustrate your vault data in a way that suits your business needs.

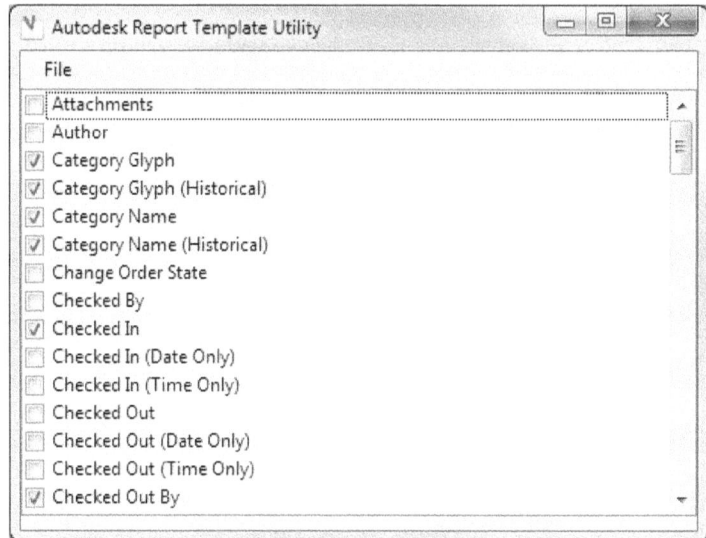

Objectives

After completing this lesson, you will be able to:

- Log in to the Autodesk Report Template Utility.

- Create and modify custom report templates.

Introduction to the Autodesk Template Authoring Utility

The Autodesk Report Template Authoring Utility is a software used to create an initial RDLC report template that contains all of the required Vault data binding information, but no formatting. You can open the RDLC file created by the Autodesk Report Template Utility in Visual Studio to specify the layout and formatting.

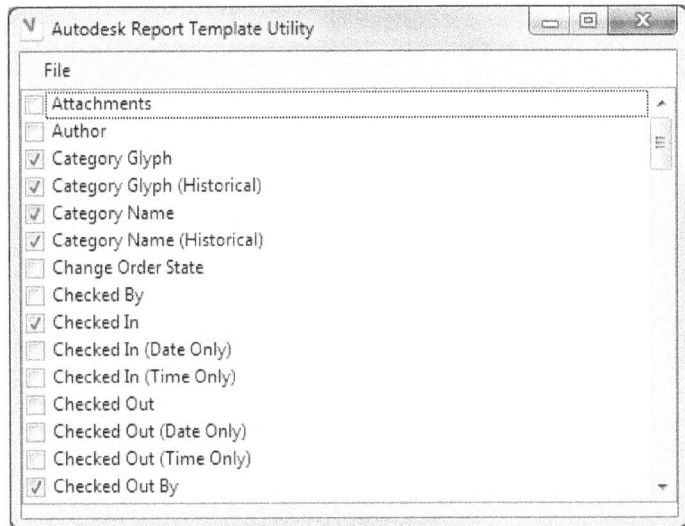

The ReportTemplateAuthoritingUtility.exe file is located in C:\Program Files\Autodesk\<*Autodesk Vault edition*> <*year*>\Explorer folder, where <Autodesk Vault edition> is the name of the Autodesk Vault edition you are using (such as, Autodesk Vault Professional) and <year> is the release year.

Report Template Authoring

Report Viewer uses the Microsoft-proposed standard Report Definition Language (RDL) to describe the format of the report. RDL is an XML schema that can contain:

- Formatting descriptions for tables, charts, images, headers, footers, and so on

- Data field definitions

- Report parameters

There are two types of RDL files supported by Report Viewer – one each for the server and local report processing mode. Vault uses the local processing mode, so you will be using the local types of RDL file – which, by convention, is stored in files with the .RDLC extension. RDL and RDLC files have the same XML schema, but RDLC files do not contain database connection information since the client application (in this case Vault) provides the data.

Although RDLC files contain XML, no knowledge of XML is required to create and edit them.

Procedure: Access the Autodesk Report Template Utility

The following steps describe how to access the Autodesk Report Template Authoring Utility.

1. Open Windows Explorer.
2. Navigate to C:\Program Files\Autodesk\<*Autodesk Vault edition*><*year*>\Explorer folder, where <Audodesk Vault edition> is the name of the Autodesk Vault edition you are using (such as Autodesk Vault Professional) and <year> is the release year.

Hint: Editing RDL Files

Detailed information on the editing of RDL files is outside the scope of this lesson, but Microsoft provides a good overview here: http://msdn.microsoft.com/en-us/library/ms159267.aspx, and a tutorial here: http://msdn.microsoft.com/en-us/library/ms167305.aspx.

There are also a number of books available on the subject of SQL Server Reporting Services that have sections covering RDLC report template creation and editing.

Creating a New Report Template

You create a new report template in three steps:

- Create a preliminary template in the Autodesk Report Template Utility with the properties you want to show in the report

- Customize the template layout using Microsoft Visual Studio.

- Test the template by generating a sample report.

Example of Using the Autodesk Report Template Utility

Your manager asks you to print a comprehensive report about files in all existing projects which have been released. She requests that the report include the file's state, revision ID, originator, and relative project. With these properties in mind, you open the Autodesk Report Template Utility and generate a preliminary template that meets your manager's criteria.

Then, using Microsoft Visual Studio, you modify the layout of the template to show the files in a bar chart based on project. Afterward, you create a search that returns all released files across all projects and then run the report using the newly created template.

Procedure: Creating a Preliminary Report Template

The following steps describe how to create a custom report template.

1. Open Windows Explorer.
2. Navigate to C:\Program Files\Autodesk\<*Autodesk Vault edition*><*year*>\Explorer folder, where <Audodesk Vault edition> is the name of the Autodesk Vault edition you are using (such as Autodesk Vault Professional) and <year> is the release year.
3. Launch the ReportTemplateAuthoringUtility.exe file. The Login dialog box displays.
4. Enter your login data and click OK. The Autodesk report Template Utility dialog box displays.
5. Select File>New.
6. Select the type of report template that you want to create from the Report Type drop-down list.
7. Select the report properties that you want to include in your report template from the Report Properties list.
8. Select File>Save As. The Save Template dialog box displays.
9. Navigate to the local folder or vault folder where you want the report template file to be saved and enter a filename in the File name field.
10. Click Save to save the file.

   Note: The report template is blank as the Autodesk Report Template Authoring Utility did not add any layout or format information to the RDLC file.

Procedure: Customizing the Layout of a New Report Template

The following steps describe how to create a custom report template.

1. Open Visual Studio and load the RDLC file you created using the Autodesk Report Template Utility.

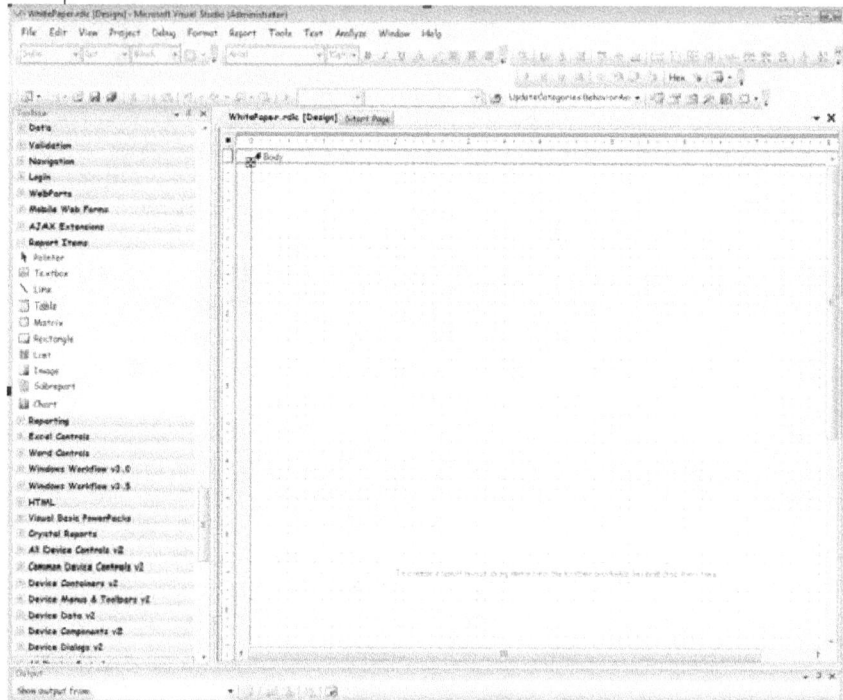

2. Add controls from the toolbox to the report template.
3. Once a control is placed in a report template the control can be configured to display the value of a Vault property. Right-click on the control and select Expression in the context menu. In the Expression dialog box, select Fields from the Category list to display all of the property names checked in step 1. Double-click on a property name to fill in the expression text box. Click OK.

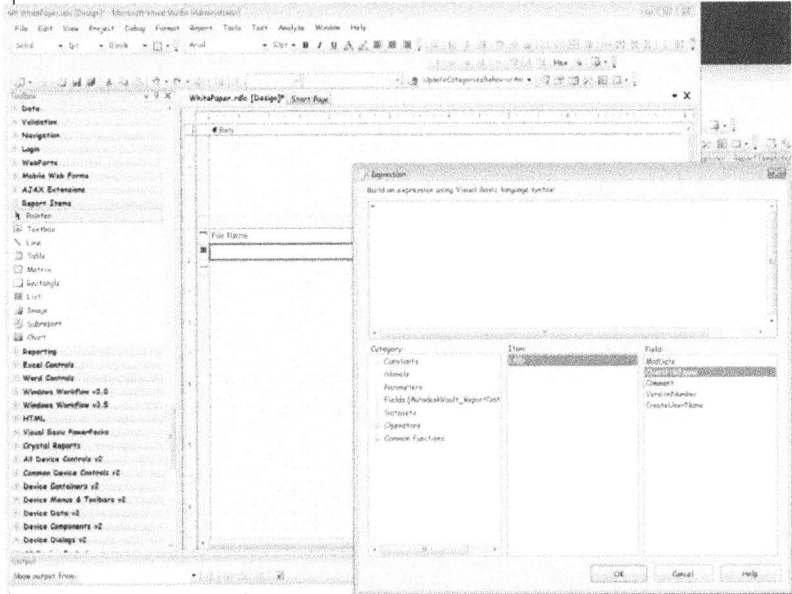

The field expression is now associated with the report control. When the report is generated, this control will be filled with the specified property for each Vault object processed.

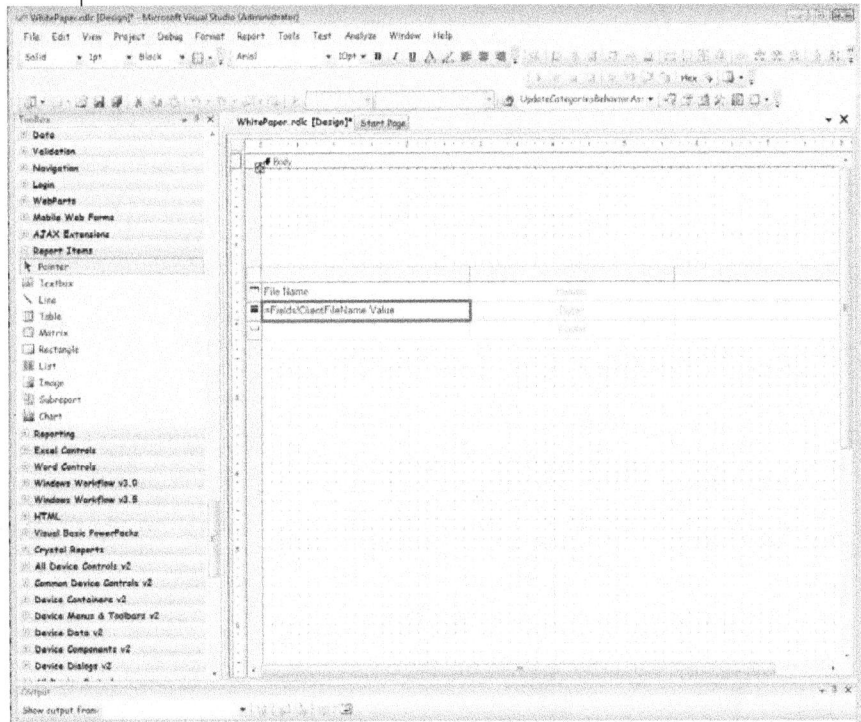

4. Save the template as an .RDLC file.

Procedure: Test the Report Template in Vault

1. Without exiting Visual Studio, start Vault and then run a report.
2. Specify the new created template in the report template dialog box.
3. View the results.
4. Modify the template in Visual Studio, as required.
5. Save the template.
6. Repeat, as required.

Including Non-property Vault Data in a Report

There is information relevant to a report that is not stored as properties in Autodesk Vault. To display this information in a report, a number of RDL-defined parameters must be supplied with values by the Vault prior to report processing. This process enables the template author to place and format these values in a report.

The following report parameters are supplied with values by Vault:

Template Parameter Name	Value
Vault_UserName	The name of the Vault user who generated the report.
Vault_VaultName	The name of the vault that provided data for the report. This is the vault that the user who generates the report is logged into.
Vault_SearchRoot	The name of the folder(s) specified in the Look in control located in the Find dialog box in Autodesk Vault.
Vault_LatestVersionOnly	The state of the Find latest versions only checkbox in the Options tab of the Find dialog box in Autodesk Vault.
Vault_SearchSubFolders	The state of the Search Subfolders" checkbox in the Options tab of the Find dialog box in Autodesk Vault.
Vault_SearchFileContent	The state of the Search file content checkbox in the Basic tab of the Find dialog box in Autodesk Vault.
Vault_SearchConditions	A string representation of the search conditions specified in the Advanced tab of the Find dialog box in Autodesk Vault.

Creating Reports with Non-property Vault Data

To use one or more of these parameters in your report, create a parameter of the same name in your template by loading the template in Visual Studio, right-clicking outside of the report template, and selecting Report Parameters.

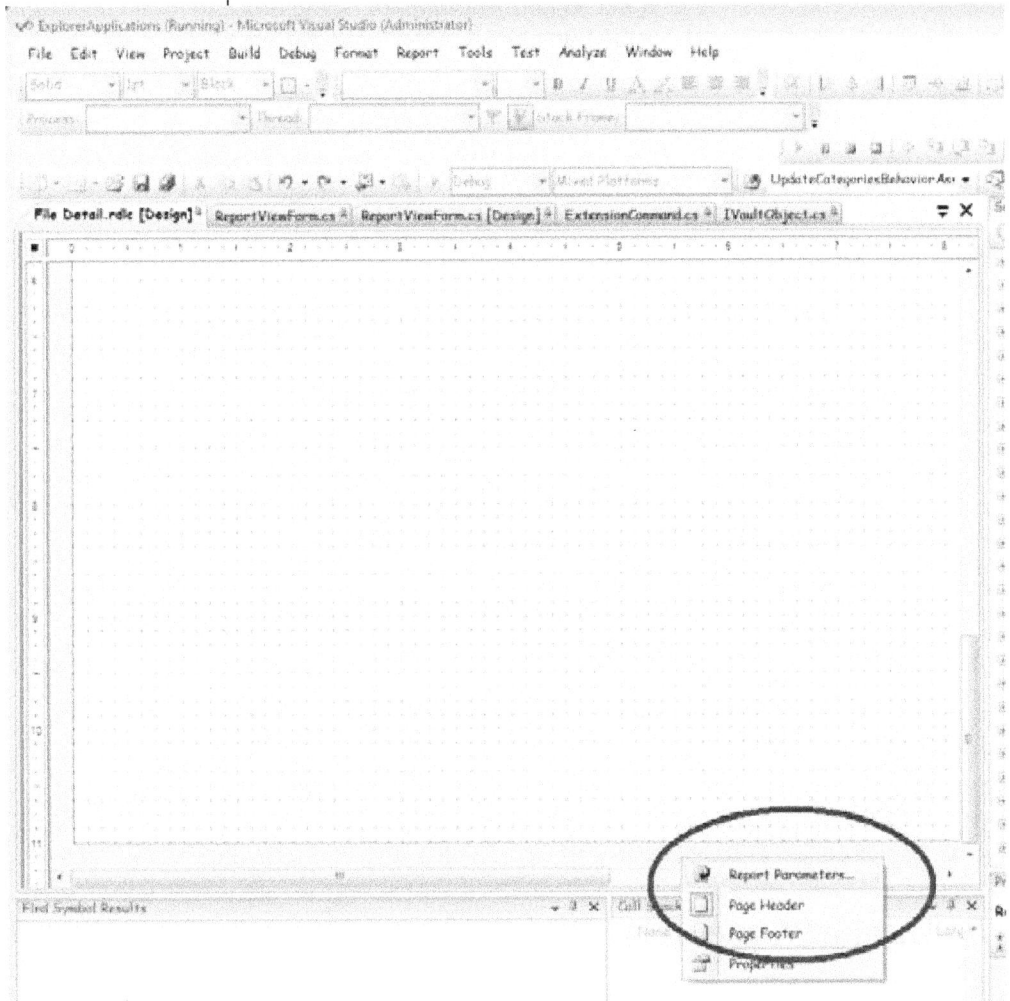

In the Report Parameters dialog box, you specify the parameters you want to include in your report. If you specify any of the reserved report parameter names listed above, the Vault reporting engine will supply a value for that parameter at runtime. Reserved parameter names must be spelled exactly as displayed in the table for the report engine to find them. Parameter names are case sensitive. The remainder of the fields in the Report Parameters dialog box can retain their default values as shown in the example below.

Placing a parameter value in a report is similar to placing property values: right-click on a control and then select Expression… in the context menu. In the Expression dialog box, double-click on a property name to specify that the parameter value to be used for this control.

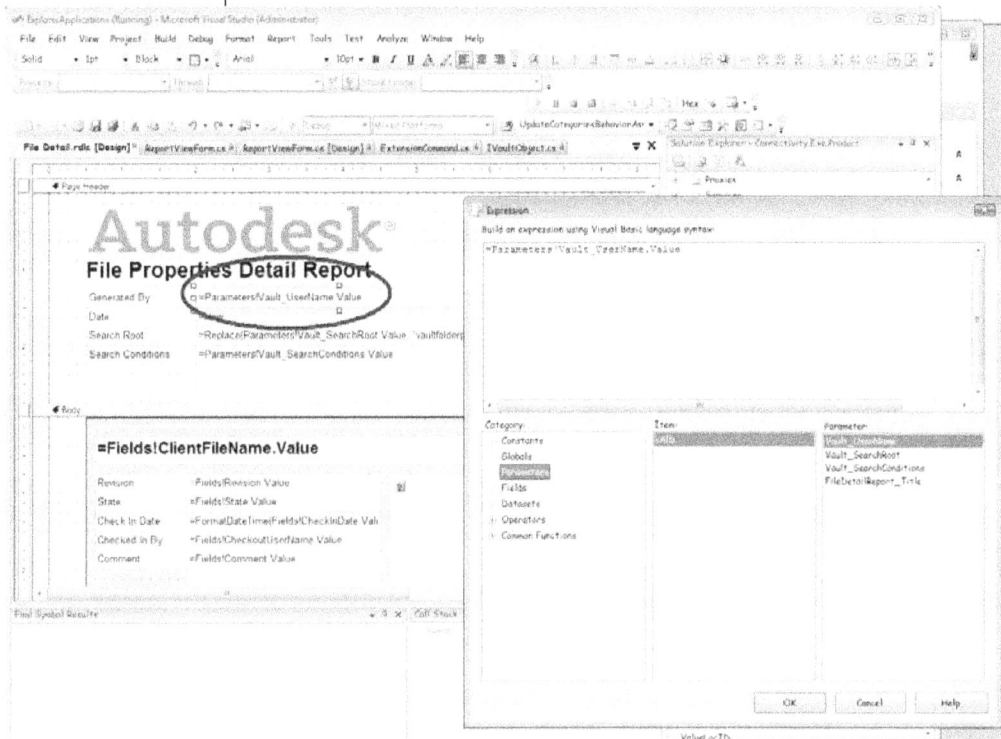

You can use parameter values in expressions just like field value. All of the sample templates included with Vault do parameter formatting in this way.

7.3 Chapter Summary

All Autodesk Vault Workgroup and Autodesk Vault Professional users can create reports to illustrate file details. These reports are useful in understanding design statuses by visually organizing file data based on specified properties.

You can use existing report templates to display your data in the form of charts, graphs, and tables. Or you can create and customize your own report template using the Autodesk Report Template Utility.

Having completed this chapter, you can:

- Create reports from an advanced search and configure how the data displays.

- Identify the different out-of-the box report templates and the information they are formatted to display.

- Create new report templates using the Autodesk Template Utility (for advanced users).

Autodesk Inventor In-CAD Data Management

You can manage and evaluate your vault file data from within the Autodesk® Inventor® software by using the Data Cards and Data Mapping features. Data Cards lets you examine pertinent vault details about a model, and modify property information for individual or multiple files. Data Mapping lets you generate report data for a model and publish the results as a chart. You can also map the report results onto the open model to better evaluate your design.

Both of these features give you an advantage in understanding and managing your design without ever having to leave the Autodesk Inventor software.

In this chapter, you learn how to view data cards, modify properties using data cards, generate reports, and map report data to your model.

Learning Objectives in This Chapter

- Enable and access both data card views.
- Build and navigate a data card deck, isolate a card, and remove a card from a card deck.
- Edit properties and track changes with data cards.
- Generate a report based on an open model.
- Map data in a report to the open model.

8.1 Working with Data Cards

Overview

Data Cards provide convenient summaries of the metadata assigned to a file or group of files through a single point of access. With data cards, you can determine a file's vault status, see a thumbnail of the file, and review and modify property information without leaving the Inventor application.

In this lesson, you learn how to enable the Data Cards feature, and view file properties in fingertip view and full data card view. You also learn how to build and manage a card deck, and use single or multiple data cards to manage file properties.

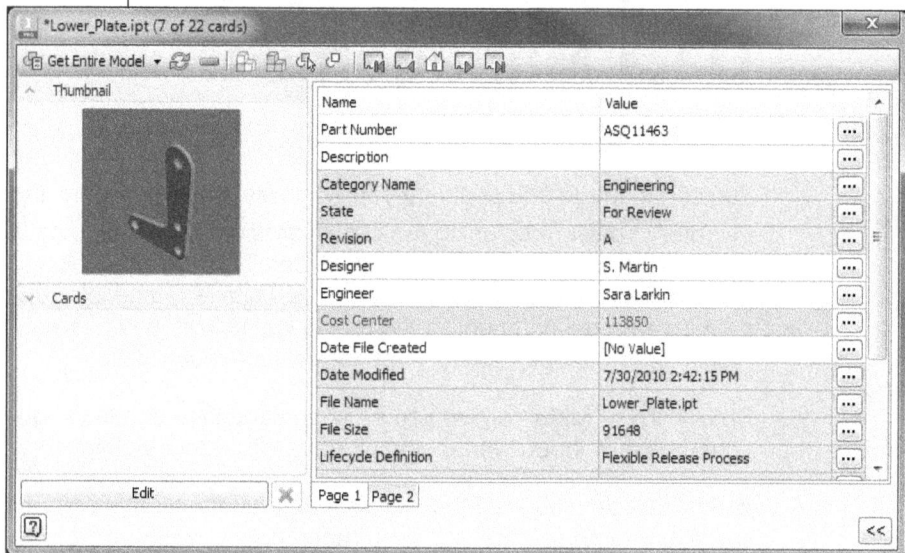

Objectives

After completing this lesson, you will be able to:

- Enable the Data Cards feature and view file properties.

- Switch between Fingertip view and Full Data Card view.

- Build and navigate a Data Card deck, including locating the Home Card in a deck.

- Isolate and remove a data card from a Data Card deck.

- Modify component properties using Data Cards.

About Data Card Views

Data Cards let you view pertinent vault details and properties for specified files. This insight into the statuses and properties of your model files makes it easier to manage the files throughout the lifecycle of the model.

Whenever a part is selected on the CAD canvas or in the Model or Vault browser list, the part is highlighted on the canvas, in the list, and the data card automatically updates to show the relevant information for that part.

Data cards can be displayed in two different ways: the fingertip view and the full data card view.

Access the Data Cards feature by clicking Data Cards in the Autodesk® Vault ribbon.

Fingertip View

The fingertip view is the default view for Data Cards. This view is a collapsed, read-only version of the full data card.

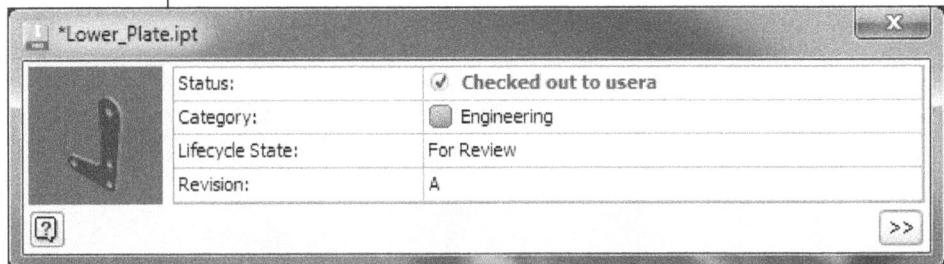

When a file is selected and the data card feature enabled, the fingertip displays the following information:

- Thumbnail
- Component name
- Status
- Category
- Lifecycle State
- Revision

Click Expand (>>) to switch from Fingertip view to Full Data Card view.

Full Data Card View

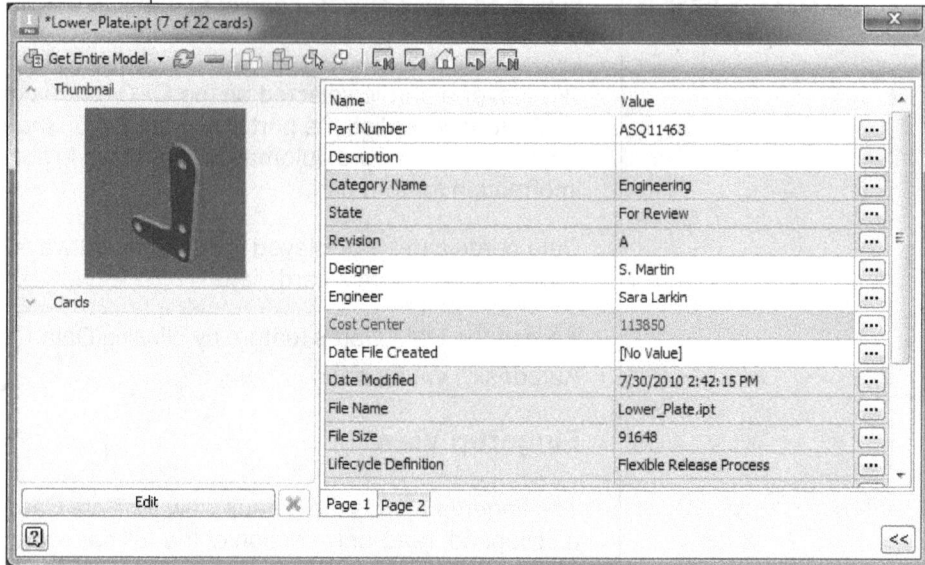

The fingertip can be expanded into a full data card which displays all of the information in the fingertip view and certain property information. The CAD administrator can determine which properties display in the Configure Data Card dialog box, which is accessed through the Vault Settings dialog box in the Autodesk Vault client.

The tasks you can perform with the data card depend on whether the data card is in read-only mode or edit mode.

Read-Only Mode

The read-only mode is the default mode for viewing the full data card. This mode enables you to compare selected files and to filter the property values based on your needs.

When a data card opens for a selected file or when a Refresh command is performed, the values for the properties are grabbed from the server and displayed. A pending icon displays next to the property name when the retrieval is in process. The pending icon disappears once the value is received for that property.

Edit Mode

The property grid can be changed to edit mode by clicking Edit. When in edit mode, the file is automatically checked out of the vault and you can edit the displayed property values. When you are finished editing, the new values are written to the local file and to the server file. These edits are made permanent when the file is checked into the vault. All actions performed on an individual card affect only the component associated with the card.

Example of Using a Data Card to Examine File Information

You just found out that one of the parts you are working with in your model has been set from Released back to Work in Progress. You need to find out who last checked in the part so that you can talk to that person about the changes he or she made.

You select the part in the model and then click Data Cards to enable the fingertip view for that part. You can see the lifecycle state is set to Work in Progress and that a revision bump has occurred, but you still need to know which engineer last made changes. You click the expand button and discover that it was your colleague Tim Smith who altered the part. Now you can talk to him about why the part was returned to Work in Progress.

Procedure: Enable Data Cards

- Click Data Cards in the Autodesk Vault ribbon. The data card for the selected file displays in fingertip view.

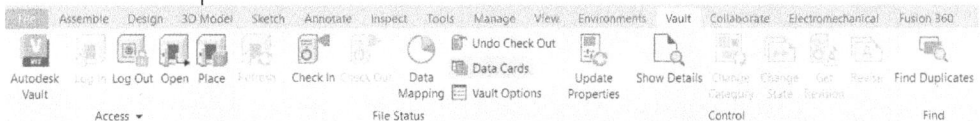

Procedure: View Fingertip Information

1. Enable data cards by clicking Data Cards in the Autodesk Vault ribbon.
   The data card window displays.
2. Select a part in the model.

   The data card grid updates automatically to show the part's filename, a thumbnail, revision, state, category, and vault status.

Procedure: View Full Data Card Information

1. Click Expand (>>) in the lower right-hand corner of the data card to switch between the fingertip view and the full data card view.
   The data card expands to display the properties. Some properties will show a pending icon until the value is retrieved from the server.

2. Click the tabs at the bottom of the grid to see additional properties.

Property information displayed on the data card is determined by the administrator in the Configure Data Card dialog box in the Autodesk Vault client.

Understanding Data Card Decks

Multiple data cards can be retrieved to create a card deck. You can specify the scope of the card deck by selecting individual files or an entire open model. A card deck contains one data card for each file specified in the scope and a Home card which lists the data cards in the card deck.

Data Card Deck Controls

At the top of the card deck, a toolbar has been provided for navigating and managing the data cards in the card deck. These commands enable you to retrieve the data cards for a model or a specified group of files and place them into a deck, refresh the data card values, remove a card from the deck, and isolate a card from the deck. There are also navigation buttons that enable you to move through the deck to the data card you want to review.

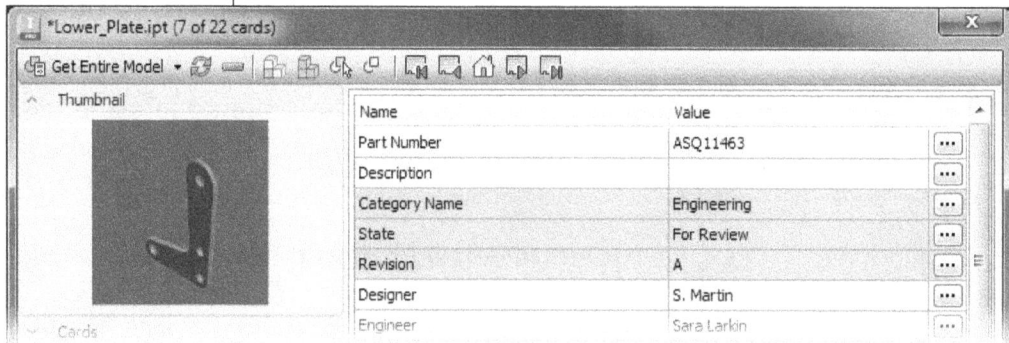

The following table defines each of the icons located in the data card navigation toolbar.

Icon	Command	Definition
Get CAD Selection ▾ / Get CAD Selection / Get Entire Model	Get Data Cards (Get CAD Files or Get Entire Model)	Retrieves either the selected CAD files or all the files in the open model and creates a card deck. Whichever Get Data Cards command is used last remains displayed.
	Refresh	If a single data card displays; the property values for that card are retrieved from the server. If the Summary card is selected, the property values for all data cards defined by the current Get command are retrieved from the server.
	Remove Card	Removes the current card or selected cards from the deck.
	Isolate On	Toggles on Isolation mode for the selected card or cards. Only the files for the selected data cards remain displayed and all other files in the card deck are rendered transparent on the canvas.
	Isolate Off	Toggles off Isolation mode for the selected card or cards. All files that were transparent when Isolate was toggled on, are displayed again.
	Select in CAD	Sends the current card selection to the CAD environment as a selection set.
	Clear CAD Selection	Clears the current CAD selection set.
	First	Goes to the first card in the card deck (also referred to as the Home card).
	Back	Goes back one card in the deck.
	Next	Goes to the next card in the deck.
	Home	Goes to the Home card.
	Last	Goes to the last card in the deck.

Procedure: Build a Data Card Deck

You can create a deck of data cards for faster referencing of properties and vault status information. Data cards are gathered from the open model or from a selection set and placed into a card deck. A home card is added as a summary card of the card deck contents.

1. Enable the data cards feature by selecting Data Cards in the Autodesk Vault ribbon.
2. Select a model or selection set in Inventor.
3. Click >> at the bottom of the data card to expand the data card from fingertip view to full view.
4. In the data card deck control toolbar, click the Get drop-down arrow and select either Get CAD Selection or Get Entire Model.
5. The data is retrieved from the vault. Depending on the size of the deck being created, the updates might take some time. You can continue working until all property values have been retrieved.
6. When all the data is retrieved, the home card displays and the navigation controls on the data card deck toolbar are activated.

Procedure: Remove Data Cards from a Card Deck

Refine your card deck by removing a data card or group of data cards from the card deck.

Remove an individual data card from a Card Deck

1. Select the data card you want to remove from the card deck.
2. Right-click and select Remove Card. The card is removed from the card deck.

Remove multiple data cards from a Card Deck

1. Click the home button to go to the home card in the card deck.
2. Select the data cards that you want to remove from the card deck from the data card list.
3. Right-click and select Remove Card. The cards are removed from the card deck.

Home Card

The home card displays the list of the files in the card deck and their property attributes. The property values that display depend on whether a single data card, multiple data cards, or no data cards are selected from the data card list.

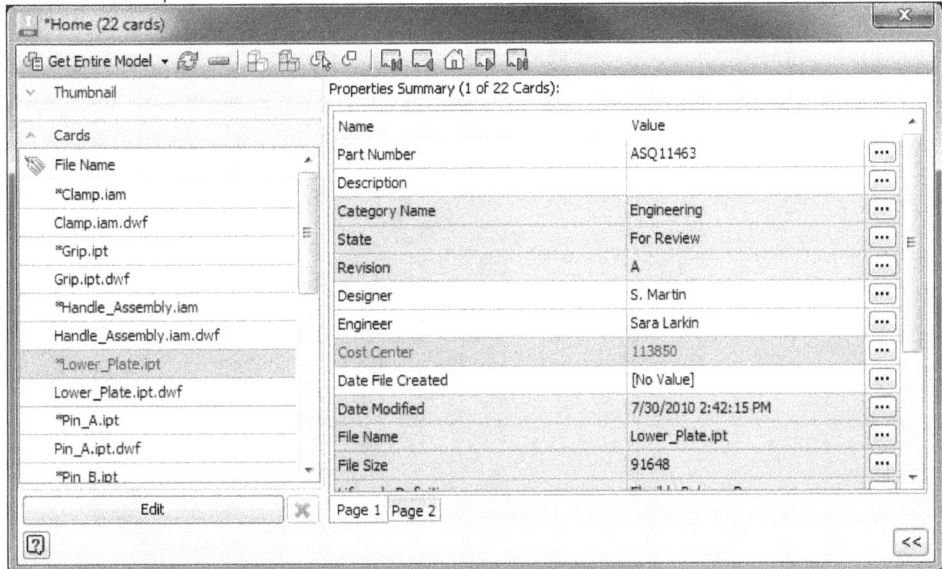

Home Card with 1 File Selected

Home Card Display Rules

1. If a single data card is selected, then the property values for that data card display on the home card.
2. If multiple data cards are selected, then the property values shared across the selected data cards display. If the values differ, then the word VARIES displays.
3. If no data cards are selected in the data card list, then all the property values shared across the entire deck display. If the values differ, then the word VARIES displays.

You can make edits with individual data cards or use the Home card to make bulk edits throughout the entire card deck. When making bulk edits for properties with different values throughout the deck, a value collector is used to list the different values associated with that property.

At the top of the home card, the number of cards in the deck and the number of cards selected for comparison display.

Isolation Mode

Sometimes, in models with many parts, it is necessary to isolate a part for easier examination. The isolation feature enables you to distinguish specified parts in a model. Select the data card(s) for the part(s) which you want to view and click Isolate On from the data card deck controls. The selected parts remain visible on the CAD canvas while all other parts in the card deck become transparent.

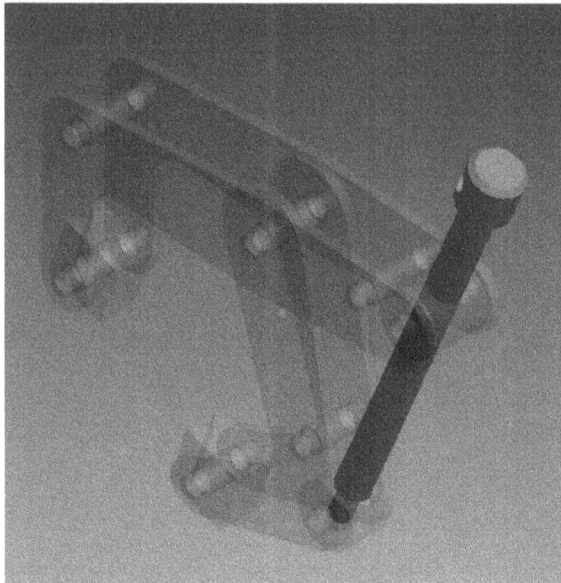

Click Isolate Off on the data card deck controls to make all parts on the CAD canvas visible again.

Procedure: Isolating Parts in Autodesk Inventor

You can isolate a part or parts for easier examination by enabling the Isolation feature.

Toggling Isolation On

1. Click Home in the data card deck toolbar to go to the home card.
2. Select the data cards for the parts which you want to isolate on the CAD canvas.
3. Click Isolate in the data card deck toolbar.

   The parts remain viewable on the CAD canvas and all other parts with unselected data cards in the card deck become transparent.

Toggling Isolation Off

- Click Isolate Off in the data card deck toolbar to make all parts on the CAD canvas visible again.

Editing Properties with Data Cards

Properties can be edited on both the full data card and in a card deck. Changes with data cards can only be made when the data card is in edit mode. Click Edit to begin changing property values.

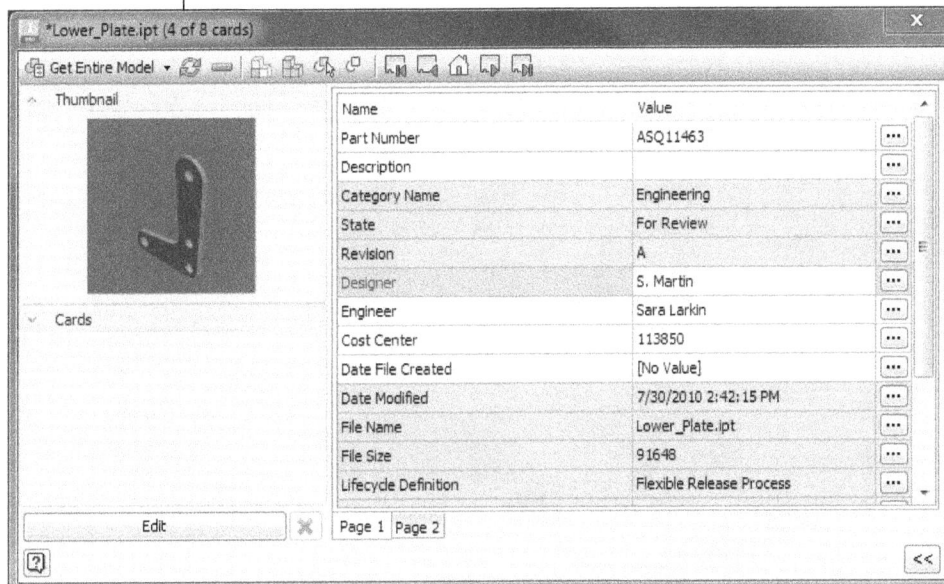

Files must be checked out before changing anything. If any files in the card deck are not checked out or if a data card is not available for editing, you will receive a message asking you to check out the files or to remove any invalid cards from the card deck. When a property is edited, click Save to commit the changes. An asterisk displays beside the filename to indicate that the data card has been modified.

Autodesk Vault operations are disabled when a data card is in edit mode.

Modified files must be checked back into the vault for the changes to become permanent. If you attempt to close the card deck or to change the data card view while a modified file is checked out, you will be prompted to check the file in or discard your changes before proceeding.

Tracking Edits

Since edits are not immediately permanent, you can track edits and review them before checking the modified files into the vault. If a property has been modified, an asterisk (*) displays beside the filename on the data card and beside the filenames in the data list on the home card if you are using a card deck.

Additionally, the font changes for property values that have been modified.

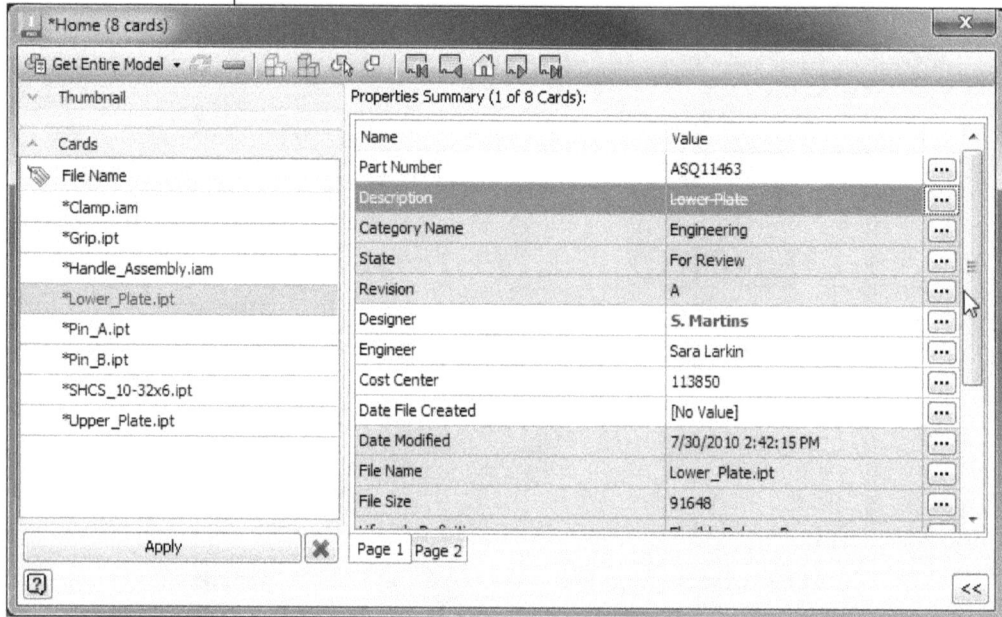

The following table explains the different text effects and their significance.

Text	Meaning	Edit
Normal font	Same as original value (no change)	The value is the same as the original value or has been reset before checking the file back in.
Normal font with gray background	Read-Only	The property cannot be altered even in Edit mode.
Strikethrough Font	Deleted Value	The original value was deleted. When the file is checked back into the vault, this value is blank.
Blue Font	Edited Value	The original value has changed but the file has not been checked back into the vault to commit the change.

Undoing Changes

During the editing process, you can choose to undo a single property change or to undo all changes as long as the current changes have not been committed.

Right-click on the property on the data card to open a context menu. Select Revert to reset the selected property to its original value. Select Revert Selected Files to reset the properties of the selected files to their original values.

Compliance Rules

Compliance is a key component in managing properties. When a property is non-compliant, a red exclamation icon is inserted into the value field on the data card. On the home card, a non-compliant icon displays beside the filename to let you know that one of the properties for that file is non-compliant.

Hover the cursor over the exclamation icon to see a tooltip describing the reason why the property is not compliant. Since some data cards contain multiple tabs of properties, the icon will also display on the tab to indicate if there is a non-compliant property not displayed on the data card. There is also a tab that shows all non-compliant properties in one list.

In the illustration below, the Cost Center value for Lower_Plate.ipt is not compliant because it requires a minimum of six characters and only five have been entered.

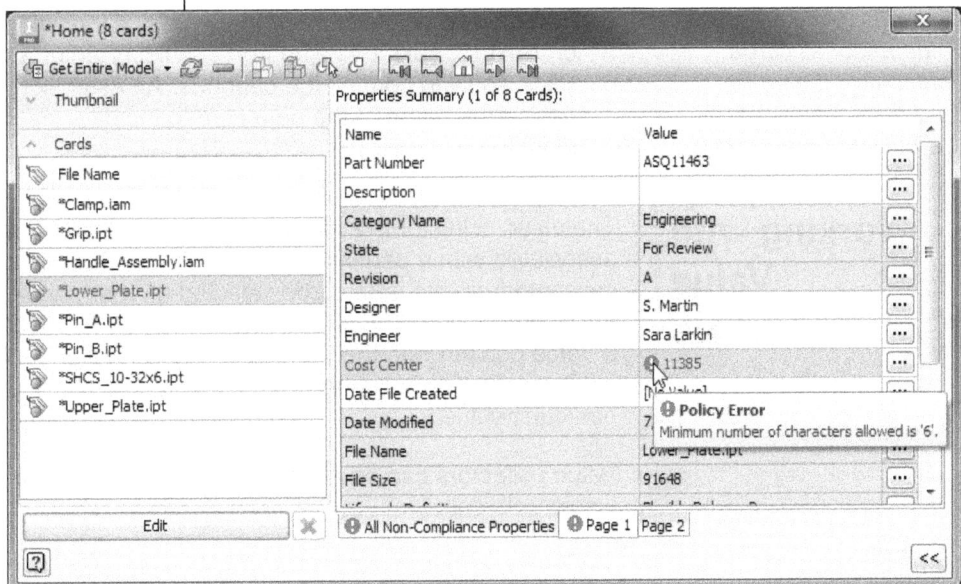

Procedure: Edit a Single Data Card

1. Go to the data card for which you want to change a property value.
2. Click Edit to enter edit mode. Properties that cannot be edited are disabled.
3. Locate the property you want to change. Use the tabs at the bottom of the values grid to navigate through all available properties.
4. Enter a new value in the property field.
   OR
   Right-click on the field and select Undo in the context menu to undo any previous changes.
5. Click Apply to commit the changes. An asterisk (*) displays beside the name of the data card to indicate that it has been modified.

Changes made to property values are not permanent until the affected files are checked back into the vault. If you attempt to resize the data card or close the data card feature, you will be prompted to check in changed files first.

Procedure: Edit Properties for Multiple Data Cards

1. Go to the home card.
2. Click Edit. Properties that cannot be edited are disabled.
3. Select the data cards in the data card list for which you want to edit property values.

   Alternatively, clear all selections to change values from the whole deck.

4. Locate the property that you want to change. Use the tabs at the bottom of the values grid to navigate through all available properties.
5. Enter a new value in the property field. If the field has a value of VARIES, select a value from the list or enter a new one.
6. Click Apply to commit the changes. An asterisk (*) displays beside the name of the data card to indicate that it has been modified.

Changes to the property value affect all cards selected or the entire card deck if no cards are selected.

Working with Value Collectors

The value collector is a dialog box that lists the different values associated with a particular property. The values listed are collected from the data cards selected on the home card or the entire deck if no cards are selected. The value collector contains a Value column with the list of property values and a Usage column which displays how many data cards share that particular value.

Value collectors can be accessed from the home card or from a single data card.

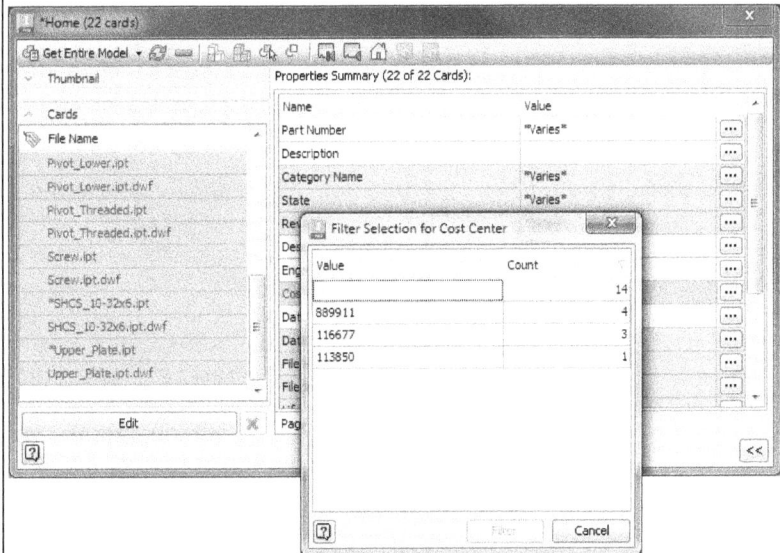

Using a Value Collector with the Home Card

In a card deck, the same properties are repeated for each card. If the selection of data cards shares the same value for that property, then that value displays next to the property name on the home card. However, if the property values differ, then the word VARIES displays next to the property. Properties with a value of VARIES display with a small ellipses icon (…). Click the icon to access the value collector.

You can filter property values for review in read-only mode or change them in edit mode.

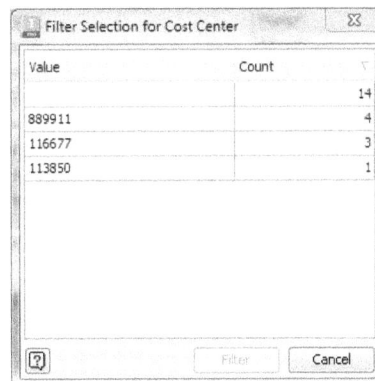

Read-Only Mode

In read-only mode, you can filter values collected. Select a value in the value collector and click Filter to select the cards in the card list that contain that property value.

The file associated with a data card must be checked out before editing any properties.

For example, the value collector for the Cost Center property lists all of the values for Cost Centers in the deck. If you select 324657 from the collector and click OK, the five cards with 324657 as the value for Cost Center are selected in the card list.

This process can be repeated for additional properties, enabling you to refine the data card selection each time.

In edit mode, you can change the values for a file associated with a particular data card or make bulk changes to all cards associated with that value.

The value collector has both a Values and a Count column. However, unlike read-only mode, an editing field at the top of the value collector enables you to adjust values for the data cards that use that property.

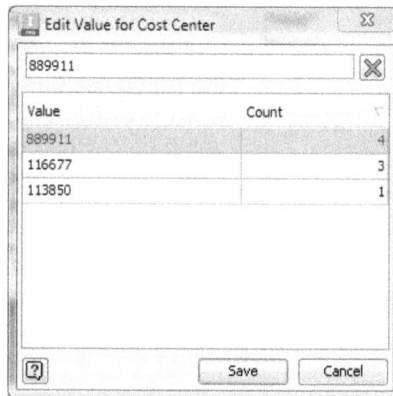

Edit Value for Cost Center		⊠
889911		
Value	Count	
889911		4
116677		3
113850		1
	Save	Cancel

For example, the value collector for the Cost Center property lists all of the values for Cost Center in the deck. If you select 889911 in the collector, 889911 displays for editing at the top of the dialog box. The value can then be cleared or modified. Click Save to commit any changes.

Using a Value Collector with a Single Data Card

On a single data card, the properties are the same as those on every other card in the deck. However, only the property values for the selected data card display. A small ellipses icon (...) displays next to each property. Click the icon to access the value collector.

Read-Only Mode

In read-only mode, the value collector displays a list of available values in the card deck. These values do not impact the card.

Edit Mode

In edit mode, the value collector displays a list of available values in the card deck. A value can be selected from the list and applied to the file associated with the current data card.

Procedure: Use a Value Collector to Filter Property Values (Read-Only)

From the Home Card

1. Go to the home card. Ensure that you are in read-only mode. (Edit should be visible.)
2. Select the data cards in the data card list for which you want to collect property values. Alternatively, clear all selections to collect values from the whole deck.
3. Click the ellipses (...) next to the property value you want to review. The icon is only available for properties displaying a value of VARIES.
4. In the Filter Selection dialog box, select the value you want to use to filter your data card selection. The data card list is updated to display only those data cards containing that property value.
5. Continue filtering the data card selection using other properties, if required.

From a Single Data Card

1. Select a data card in the card deck to review its property values.
2. Ensure that the card deck is in read-only mode. (Edit should be visible.)
3. Click the ellipses (...) next to the property value you want to review. A list of values that already exist in the card deck for that property displays.

Procedure: Use a Value Collector to Edit Property Values

From the Home Card

The file associated with a data card must be checked out before editing any properties.

1. Go to the home card.
2. Click Edit.
3. Select the data cards in the data card list for which you want to collect property values. Alternatively, clear all selections to collect values from the whole deck.
4. Click the ellipses (...) next to the property value you want to change. The icon is only available for properties displaying a value of VARIES.
5. In the Edit Value dialog box, select a new value for the selected property from the Values list or enter a value in the Editing field.
6. Any changes made to a value affect all data cards using that property value. Refer to the Usage column for the number of data cards affected. If required, refine your data card selection using the steps described in the read-only section before continuing.
7. Click Save to commit the changes and close the Edit Value dialog box. An asterisk (*) displays beside the name of the data card to indicate that it has been modified.

From a Single Data Card

Changes made to property values are not permanent until the affected files are checked back into the vault. If you attempt to resize the data card or close the data card feature, you will be prompted to check in changed files first.

1. Select a data card in the card deck for which you want to edit property values.
2. Click Edit.
3. Click the ellipses (...) next to the property value you want to change.
4. A list of values that already exist in the card deck for that property displays.
5. Select a new value for the selected property from the Values list or enter a value in the Editing field. Click Save to commit the changes and close the Edit Value dialog box. An asterisk (*) displays beside the name of the data card to indicate that it has been modified.

Managing the Data Card Layout

Administrators can streamline property management with data cards by customizing the data card layout. In the Configure Data Card dialog box in the Vault Settings of the client, administrators can determine how many pages a data card uses and which properties display.

Select Tools>Administration>Vault Settings>Behaviors tab and click Data Card to access the Configure Data Card dialog box.

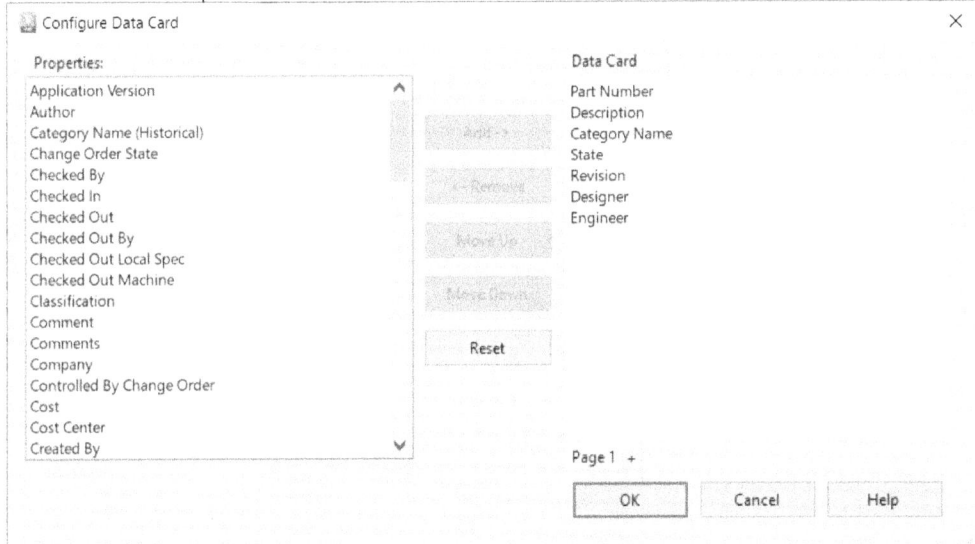

You can manage tabs and determine which properties are available for the CAD user to modify in the Configure Data Card dialog box. A properties list displays all of the properties that can be added to the selected tab. A property can be added to a single tab only once. Several different tabs, however, can list the same property.

Actions	Description
Add	Select one or more properties from the properties list and click Add to include them in the selected data card tab.
Remove	Select a property already assigned to a tab and click Remove to delete it from that tab.
Move Up	Moves a property up in the selected tab.
Move Down	Moves a property down in the selected tab.
Reset	Returns the current tab to the last layout.
Rename tab	Double-click on the tab to rename it.
Add new tab	Click the small tab with a plus sign (+) to add a new tab to the data card. By default, the tabs are numbered sequentially.
Delete a tab	Click the X in the selected tab to delete the tab itself.
OK	Saves the changes to the data card layout and closes the dialog box.

Procedure: Configure Data Card Layout

1. Select Tools>Administration>Vault Settings>Behaviors tab. Click Data Card.
2. In the Configure Data Card dialog box, select one or more properties from the properties list and click Add to add them to the selected tab.

   Select a property and click Remove at any time to refine the properties in the selected tabs.

3. If required, click Move Up or Move Down to reorganize the properties in the tab, as required.
4. Double-click on the selected tab and rename it.
5. Click the + tab to create a new tab.
6. Click the x tab to delete a tab.
7. When finished, click OK to save your settings and close the dialog box.
8. Click Reset at any time to restore the dialog box to the last saved layout.

Practice 8a

Manage a Card Deck

In this practice, you create a custom data card deck for a design.

Task 1 - Create a card deck.

1. Start Autodesk® Vault Workgroup software. Log in using the following information:

   - User Name: **usera**
   - Password: **vault**
   - Vault: Data Card and Mapping Vault

2. In the Navigation pane, click Project Explorer ($).

3. Click Find in the toolbar.

4. In the Find dialog box, search for Clamp.iam.

5. Right-click on Clamp.iam and select Open to launch it in Autodesk Inventor software. Select the Data Cards and Data Mapping Exercise project file.

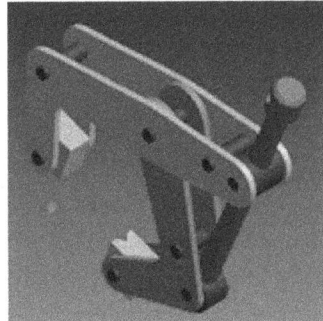

6. Log in to Vault as usera, if required.

7. In the Autodesk Vault ribbon, click Data Cards.

8. The Fingertip view of the data card for the clamp displays.

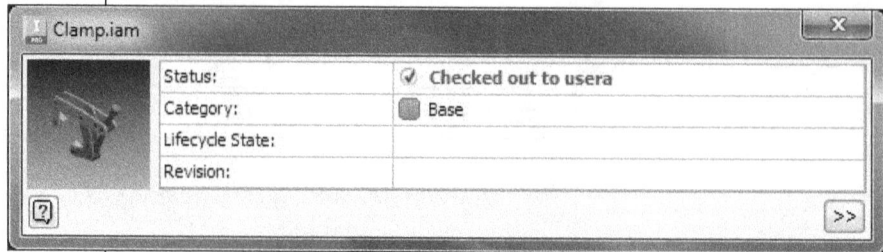

Clamp.iam

Status:	☑ Checked out to usera
Category:	🗋 Base
Lifecycle State:	
Revision:	

9. Click the expand button on the fingertip view to switch to full data card view.

10. Note that the title says Home and that there is only 1 card in the deck. Now you will add data cards for referenced parts.

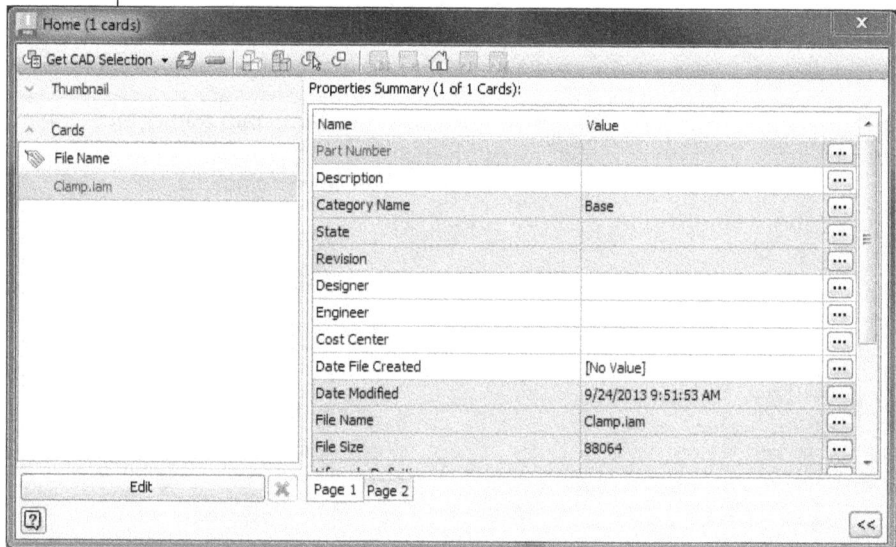

Home (1 cards)

Get CAD Selection ▾

Thumbnail

Cards
  File Name
    Clamp.iam

Properties Summary (1 of 1 Cards):

Name	Value
Part Number	
Description	
Category Name	Base
State	
Revision	
Designer	
Engineer	
Cost Center	
Date File Created	[No Value]
Date Modified	9/24/2013 9:51:53 AM
File Name	Clamp.iam
File Size	88064

Edit

Page 1 Page 2

11. At the top of the full data card view, click Get Entire Model from the drop-down list in the toolbar.

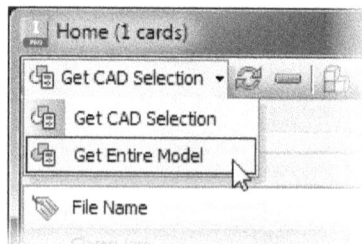

Home (1 cards)

Get CAD Selection ▾
  Get CAD Selection
  Get Entire Model
File Name

Data Cards for all of the design components are retrieved.

Task 2 - Edit Properties for a Single Data Card

You now have a card deck consisting of data cards for all of the components in the Clamp.iam design.

Note that one of the cards has a non-compliant icon next to it.

1. Click the Lower_Plate.ipt name in the card list to go directly to that card.

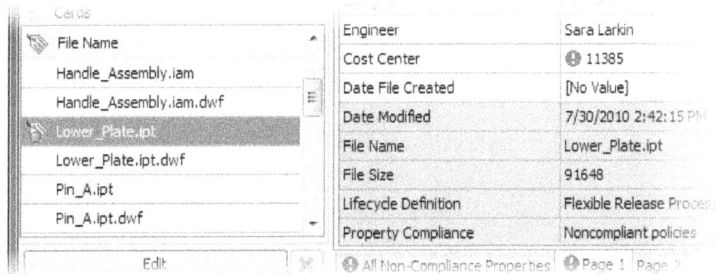

2. The Cost Center property for the Lower_Plate.ipt does not comply with property policy. In this case, the minimum character length for cost center is six characters.

3. Click Edit to enter editing mode.

4. Click the ellipses icon in the value field for Cost Center.

5. The Edit Value for Cost Center dialog box opens.

6. Note that only one card is using the 11385 cost center but no other cards in the deck are using a cost center. You will fix this in a few steps.

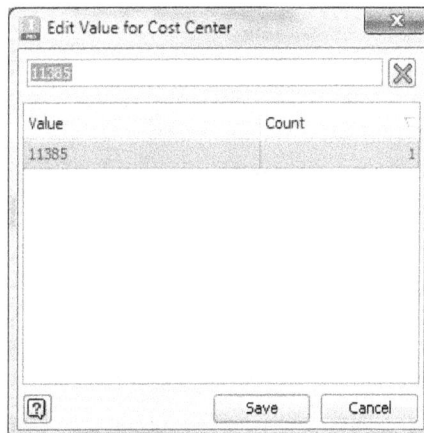

7. Enter **113850** in the entry field at the top of the dialog box and click Save.

8. The Cost Center value has been updated. Note that the new value is in bold blue in the Data Card field.

9. This means that the value has been changed but it has not applied yet.

10. Click Apply on the data card to commit the change. A Property Edit Result dialog box displays whether the change was a success. Click close to exit this dialog box.

11. Click Home in the data card toolbar to return to the home card in the card deck.

12. Note that the compliance error has been resolved.

13. Double-click on the Upper_Plate.ipt file in the card list to go directly to that card.

14. Since this part is from the same cost center as the Lower_Plate.ipt, ensure that this card is updated as well.

15. To do so, click Edit.

16. Click the ellipses button beside the Cost Center Value.

17. All available values are listed or you can enter one manually.

18. Since you know that this part shares the same cost center as the previous part, simply double-click on the 113850 value and it enters that same value in the entry field.

19. Click Save to close the dialog box.

20. Click Apply on the Upper_Plate.ipt data card to commit the changes.

21. Click Close in the Property Edit Result dialog box.

22. Click Home to return to the Home card.

Task 3 - Edit properties for multiple data cards.

Pin_A.ipt, Pin_B.ipt, and Grip.ipt all share the same cost center but it's different from the one you just did. Rather than edit them one at a time, you can make a mass edit from the home card.

1. Select Grip.ipt, Pin_A.ipt, and Pin_B.ipt in the Data Cards list by holding <Ctrl> as you click on the filenames.

2. Click Edit in the Home card.

3. Click the ellipses button next to the value for Cost Center.

4. In the Edit Value for Cost Center dialog box, enter **116677** and click Save.

5. Click Apply to commit the changes.

6. The Property Edit Result dialog box shows the multiple changes and whether they were saved to the server successfully.

7. Click Close to exit the dialog box.

8. In the Home card, select all of the cards in the card list.

9. Note that the Cost Center says Varies. This means that more than one value exists for Cost Center in the selected group of cards.

10. Click the ellipses button to review the different values for Cost Center in the deck. Note that the Count column indicates how many cards share each value.

11. Double click the value that is blank and click Filter.

12. The data cards with the empty (blank) value are automatically highlighted in the Home card list.

13. Click Edit.

14. Click the ellipses button beside the Cost Center value.

15. Enter **889921** in the Edit Value for Cost Center dialog box and click Save.

16. Click Apply to commit the changes.

17. Click Close in the Property Edit Result dialog box.

18. All cost center values are now updated.

8.2 Data Mapping and Report Generation

Overview

The Data Mapping feature enables you to easily assess important business data for your model. Report data is mapped on to the model to provide visual output of the correlation between report results and the open model. Mapping the report to the model colors the model to match the corresponding chart elements. The entire chart can be mapped onto the model, or you can choose which chart elements to map.

Use data mapping to visually evaluate your design.

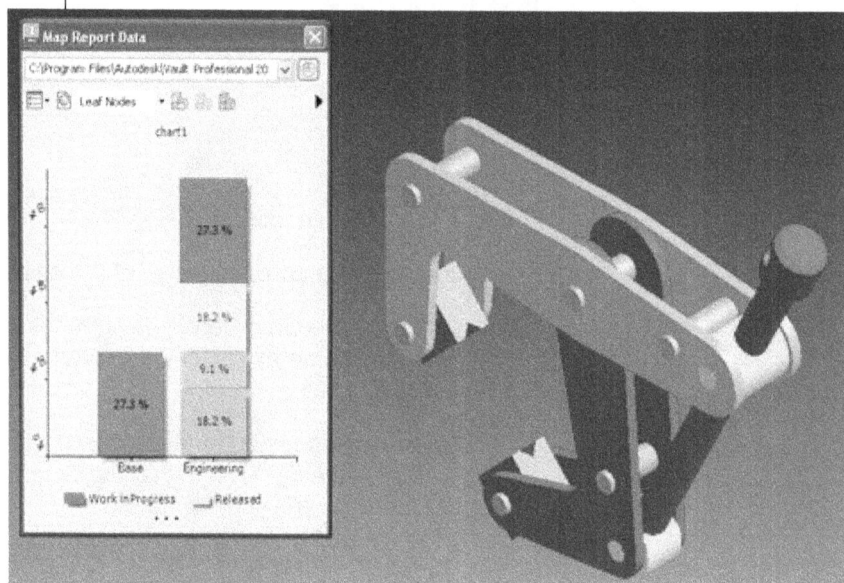

Objectives

After completing this lesson, you will be able to:

- Map your data onto a model

- Generate a report based on your data mapping results

- Manage chart elements

- Configure the color assignments for your reports

Introduction to the Data Mapping

Data Mapping is not available in sketch mode.

Data mapping is a useful tool for viewing different levels of data in a model. However, because the model hierarchy can be mapped at different levels, it is important to know from where the data is being collected to accurately interpret the results. Additionally, you should also know how file attachments affect the report results.

Procedure: Enable Data Mapping

Data Mapping must be enabled before you can generate reports or map any model data for review.

- In the Autodesk Vault ribbon, click Data Mapping to launch the Map Report Data dialog box.

File Attachments

A report is generated using all of the files in the current model, including attachments. As a result, the chart might not have a 1:1 correlation with the files displayed in the canvas.

For example, a pie chart slice can indicate that a large percentage of files are currently in the Work in Progress (WIP) state. However, when mapping the data onto the model, only a small number of files are color coded to the WIP slice. This difference in display is because the slice is taking into account the attached files and the part files, but only the part files display on canvas. You can view the full report to see a complete list of files that make up a pie slice.

Mapping Report Data to the Model Hierarchy

When a report is generated, the reporting system evaluates the files without knowledge of their relationships. The resulting chart represents actual flat data. Since a model has several levels to it, you have the option of mapping your data as three different levels to better understand the report data. This versatility enables you to examine model data at the parts level, the assemblies' level, and the first children level. By examining all three levels, you will have the most complete picture of the report results.

Leaf Node Mapping

Leaf Node mapping is the most granular view of the model. Only parts in assemblies are mapped. This level is used most often early in a project to see where components are in the development process.

All Assemblies Mapping

All Assemblies mapping provides a perspective of the report results as they relate to the assembly level and first level parts. The color of an assembly determines the color of its parts but subassemblies are assigned their own colors.

First Level Children Mapping

First level children mapping is the least granular view. All parts and assemblies within each first level child are given the same color as the first level child.

Mapping Your Data

The Map Report Data dialog box contains several features that enable you to generate reports, map report results, and manage chart elements. The Map Report Data dialog box turns opaque when the mouse moves over it and transparent when the mouse moves away. The chart legend can be toggled on or off to further reduce the size of the dialog box and conserve canvas space.

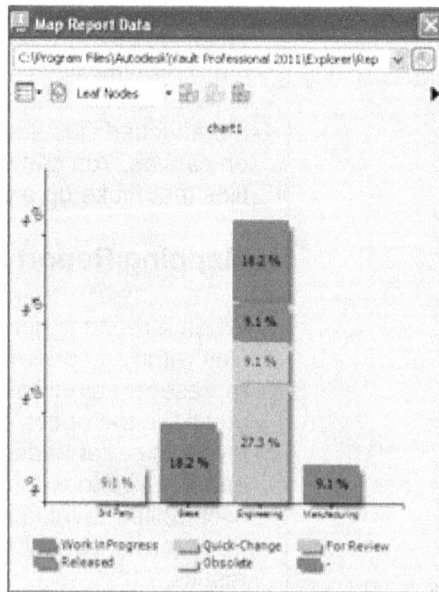

When the Map Report Data dialog box first opens, only the Report Template menu and the Generate Report button are enabled. All other controls are disabled until a report is generated.

Since the Map Report Data dialog box is document-based, each document can have its own dialog box.

Understanding the Map Report Dialog Box

The following table describes each of the features available in the Map Report Data dialog box.

	Feature	Description
no icon	Report Template menu	The report template drop-down list contains a list of the most recently used templates and the options for opening an existing template from either a local folder or the vault. **Note:** Opening a template from the vault checks that file out of the vault. The file is checked in after it is saved.
	Generate Report	Creates a report based on the selected template. Click the button again to refresh report results after making changes.
	Display Options	Enables or disables chart labels and the chart legend.
	View Full Report	Displays the full report in a report viewer.
Leaf Nodes	Mapping Method menu	Enables you to select which of the three mapping methods to use when mapping chart data or isolating files. The three options are: leaf nodes, all assemblies, and first level children.
	Apply Color Mapping	Assigns the chart element colors to the corresponding model components based on the selected mapping method. This button is a toggle and can be clicked again to toggle off color assignments.

	Apply Isolation	Dims the files that are not represented by the chart elements and leaves the selected chart data mapped on the screen at full visibility. The data is isolated based on the current mapping method.
		This button is a toggle and can be clicked again to toggle off isolation and restore all files to full visibility.
	Clear Color Mapping or Isolation	Updates the current mapping and isolation display if any changes are made to the chart element selection.
		Note: If new data is added to the vault, the report must be regenerated. This button does not re-run the report.
	Chart Selector	Enables you to select which chart to use for data mapping if more than one chart exists for the template.
		If data is currently mapped when a new chart is selected, the data is cleared. Click Data Mapping to map the data from the new chart.
Override Color Reset Selection Set Add to Selection Set Get Data Cards	Chart element context menu	Enables you to select and manage chart elements for custom data mapping. Access the menu by right-clicking on any of the elements in the.
		By default, all chart elements are mapped to the model.
Work in Progress Quick-Change Released Obsolete	Chart Legend	Displays the chart elements and associated color map data graph assignments in a colorful graph.

Procedure: Map Report Data

After generating a report, you can map the results onto the open model in Inventor.

The report is generated using all of the files in the current model, including attachments. The resulting chart might not have a 1:1 correlation with the files displayed in the canvas. View the full report to see a complete list of files that make up the pie slice.

1. Generate a report. See the previous section for more information on generating a report.
2. Once the report is generated, select one of the three mapping methods.
3. Click Map Report. The model is colored relative to the report displayed in the data map control.

Creating Reports for Your Model

The reporting feature, when used in conjunction with data mapping, lets you map report data to the canvas for visual overview of a model's status and development. This information makes it easier to track designs and projects throughout their lifecycles. You can generate reports of model data based on any of the templates supplied with the client. The report feature is accessed from the Data Mapping dialog box.

AUTODESK.

System File Properties by Category Report

Folder Name   :
Generated By   :
Date   : 7/15/2015 4:52:05 PM
Search Root   :
Search Conditions :

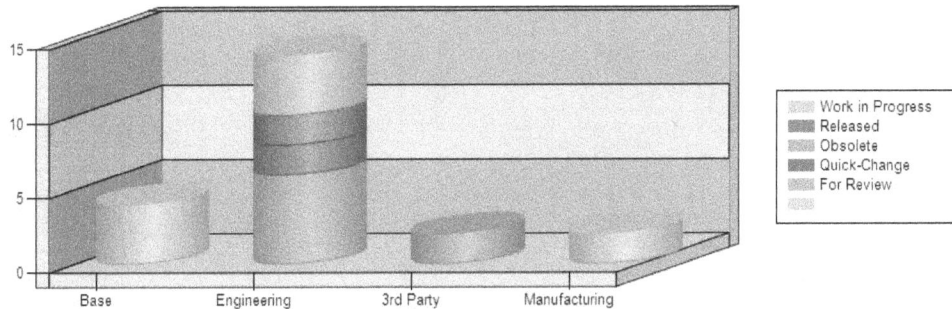

Report Templates

Refer to the chapter on Reporting for more information on working with report templates.

Several report templates are provided with the Autodesk Vault client. These report templates contain a color palette for a chart, but the templates do not specify which color is assigned to which chart element. You can specify how chart elements are color coded when you use the data mapping feature. Color coding chart elements enables quick, repeatable viewing of model data.

You can assign standard color mapping in the Assign Color dialog box in the Autodesk Vault client. Access the dialog by selecting Tools>Administration>Vault Settings. Select the Behaviors tab and then click Define under Report Management.

Report Charts

The in-CAD report feature can display data in four different charts:

- Pie chart

- Doughnut chart

- Column chart

- Stacked column chart

If a report contains a chart type not supported by the in-CAD report control, the chart is not displayed on the CAD canvas. The report can be viewed outside the application with a report viewer.

Procedure: View the Full Report

In addition to mapping the data from the report onto the Inventor model, you can view the complete report including any tables and additional layout and formatting.

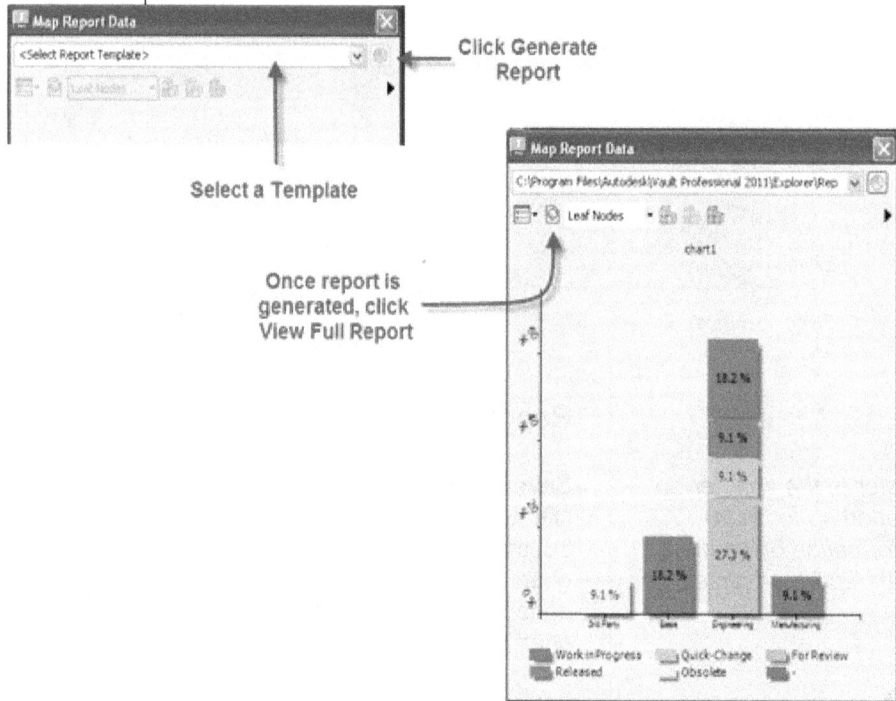

Select a Template

Click Generate Report

Once report is generated, click View Full Report

1. Enable report control by clicking Data Mapping in the Autodesk Vault ribbon. The Map Report Data dialog box displays.
2. In the Map Report Data dialog box, select a report template from the drop-down list, or open a new template from a local folder or the vault.

3. Click the Generate Report icon. A progress bar displays with the status of the report. Depending on the size of your model, this process can take a few minutes. You can continue to work while the report is being generated.

   Once the report has been generated, the report chart displays in the data mapping control.

4. Click the View Full Report icon to display the full report.

Managing Chart Elements

The ability to manipulate chart elements makes it easier to customize how you view your report data when it is mapped. The chart control enables you to override chart colors, create a selection set of files in Inventor based on chart elements and the mapped components, and retrieve a data card deck for the mapped components through a convenient context menu.

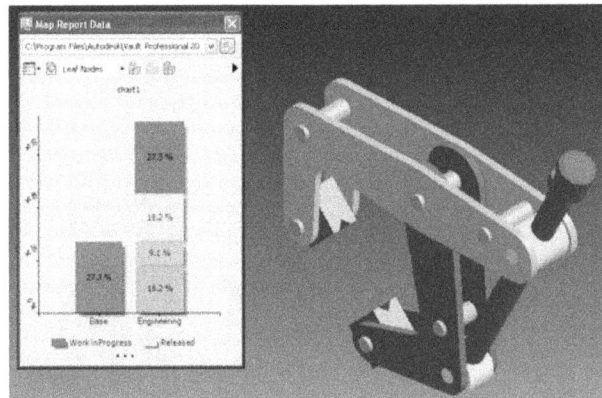

Selecting Chart Elements

When you map report data, all chart elements are mapped to the model by default. However, you can select individual chart elements in the report and map only those elements. Additionally, you can manipulate the way the data displays on the open model.

There are three ways to select chart elements. Once the chart elements are selected, use the context menu to customize how the data is mapped or viewed.

- Click a single element in the chart to select it. The element is outlined in red.

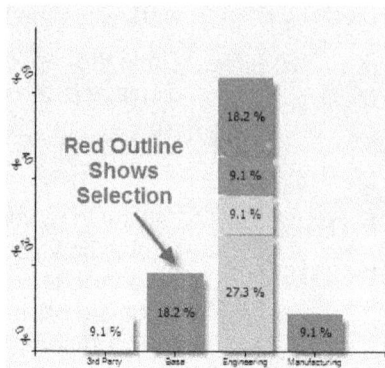

- Hold Control and click multiple chart elements to select multiple chart elements and act on those elements using the context menu.

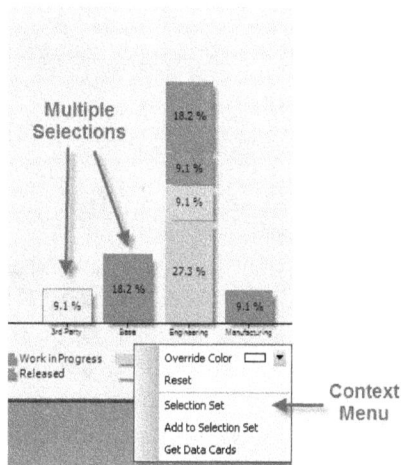

- Double-click on different chart elements to separate them from the chart. When Map Data is toggled on or the data mapping is refreshed, the selected pieces are mapped on the model.

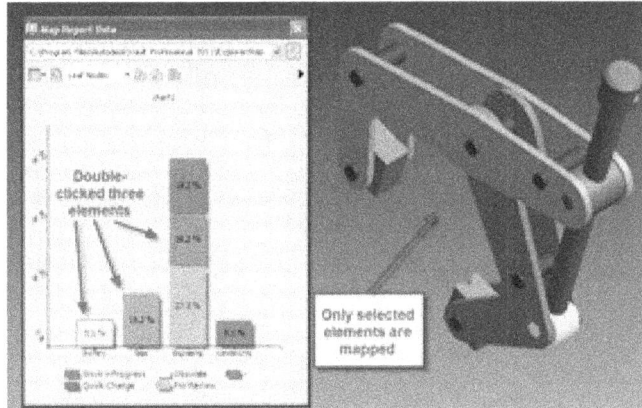

Changes to element selection and color overrides are not mapped onto the model until you update the mapping.

- Once a selection is made, click Clear Color Mapping or Isolation to update the data mapping or to update the isolation.

Chart Context Menu

A context menu provides additional options for manipulating mapped data and customizing the view.

Command	Definition
Override Color	Enables you to specify a different color for a chart element.
Reset	Removes a color override.
Selection Set	Creates a selection set from the components corresponding to the selected chart elements. The corresponding components are selected in the browser and the canvas.
Add to Selection Set	Includes the components corresponding to the chart element to the current selection set.
Get Data Cards	Retrieves data cards for each of the currently mapped components.

Managing Data Mapping Reports

The report management feature enables the administrator to assign colors to values in a report template. When the template is used by the report generation feature in the CAD application, the colors are automatically assigned to their associated values.

The administrator can also remove unused or outdated values from the report template.

When a report is generated that returns a value for which a color has not yet been assigned, the report control will assign a color to the new value from a predetermined list of colors and write back the report template a name and value pair for the new color. The new value and default color assignment display in the Assign Color dialog box, where the administrator can update the template by assigning a color to this new value.

The Assign Color Dialog Box

When a template is opened in the Assign Color dialog box, the chart elements contained in the template are listed along with the currently assigned color for each element. If the template contains more than one chart, the chart elements are grouped by chart.

Templates can be opened from a local folder or from Autodesk Vault. The Value column will be populated with the names of chart elements only if a report has already been generated. If no report has been generated, the fields in the Value column are blank.

By default, the Assign Color dialog box displays a default palette of eight colors. Unless specified in the template, the colors are assigned to chart elements in this order:

- Grey

- Red

- Orange

- Yellow

- Light Green

- Cyan

- Blue

- Violet

You can enter the exact chart element name in the Value field and then select a color to assign that color to the chart element.

Remember to save the template to commit the changes.

Procedure: Manage Report Templates

1. Click Tools>Administration>Vault Settings.
2. In the Vault Settings dialog box, select the Behaviors tab.
3. Click Define under Report Management to open the Assign Color dialog box.
4. From the File menu, open a report template from either the vault or a local folder.

   Note: If the template is stored in the vault and the administrator has write-permission on the current file, the template is checked out of the vault.

5. If the template does not contain any custom color properties, the default color palette displays.
6. If the custom color properties have already been added to the template, the value names are extracted and displayed with their assigned color in the dialog box. Any new values without an assigned color display with the next available color in the default list.
7. Do one of the following:
   - Specify a new color assignment for an existing property by selecting a new color in the Color field.
   - Enter the exact value name for a new property in the Value field.
   - Select a color to assign to the property from the Color field.
8. Select File>Save to commit the changes. If the template was checked out of the vault, it is checked back in after being saved.

Practice 8b

Map Your Data

In this practice, you learn to generate a report based on your model's data and map report data to the open model.

Task 1 - Create a full report.

1. Start Autodesk Vault Workgroup software. Log in using the following information:

   - User Name: **usera**
   - Password: **vault**
   - Vault: Data Card and Mapping Vault

2. In the Navigation pane, click Project Explorer ($).

3. Click Find in the toolbar.

4. In the Find dialog box, search for Clamp.iam.

5. Right-click on Clamp.iam and select Open to launch it in Autodesk Inventor.

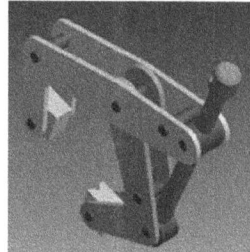

6. In the Autodesk Vault ribbon, click Data Mapping.

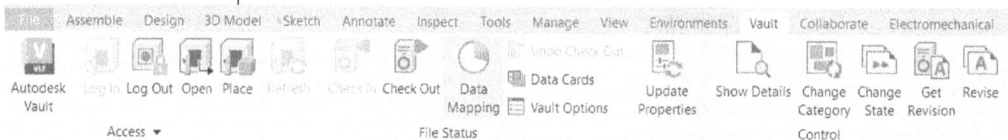

7. The Map Report Data dialog box opens. Select Open Local Template from the Select Report Template drop-down list.

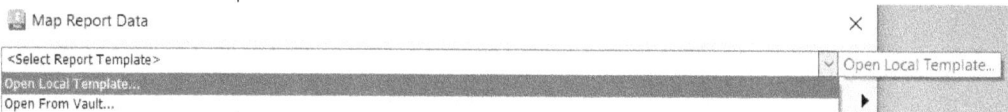

8. Navigate to *C:\Program Files\Autodesk\Vault edition\ Explorer\Report Templates* and select the File By Category.rdlc report template.

    Note: If you receive a warning indicating the template is read-only, a workaround is to check in the File By Category.rdlc template file to the vault and use the Open from Vault command instead of Open Local Template.

9. Click Open.

10. In the Map Report Data dialog box, click Generate Report.

11. A Bar Graph report displays in the Map Report Data dialog box. The graph shows a percentage breakdown of files in each category based on state. The available states in the example below are Work in Progress, Quick-Change, For Review, Released, Obsolete, or no state.

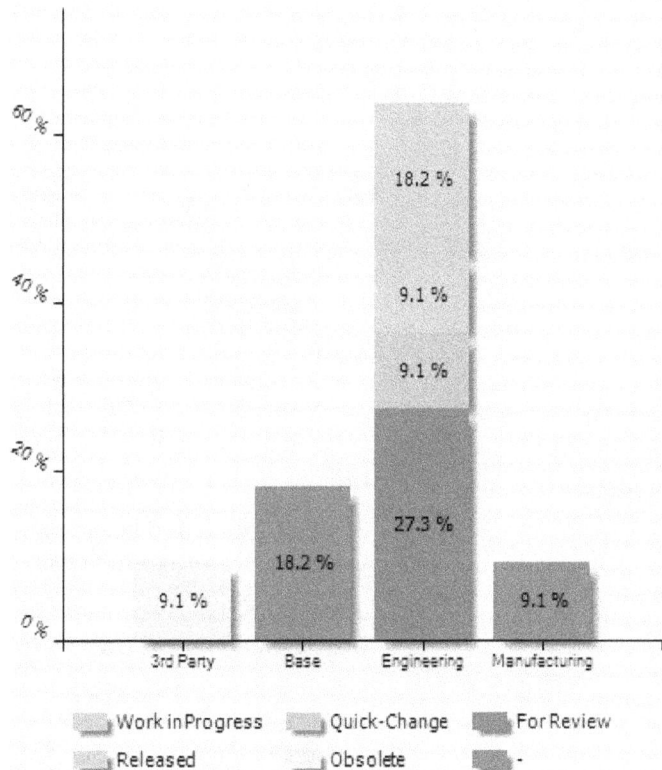

12. Click View Full Report to see the report in printable format.

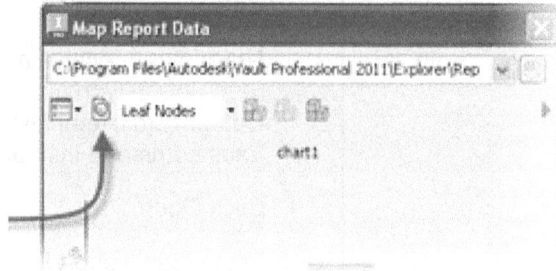

The report automatically launches in Microsoft Viewer.

AUTODESK.

System File Properties by Category Report

Folder Name   :
Generated By   :
Date   : 7/15/2015 4:52:05 PM
Search Root   :
Search Conditions   :

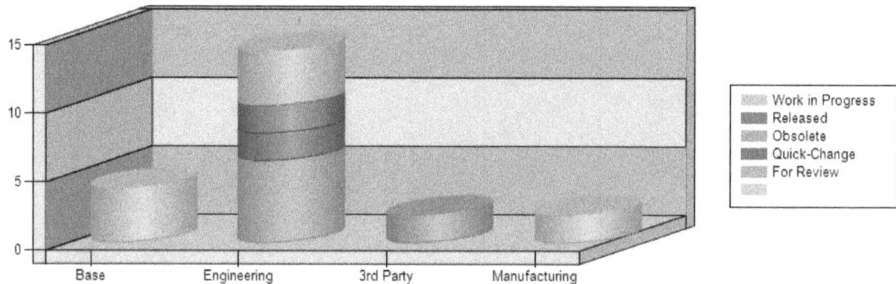

13. Click Export and select PDF to save the file to a local folder as a PDF. The file can then be emailed or stored in a vault.

Task 2 - Map report data to the model.

It can be useful to view the report data on the model for an easier understanding of the state of the design.

1. Go to the Map Report Data dialog box that is still open from the previous section. If you closed the dialog box, simply click Data Mapping and generate the report once more.

2. Click Apply Color Mapping to map the report data to the model in its entirety.

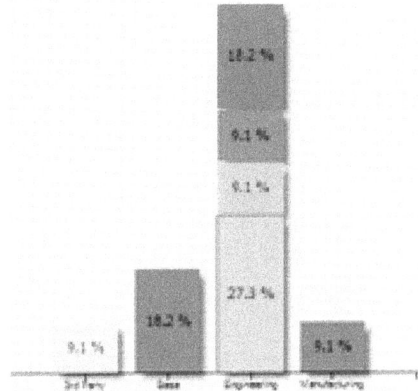

By examining the model and referencing the Map Report legend, you can determine the state of each component. For example, the Lower_Plate.ipt is in the For Review state.

3. In the Map Report Data dialog box, double-click on the For Review section of the Engineering bar.

4. In the Map Report Data toolbar, click Apply Isolation to show only the For Review pieces in the model.

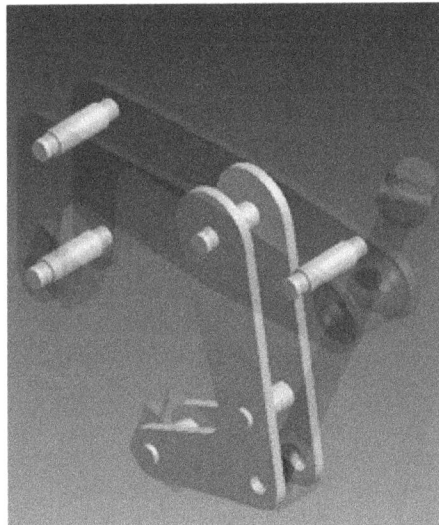

5. Examine the components in Released and Quick-Change states. In the Map Report Data dialog box, double-click on the Released and Quick-Change pieces as well.

6. The components are mapped on the model and all other components are transparent.

8.3 Sheet Set Manager Integration

Overview

Autodesk Vault Workgroup and Autodesk Vault Professional integrate with the AutoCAD Sheet Set Manager (SSM) for supported AutoCAD products. This integration enables you to add, access, and modify the sheet sets to Vault. You can also access and modify sheet sets in a collaborative environment. In addition, users can rely on up-to-date Vault status on sheet drawings in Sheet Set Manager.

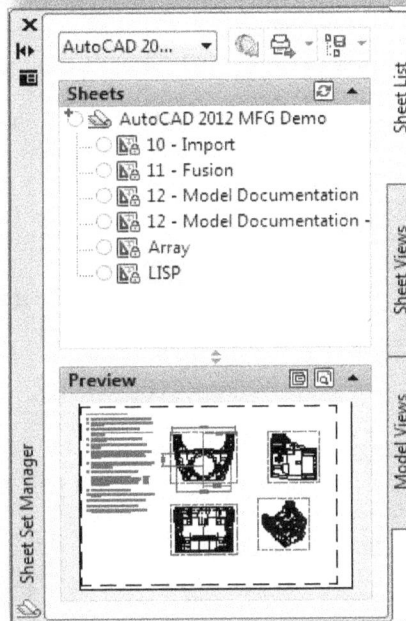

Vault also supports all sheet set functionality, including property management, plotting, and publishing tasks. In Vault Explorer, you can use search capabilities to find sheets and sheet sets based on properties inside the sheet set manager. Sheets are represented as files in the Vault which gives you the relationship between sheets and associated drawings.

Once you start working on a Sheet Set in a Vault environment, there are some changes to how certain Sheet Set commands work.

Objectives

After completing this lesson, you will be able to:

- Understand how to work on a sheet set with Autodesk Vault.

Resave All Sheets

When you work on a sheet set with Vault, you are working in a collaborative environment. When you resave all sheets, note the differences when:

- Working in a shared sandbox environment, you can Resave All as long as none of the sheets/files involved is currently checked out by other users. The Resave All command gets aborted if there are files that cannot be checked out and, therefore, saved. A file might not be available for check out if it is currently checked out to another user or if vault constraints restrict access to the file.

- Working in a non-shared sandbox environment, you can Resave All even if some of the files are checked out by other users. You get a list of files that are not available for saving when the sheet set command is completed.

Remove Sheet or Sheet Subset

When you remove a sheet or subset from a vaulted sheet set, its equivalent vaulted copy is NOT removed automatically. As a result, if you were to re-use the same sheet or sheet subset name, you are informed that the files already exist in the Vault.

Historical references from sheets or sheet set files are lost when they are removed with Vault Explorer.

If the removed sheet or sheet subset files are expired or redundant, you can remove them via Vault Explorer.

Move, Rename, and Copy Design in the Vault Client

Move, Rename, and Copy Design changes made in the Vault Client are ignored when you open the edited sheet set in SSM.

8.4 Chapter Summary

Data Cards and Data Mapping make it easy for you to track and evaluate your design. You can examine pertinent vault details about a model, modify property information for individual or multiple files, generate reports for a model and publish the results as a chart, and map the report results onto the open model. The AutoCAD Sheet Set Manager integration enables you to add, access, and modify sheet sets in a collaborative Vault environment.

Having completed this chapter, you can:

- Enable and access both data card views.

- Build and navigate a data card deck, isolate a card, and remove a card from a card deck.

- Edit properties and track changes with data cards.

- Generate a report based on open model data.

- Map data in a report to the open model.

- Understand how to work on a sheet set with Autodesk Vault.

Copy Design, Job Server, Vault Revision Tables, and Backups

The Copy Design feature helps you save time by creating new designs based on existing ones. Other topics covered in this chapter include the Job Server, Revision Tables, and Backups. The process of creating and checking in visualization files manually can be time-intensive for some users, especially those responsible for managing large assemblies. The Job Server utility enables users to automatically create and check-in visualization files from their local workstation. The Vault Revision Table feature enables you to automatically update a drawing's revision table with Vault data when properties are synchronized through the Job Server. To prevent data loss, you can use the Backup and Restore functionality.

Learning Objectives in This Chapter

- Create new designs from existing ones using the Copy Design feature.
- Differentiate between the Job Server and Job Processor.
- Enable the Job Server.
- Administrate the Job Server.
- Log in to the Job Processor to view Jobs.
- Enable the Vault Revision Table functionality.
- Understand the Vault Revision Table settings.
- Backup and Restore your Autodesk Vault Machine.

9.1 Copy Design

Overview

Create new design objects by copying existing data in a vault with the Copy Design feature. Depending on which design application you are using, copying a design involves copying a drawing and its related files, copying an entire design structure along with the related 2D drawings for 3D models, or copying components of a design. The Copy Design command can be launched from several menus, such as the Edit menu and the right-click menu in the main table and preview pane. It can also be launched in Inventor from the right-click menu in the Vault Browser and Show Details dialog box.

Objectives

After completing this lesson, you will be able to:

- Create new designs from existing ones using the Copy Design feature

Copy Design Interface

There are three major sections of the Copy Design interface: Tool Bar, Main View and Navigation Panel.

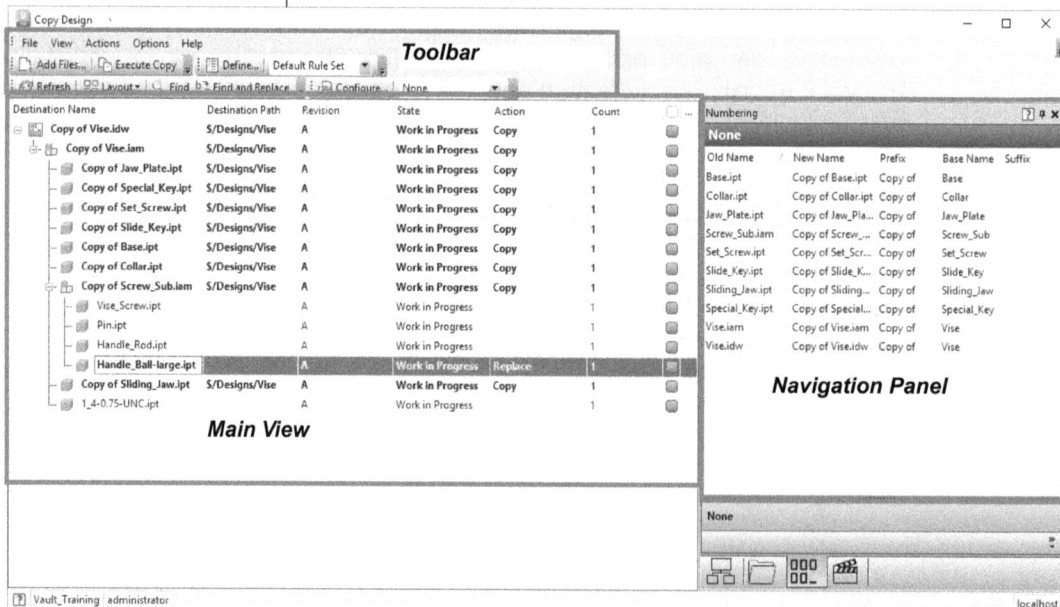

The Toolbar

The Toolbar consists of five menus: File, View, Actions, Options, and Help menu.

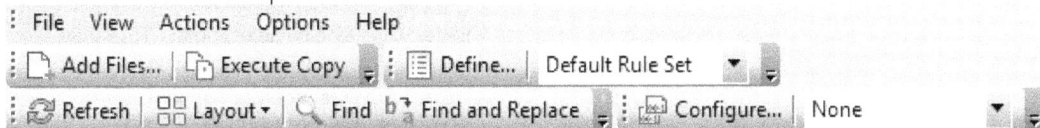

Use the toolbar to log in and out of a vault, access administrative options like numbering schemes, add objects to the main view, control copy settings and rule sets, and create copies.

File Menu	
Export	Export to a desired location. Specify the location and format in the Save as dialog.
Add Files	Add the files that you want to copy to the main view.
Clear Root Node	You can remove the node and all children from the dialog using the Clear Root Node option from the right-click menu. This option is only available if you select the root node.
Execute Copy	Once everything is configured, click Create Copy to begin the copy operation. Before you perform the copy operation, Copy Design checks the file name duplicates and user permission for the folder.
Exit	Click to exit the Copy Design dialog.
View Menu	
Panels	Select which panels you want to display in the Copy Design dialog.
Layout	Customize how the main grid looks. You can select from three views: Tree View List View Folder View
Show Grid Lines	Select to toggle the display of grid lines on or off in the grid.
Show Banding	Select to toggle the display of alternating color bands on or off in the grid.

Show Drawing View	By default, the selected model and any associated drawings are copied. When Drawing View is turned on, the view mode displays all associated drawings and you can configure the copy operation based on the drawings.
	Drawings are now visible in the Documentation folder. Display it by selecting the Tree View.
	Note: A status of Auto indicates that the drawing linked to the file receives the same action as the associated file. For example, if a file is marked for copy, the associated drawing receives the same new file name and save location during the copy event.
Show Children	Select whether to show or hide the model attachments and library files in the copy view.
	By default, all library files and attachments are set for copy. However, you can assign different copy actions to children files by displaying them in the Copy Design view.
	In the Show Children menu, select which types of children files to show by choosing one or both of the following check-boxes:
	Attachments
	Select Attachments to show all file attachments.
	Note: All file types are shown, including generic file attachments.
	Include Library Files
	Select Include Library Files to show all associated library files.
Automatic Column Sizing	Select to toggle whether or not columns adjust automatically to fit within the available view area.
Find	Select to find the text. You can search for the text in the main grid or the numbering panel.
Find and Replace	Enables you to find a desired text and replace it with a desired one. You can perform the operation in the main window or the numbering panel.
Refresh	Refresh the Copy Design main view to see the most recent changes to files or the design structure.
	Note: If dependent files are cloaked, the following message displays: "Some of the children of the added object are inaccessible." An administrator must provide access to the dependent files. After obtaining access, refresh the Copy Design main view.

Actions Menu	
Copy All	Select Copy All to designate all files in the main view for copy.
Copy Top Nodes	You can copy multiple design trees with one command. Selecting Copy Top Nodes sets all top level components to copy.
Copy	Select to copy selected files from the main grid. Hold the Ctrl key to select multiple files at once.
Copy To	Select to copy selected files from the main grid to a specified location. Hold the Ctrl key to select multiple files at once.
Copy Branch	Enables you to copy a complete branch with all files maintaining the original folder structure.
Copy Branch To	Enables you to copy a complete branch to a specific folder maintaining the original folder structure.
Reuse	The file is reused without creating a copy. This is a great way to minimize duplicates of a file that must be used in more than one location of a design. **Note:** If a file is changed to Reuse, the parent file also changes to Reuse.
Reuse All	Applies the reuse action to all the files in the main grid.
Reuse Branch	Applies the reuse action to the selected file and the entire file structure beneath it. The specified files are reused in the destination structure and no copies are created. Note: If a file is changed to Reuse, the parent file also changes to Reuse.
Replace	Replaces the selected file with another file. The name of the copied file changes to the replacement file's name. Note: The pending copy of a file can be used as a replacement.
Exclude	Exclude selected item from the copy operation.
Go To	After the Copy operation, you can open the Source Folder, or Destination folder using the options in the right-click menu.

Options Menu	
Numbering Schemes	Select Numbering Schemes to set which naming schemes are valid for use in your copy design configuration. You can also set the default numbering scheme.
Action Rules	Select to create, edit, and delete rules that apply to your copy operations. Each Rule Set contains a number of file behavior and property settings that can be applied to the copied file based on the source file.
Automatically Copy Parents	When Automatically Copy Parents is turned on, the parent of each copied component is also copied. Note: Disabling this option results in source assemblies being edited to include the new copied part.
Link Drawings with Models	When Link Drawings with Model is turned on, each drawing connected to a model is copied to the same location and shares the same new file name as the model. Note: Changes in the model behavior are applied immediately to the file.
Remove All Attachments	By default, all file attachments are copied. Removes attachments of the files during the copy operation.
Remove BOM Objects	Removes BOM objects from the copy operation.
Select References	By default, all component references are copied. When Select References is turned on, you can choose which references of a component are copied instead of using the legacy configuration where all component references are copied. Note: Multi-select is not enabled when using Select References view. Any reference that is selected must have its own unique action. See Select References for more information about creating and editing rules.

The Main View Grid

The main Copy Design view shows the name of the files available for copy, the file identification number, the destination folder, the action that will be performed on the file, the revision and state of the file, and how many instances (Count) of the file occur in the current list.

Tip: By default, reference filenames are set to the destination file name when an action is assigned. You can view the Numbering Panel to identify files by original name or add File Name (Historical) to the main view.

You can also manage copy actions and customize the view from the main view.

Destination Name	Destination Path /	Revision	State	Action	Count		...
⊟ Copy of DECIN-00000.Ru...	$/Inventor/Ja... ...			Copy	1	☐	
pipipe.1548344949338.ipt					1	☐	
DECIN-00000.Route01.ipt					1	☐	
pipipe.1548344946030.ipt				Exclude	1	☐	
ASME B16.11 90 Deg El...					1	☐	
Copy of pipipe.15483...	$/Inventor/JanP			Copy	1	☐	
Copy of pipipe.15483...	$/Inventor/JanP...			Copy	1	☐	
Copy of pipipe.15483...	$/Inventor/JanP...			Copy	1	☐	

The Navigation Panel

There are four different navigation panels: Where Used, Actions, Numbering and Folders. Each has its own tab. The Actions panel is shown with its tab selected in the image below.

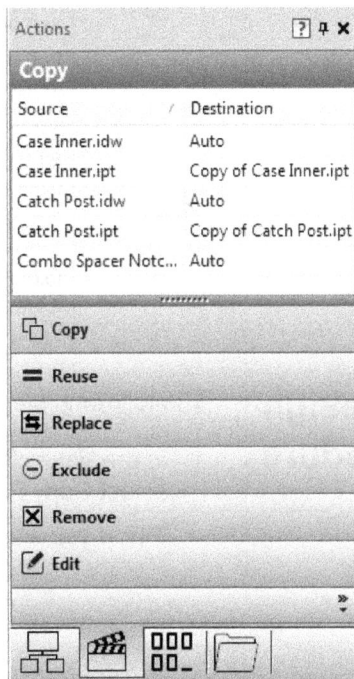

The functionality provided in the four navigation panels is described in the following table.

Panel	Details
Where Used	The Where Used panel lets users track the origin of the copy objects and their destination.
	Since you can replace existing files with uncommitted instances of files that are being copied, this means that the copied instance can have numerous destinations. Use the Where Used tab to ensure that the files are copied to the right locations.
Actions	The Actions Panel enables you to review which operations are assigned to be performed on files in the main view.
	Once you have configured the files in the main view, you can use the Actions Panel to filter the files based on their assigned operation. Assigned operations include copied, reused, replaced, excluded, removed, or edited.
	Use the Actions Panel to verify the copy design configuration in the main view and to make changes.
	Note: You can also set Action operations by dragging and dropping files from the main grid onto the required operation button in the Actions Panel.
Numbering	The Numbering Panel lists all of the files selected for copy. It also shows the original and new name for each selected file.
	The grid displays the renaming options based on available numbering schemes.
	In the Numbering Panel grid, you can edit certain fields and individual numbering schemes.
Folders	The Folders Panel lets you review the source and destination folders for the copy design operation. This is a great way to verify that the required files are selected and will be copied to the correct location.
	You can group selected files for operations based on the folder location. You can also drag-and-drop files between folders or from the main grid to perform a copy.

Copy Design Procedure

The following steps outline a typical copy design workflow.

1. In the Vault client, right-click on the file you want to copy and select Copy Design. The Copy Design dialog box opens.

   Tip: If you want to copy a particular version of a file, in the History tab, right-click on the version and select Copy Design.

Note: If dependent files are cloaked, the following message displays: "Some of the children of the added object are inaccessible." An administrator must provide access to the dependent files. After obtaining access, refresh the Copy Design main view.

2. Click Add Files from the File menu on the toolbar to add additional files for copying.

   Important: AutoCAD Electrical users should select the electrical project (WDP) and not just the drawings. In addition, all project support files (WDT, WDL, AEPX) should have the same name as the project file.

   The files are added to the main view of the Copy Design dialog.

3. In the toolbar, click Actions, and select the desired operation for the files listed in the main view.
4. If you want to perform a different action on a file, right-click on the file and select the action from the context menu.

   Tip: Click Refresh at any time to capture the latest version of the listed files and file structure.

5. To select the rule set that you want to apply to the copy operation, click Options > Action Rules, and select a desired rule from the list. Or, click Define to define a new action rule.

6. Once everything is configured, click Execute Copy on the toolbar to start the copy operation.

   Several pre-checks are performed to ensure that:

   - All files have unique names (by Folder)
   - Vault unique file name rules are met
   - Selected files still exist
   - Files requiring edits are write-enabled
   - Files requiring edits are owned by the workgroup site

   All successful copy operations receive a green check in the main view. If a copy operation failed, a red cross is displayed.

   To perform another copy operation, modify your settings and click Execute Copy.

Practice 9a

Copy Design

In this practice, you create a new design by copying an existing design using the Copy Design feature.

1. Browse to one of the design folders, select an assembly file, right-click and select Copy Design. The files are added to the main view of the Copy Design dialog box.

2. Select the Actions menu and select Copy All to copy all of the files listed in the main view.

3. Multi-select a couple of the files using <Ctrl>, right-click and click Reuse.

4. Click the Numbering tab and change the Prefix column to AOTC_ and note that the Name column updates.

5. Click the Folders tab to see where the files will be copied, as also shown in the Destination Path column in the main view. Select the ellipses button to change the destination path of one or more files.

6. Click ⬚ Execute Copy in the toolbar to start the copy operation.

7. All successful copy operations receive a green check in the main view.

8. Return to Autodesk Vault and navigate to the folder where the copied objects are and confirm that copy was successful.

9.2 Enable the Job Server

Overview

With Autodesk® Vault Workgroup or Autodesk® Vault Professional, you can use the Job Server Utility to automate specific jobs like DWF or PDF generation when changing the state from Work in Progress to Released.

Objectives

After completing this lesson, you will be able to:

- Differentiate between the meaning of Job Server and Job Processor

- Enable the Job Server in the Global Settings

- Initiate a job

- Work with the Job Queue

Job Server vs. Job Processor

Administrators can manage the Job Server by tracking jobs, resubmitting stalled jobs, and deleting unnecessary jobs. However, the Job Server must be enabled by an administrator.

Users assign their publishing jobs to a job queue where they are stored until certain parameters are met. The Job Processor then creates the visualization files and checks them into the Vault based on the publishing properties defined in the Global Settings dialog box.

Enable the Job Server

Note: You must be an administrator to enable the Job Server.

1. Select Tools>Administration>Global Settings.
2. In the Global Settings dialog box, click the Integrations tab.
3. Select the Enable Job Server checkbox to activate the job server.

The Job Server permits for publishing jobs to be queued and processed at a later time. You must activate the Job Server prior to sending any jobs to it for publishing.

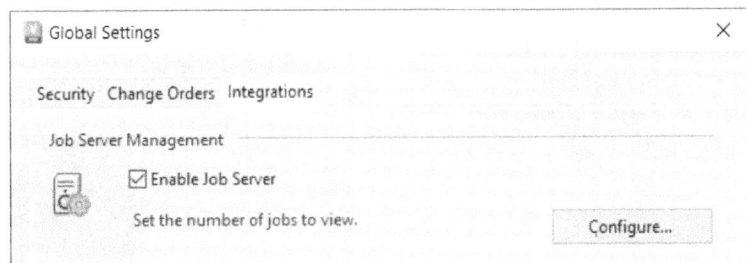

Job Processor

The job processor is installed at the same time as the Vault Client. As of the 2019 software release, the job processor has all of the required CAD applications included with it, so that it can be installed on a computer that does not otherwise have CAD tools installed.

You must have the Job Server enabled to set up jobs. Having a job processor running is not required to submit jobs. The jobs will enter a queue until a job processor comes online to request jobs.

As already explained in the section before, the Job Processor is the engine which controls and completes the jobs.

The first time you access the job processor, you must specify the user name, password, and server name. The job processor will remember these login credentials each time you log in until changed through the Administration menu.

1. On the workstation where you want jobs to be processed, select Start menu>All Programs>Autodesk Data Management>Autodesk Job Processor [Edition] for Vault to launch the Job Processor application.

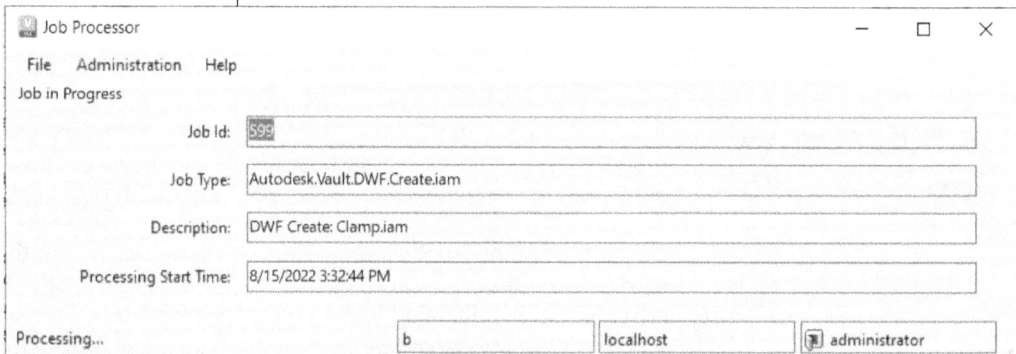

Select File>Pause at any time to halt the job processor and prevent it from processing any new jobs. If the job processor is in the middle of processing a job, it will finish the job first. The Administration>Settings are not accessible unless the job processor is paused.

2. Select Administration>Settings to display the Settings dialog box.
3. Enter the User Name and Password of the user for this workstation.
4. Specify the server from which you want the job processor to pull jobs for publishing.
5. Click OK to save your changes and close the Settings dialog box.
6. Select File>Resume to log in to the specified server.

   You can find the Job Processor in your taskbar. Click on the arrow-up symbol to see the Job Processor symbol.

You do not have to start the Job Processor each time you are starting your machine. There is a mechanism to automate this start procedure by configuration. This is handled in the Configure Job Server lesson.

Job Processor Details

See the following table for an explanation of all fields in Job Processor:

Detail	Description
Job ID	Displays the number of the job currently being processed.
Job Type	Displays a description of the job being processed.
Description	Displays more information about the job in the queue.
Status	Displays the current state of the Job Processor.
Processing Start Time	Time at which the Job Processor began working on a job.

Job Server Queue

The Job Server Queue lists all active jobs and displays the status whether the jobs were executed successfully (job is gone from list), is still pending (status = Pending) or an error has occurred (status = Error).

1. Select Tools>Job Queue.

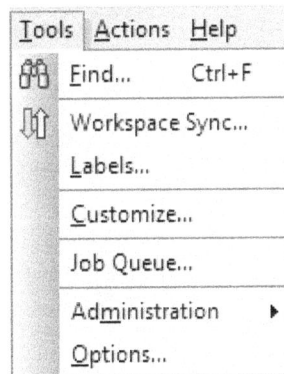

Tools	Actions	Help
🔍 Find...	Ctrl+F	
⬍ Workspace Sync...		
Labels...		
Customize...		
Job Queue...		
Administration	▶	
Options...		

2. In the Job Server Queue dialog box, you can sort the jobs by ID, Priority, Status, Description, Submitted Date, or by whom they were submitted.

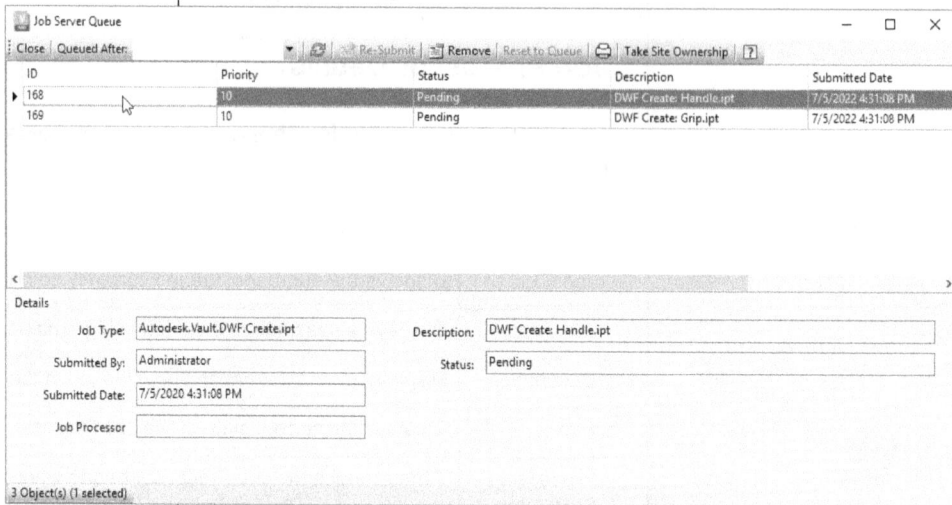

The Job Server Queue dialog box displays up to 1,000 jobs. A warning will display to inform the user if there are more than 1,000 jobs in the queue.

3. Right-click on the column heading to customize the layout and view of the queue.
   - If you want to filter the list so that it only displays the jobs queued after a specific date and time, click the Queued After list and specify when.

4. Select a job that you want to modify and perform one of the following actions:
   - If you want to delete the job from the queue, click Remove.
   - If the job has an error status, click Re-Submit to reprocess the job.
   - If you want to remove the job processor from the task and leave the job in the queue, click Reset to Queue.
   - If you want to assign the task to the job processor on your workstation, click Take Ownership.

5. Click Print to send a copy of the grid to the default printer.
6. Click Refresh at any time to update the queue.

Job Server Details

This table describes the details of the Job Server Queue dialog box.

Detail	Description
Job Type	The type of job that was submitted for processing. Visualization jobs display as Autodesk.Vault.DWF.Create {0} where {0} is the file extension.
Submitted By	Displays the name of the user who submitted the job to the queue.
Submitted Date	Displays the date and time the job was submitted to the queue.
Job Processor	Displays the name of the computer that has taken the job from the queue for processing.
Description	Displays more information about the job in the queue. This field will also display the DWF Create: filename.
Status	Displays whether the job's status is Pending, Processing, or Error.
Results	Displays information only if the job has an error status.

Job Server Commands

This table describes the commands in the Job Server Queue dialog box.

Command	Description
Close	Closes the Job Server Queue dialog box.
Queued After	Filters the list by showing the first 1,000 jobs queued after the specified date and time.
Refresh	Refreshes the queue.
Re-Submit	Reprocesses a job that has encountered an error. This button is only enabled when a job has been placed in error state.
Remove	Removes any job with the status of Error or Pending.
Reset to Queue	Removes the reservation of a job by the job processor. **Note:** This command is not in the toolbar by default. To add the command, click the toolbar list and select Add or Remove Buttons.

Take Site Ownership	Transfers ownership of the job's reservation to the current user's Job Processor. When a site that has reserved jobs is deleted, or a backup is performed but the information is restored to a different site, the pending jobs are deleted from the queue. This feature enables administrators to claim ownership for processing the job before it is deleted.
Print	Prints the current queue grid to the default printer.

Initiate a Job

In your default Autodesk Vault installation there is already a job integrated, which starts to automatically generate and save DWF files to selected elements. Use the following steps to view the current queue status:

1. Select one or more CAD files from the list in the main grid.
2. Select Actions>Update View>Queue Update to set up a DWF generation job in the Job Server Queue.

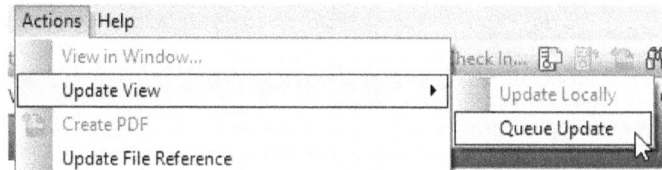

3. Now go to the Job Server Queue by selecting Tools>Job Queue.
4. You should see the new DWF Job listed as Pending.

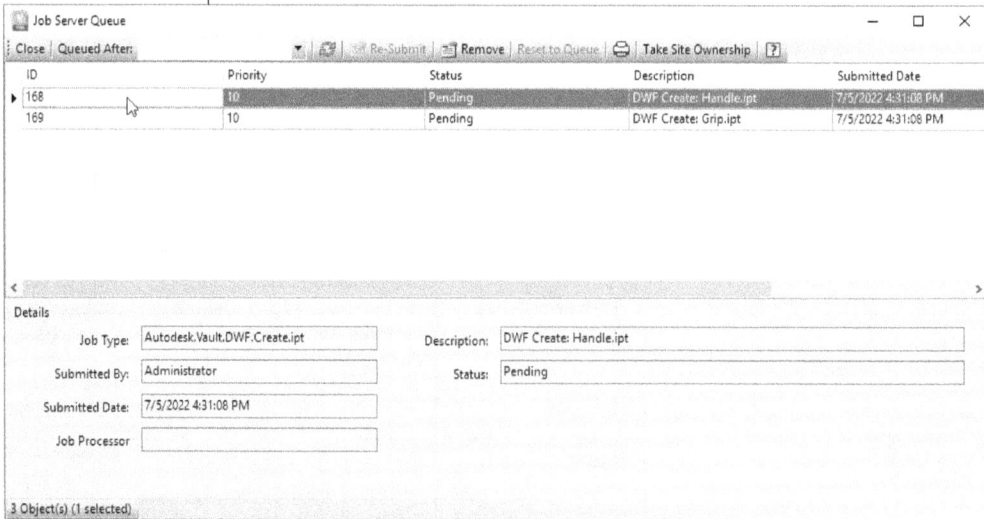

5. As soon as the DWF is generated successfully the job will disappear from the Queue.

6. Press Refresh from time to time to check whether the job is already done.

7. Have a look back to your component list and find the new generated DWF.

In case the job is still hanging in the Queue, ensure that your Job Processor is running and completing your job. You can easily check whether your Job Processor is running or not by having a look to the task bar.

Practice 9b

Run Some Jobs and Watch Them in the Job Queue

In this practice, you will first enable the Job Server and get the Job Processor run. Then select multiple CAD files and run the predefined DWF Job.

Task 1 - Enable the job server and get the job processor run.

1. Log in to Autodesk Vault as Administrator. Ensure that Designs.ipj is set as the Inventor project file.

2. Go to Tools>Administration>Global Settings.

3. Select Enable Job Server in the Integrations tab.

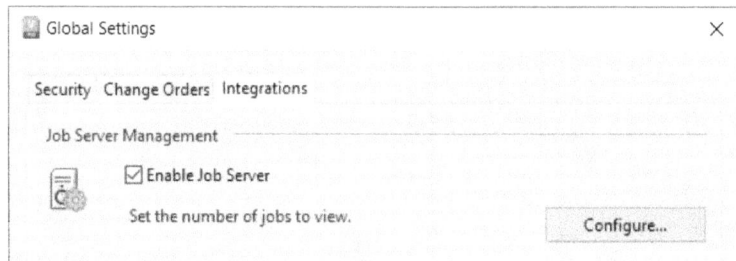

4. Open your Windows Explorer.

5. Browse to Program Files>Autodesk>Vault Client [Edition]> Explorer>and start the file JobProcessor.exe.
   OR
   Use your Windows Start menu>All Programs>Autodesk Data Management>Autodesk Job Processor [Edition] for Vault.

6. If required, enter your name, password, and server to log on.

Ensure that the required CAD Applications are installed on the same machine the Job Processor is installed.

Task 2 - Multi select some CAD files and start the automatic DWF generation.

1. Select CAD files from the main Vault grid.

2. Click Actions>Update View>Queue Update.

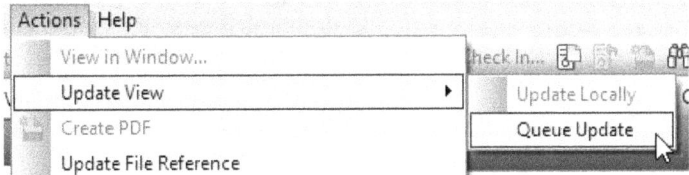

3. Open the Job Queue to watch the newly created DWF jobs and their status.

4. Go to Tools>Job Queue.

5. Select one pending job from the list and remove it by the command Remove in Job Queue dialog box.

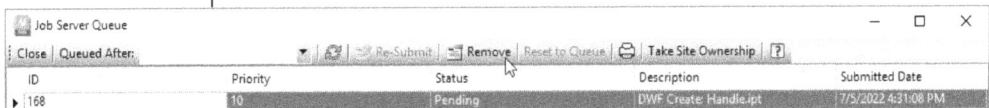

6. Wait some seconds and refresh your list by the command Refresh in Job Queue dialog box. If no error occurred and the list is empty exit the Job Queue. If the job processor is idle, it can take up to 10 minutes to evoke again.

   Tip: To facilitate the job processing, pause the job processor and resume it by selecting File>Pause and then selecting File>Resume.

7. Double check with your list in Vault whether all DWF's were generated, beside the one you removed from the Job Queue.

9.3 Configuring the Job Server

Overview

From the administrative point of view there are several tools that help you to configure and administrate the jobs and events in Vault. The Job Processor can be configured to automatically start each time your machine is started and with the LifeCycleEventEditor you have a highly flexible tool available that makes it easy to handle Lifecycle transitions automatically by generating automatic jobs.

Objectives

After completing this lesson, you will be able to:

- Configure the Job Server/Job Processor via UI.

- Understand settings in the configuration file.

- Use the LifeCycleEventEditor.

- Use the Job Server Log files for analyses.

Configuration via Job Processor UI

There are several options and commands in the Job Processor dialog box that will be explained in the following table.

Command	Definition
Pause	On Pause the Job Processor will pause, the jobs still keep in the queue. It prevents from processing any new jobs. If the job processor is in the middle of processing a job, it will finish the job first.
Resume	After you have set the Job Processor to Pause you can click Resume to go on completing the jobs in the queue.
Exit	On Exit the Job Processor will exit and close.
Start on Windows Logon	Here you can set whether the Job Processor is started automatically on Windows Logon.
Settings	In the Settings dialog box, you can enter your name, password and server.

Job Types	Displays the Job Types dialog box, which contains all available Job Types to use. If the workstation does not have the required information to process the particular type of job, that type of file is unchecked.
About Job Processor/Help	Here you can find useful Help files for handling and administrating the Job Processor

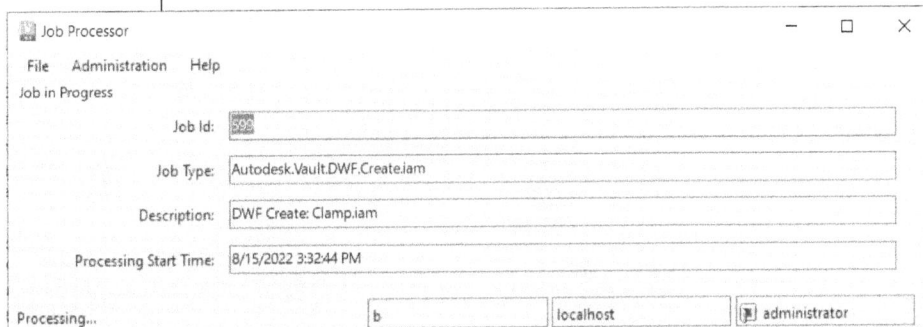

The Configuration File

In the Job Processor configuration file, you can add, edit and delete your custom jobs and so some global settings for the job services.

Name of configuration file: JobProcessor.exe.config

Location of the Configuration File

The configuration file can be found in the folder Explorer.

Path to the configuration file: Program Files>Autodesk>Vault Client [Edition]>Explorer.

Settings in the Configuration File

To add a new job to the configuration file, go to the jobHandler section in the configuration file.

<jobHandler>	Add your custom Jobs here. As soon as they are implemented correctly in this configuration file, you should check whether the Job is available and listed in the JobProcessor. Open the JobProcessor and select Administration>Job Types. The new job should be listed here and is ready to use

Log File

For analyses and control you can have a look to the Job Processor Log file which can be found in the same folder as the configuration file: **Explorer**.

Path to Log-File: Program Files>Autodesk>Vault Client [Edition]>Explorer

Here you can find useful information why your job could not be completed successfully or why the JobProcessor / JobServer does not work.

Practice 9c

Change Settings in the Job Processor

In this practice, you will change the configuration of Job Processor to start the Processor each time your machine is started. You will then set up some Jobs in Vault and Pause them in the Job Processor. Last but not least you will Resume and look at the Job Processor Log file to see whether or not all processes were successful.

Task 1 - Configure the Job Processor.

1. Start the Job Processor if it is not started yet.

2. Browse to Program Files>Autodesk>Vault Client [Edition]> Explorer>and start the file JobProcessor.exe.

   OR

   Use your Windows Start menu>All Programs> Autodesk Data Management>Autodesk Job Processor [Edition] for Vault.

3. Go to Administration menu and activate the automatic start by click Start on Windows Logon.

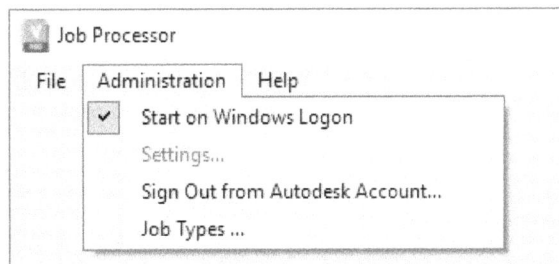

4. For your information, go to the Administration>Job Types command and get an overview of which jobs are available in this Vault installation.

Task 2 - Pause and resume the job process.

1. Select several components and create the DWF Job, explained in the first Lesson (Go to Actions>Update View>Queue Update).

2. Go to the Job Queue and watch the progress.

3. When only a few jobs are left and still pending, go to the Job Processor and select Pause from the File menu.

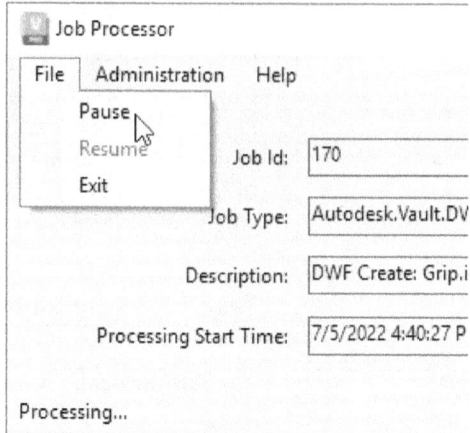

4. The progress of Job execution is paused. The job which was currently in progress will be finished. All jobs queued after this current job are paused and will not be handled as long as the Job Processor is "stopped" (paused).

5. After a while, click Resume in the File menu in the Job Processor dialog box to go on with job execution.

6. Double-check with your Job Queue whether all files were generated successfully. Exit the Job Queue and the Job Processor (File>Exit).

7. Have a look to the Job Processor Log file, which is stored in the Explorer directory of your Vault installation and analyze the content.

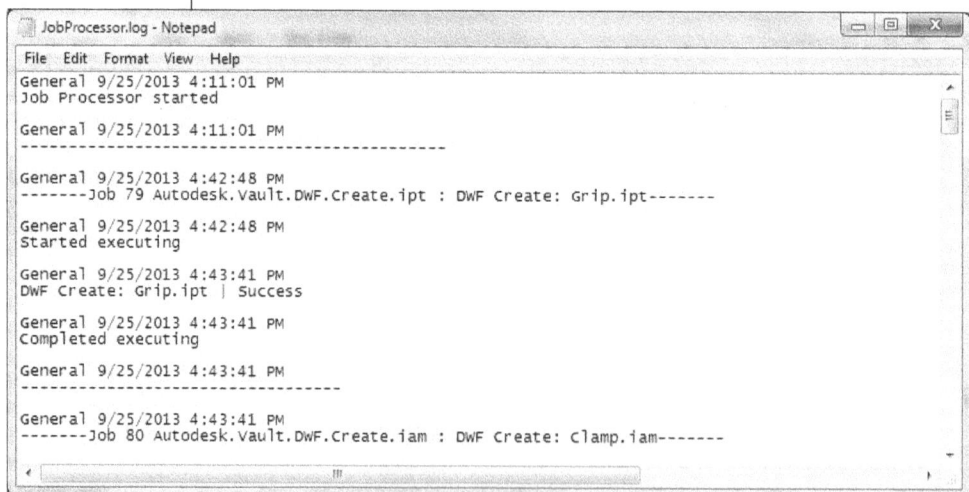

9.4 PDF Publishing

You can automatically publish and manage 2D PDF files from CAD files as documentation in the design release process at any lifecycle state.

Configuring PDF Publishing Options

Use the following steps to select the required settings for 2D AutoCAD and 2D Inventor PDF printing.

Note: You must have administrative access to perform these tasks.

1. Create a user with access to Released files. See Assign Roles to Users for more information.
2. Configure lifecycle definitions.
3. Click Tools > Administration > Vault Settings.
4. On the Vault Settings dialog, select Behaviors > Lifecycles.
5. Select the definition to be modified > Edit.
6. On the Lifecycle Definition dialog, select the Transitions tab, then (as an example) select Work in Progress to Released > Edit.
7. On the Transitions dialog, select the Actions tab.
8. From the drop-down, select one of the following options.
9. Synchronize properties, update view and PDF using Job Server.
10. Synchronize properties and update PDF using Job Server.
11. Note: Selecting one of these options from the list does not automatically select the check box as well. Make sure to select the check box beside the option, too.
12. From the Security tab, add the user created in Step 1, and allow Modify access under the Released state.
13. On the Lifecycle Definition dialog, select Design Representation Process > Edit.
14. On the Lifecycle Definition dialog, select the Released state.
15. Select the Security tab, add the user created in Step 1 and assign it Modify access. See Edit Lifecycle State Security for more information.
16. Note: You can create PDF at any life cycle state.
17. Sync state job fails if you do not have adequate permission for a particular state to be set on a PDF file, for example, you do not have the modify access on the Released state.
18. To enable the job server, click Tools > Administration > Global Settings > Integrations tab > Enable Job Server.

19. Note: For Job Processor to generate DWF and 2D PDF files, launch AutoCAD DWG Trueview at least once on the Job Processor.

2D AutoCAD PDF Publishing Options	Details
Add As An Attachment	Shows the published PDF file as an attachment to the file.
Upload to Source File Location	Automatically stores the published PDF file to the selected file location.
Upload To Selected Vault Path	Defines a specific location (using Browse) to store the published PDF file.
Sync Lifecycle State and Revision As Source	Allows both the published PDF and its source file to have the same lifecycle state and a revision value.
Use Page Settings From User DWG	Eliminates the need to reconfigure page settings in Vault if previously done in the native application. Checked and cannot be unchecked.
Include Model Space	Enables the published PDF file to contain model space view.
Include Layouts	Enables the published PDF file to contain model space view only.
Include Layer Info	Enables the published PDF to contain layer information.
Initialize Layouts	Enables support for legacy files.
Include Font Handling	Enables publishing a PDF file with font styles.

2D Inventor PDF Publishing Options	Details
Add As An Attachment	Shows the published PDF file as an attachment to the file.
Upload to Source File Location	Automatically stores the published PDF file to the selected file location.
Sync Lifecycle State and Revision As Source	Allows both the published PDF and its source file to have the same lifecycle state and a revision value.
Upload To Selected Vault Path	Defines a specific location (using Browse) to store the published PDF file.
Vector Resolution	Set as 400 DPI for managing large PDF file size and appropriate details.

Plot Object Lineweights	Enables the published PDF file to display a consistent lineweight for object and consistent lineweight for linetypes.
All Sheets	Prints all the sheets in the drawing. To print sheets for which the Exclude from Printing option is checked in the Edit Sheet dialog box, select Print Excluded Sheets.
All Colors As Black	Prints the drawing in black and white. Embedded images and shaded views are still printed in color.

Publish PDF from 2D CAD Files

Use the following steps to configure lifecycle definitions and PDF options to publish PDF from 2D CAD files.

Note: You must have administrative access to perform these tasks.

1. Create a user with access to Released files. For more information, see Assign Roles to Users.
2. Configure lifecycle definitions.
   a. Click Tools>Administration>Vault Settings.
   b. In the Vault Settings dialog box, select Behaviors>Lifecycles.
   c. Select the definition to be modified, and then select Edit.
   d. In the Lifecycle Definition dialog box, select the Transitions tab, then (as an example) select Work in Progress to Released >Edit.
   e. In the Transitions dialog box, select the Actions tab.
   f. From the drop-down, select one of the following options.
   • Synchronize properties, update view and PDF using Job Server
   • Synchronize properties and update PDF using Job Server

Note: Selecting one of these options from the list does not automatically select the checkbox as well. Ensure that the checkbox beside the option is also selected.

   g. In the Security tab, add the user created in Step 1 and enable the Modify access under the Released state.
   h. In the Lifecycle Definition dialog box, select Design Representation Process>Edit.
   i. In the Lifecycle Definition dialog box, select the Released state.
   j. Select the Security tab, add the user created in Step 1, and assign it Modify access.

Note: You can create PDF at any lifecycle state.

Sync state job fails if you do not have adequate permission for a particular state to be set on a PDF file, for example, you do not have the modify access on the Released state.

3. To enable the job server, click Tools>Administration>Global Settings>Integrations tab>Enable Job Server.

Note: For the Job Processor to generate DWF and 2D PDF files, launch AutoCAD DWG Trueview at least once on the Job Processor.

4. Click Tools>Administration>Vault Settings>PDF Options> Options to launch the PDF Options dialog box and configure the PDF publishing options.
5. Publish a PDF from a CAD file.
   a. Select any AutoCAD DWG file or Inventor 2D CAD file.
   b. Click Change Category. In the Change Category dialog box, select the Engineering category. Click OK.
   c. Click Change State. In the Change State dialog box, select Released from the lifecycle state drop-down list. Click OK.

This generates a PDF as an attachment to the selected file. Additionally, a thumbnail for the PDF displays in the Preview tab.

Note: To synchronize the revisions of the drawing file and 2D PDF file, set each file's Lifecycle Revision to be the same.

Note: To verify the Design Representation classification, click Tools>Administration>Vault Settings>Behaviors>Rules. In the Assignment Rules dialog box, view the Rule Criteria for Design Representation.

Create a PDF from 2D CAD Files

Use the following steps to create a copy of a PDF file using a 2D CAD file.

When using this command, a PDF can be created without going through a lifecycle state change for a 2D file.

Note: You must have appropriate access given by your administrator to access the Create PDF command in the different access points.

As an Administrator, you must enable the Enable Manual PDF Creation checkbox in the PDF Options section of the Settings dialog in order to use the Create PDF capability.

1. Select the 2D CAD file for which you want to manually create PDF.
2. Right-click and select Create PDF, or select the command from the Actions menu.

   IMPORTANT: The Create PDF command is available only for the latest version of the file and not for any historical version/revision of the 2D CAD files.

PDF Publish Location

Create PDF for 2D CAD files and specify a desired location outside of Vault Client.

Note: You must have administrative access to perform these tasks.

1. Click Tools > Administration > Vault Settings.

2. In the Vault Settings dialog box, click the Files tab.

3. Click the Define button next to Specify PDF Publish Location.

4. In the PDF Publish Location dialog box, select the desired option:

   a. Disable PDF Publish Folder Location: Disables to publish PDF files locally. Automatically generated PDF files are still created in the Vault Client.
   b. Flat List: Select to store all the PDF files in a single folder on the local computer.
   c. Duplicate Vault Folder Structure: Select to store local copies of the files in a folder structure that duplicates the structure used in Vault Client.
5. If you select Flat List or Duplicate Vault Folder Structure, click the Browse button and select a shared network folder which is accessible to all users.
6. Click OK.

   Note: By default, automatically generated PDF files are hidden in the file list. Select Tools > Options to enable to Show hidden files.

9.5 Vault Revision Table Administration

Overview

The process of manually updating the revision tables on drawings can be time-consuming, especially for changes that require simple property updates throughout a design's lifecycle. The Vault Revision Table feature enables you to automatically update a drawing's revision table with Vault data when properties are synchronized through the Job Server. This functionality eliminates the need to open each drawing in its native CAD application for updates.

Important: You must be an administrator with appropriate ownership privileges to enable the Vault Revision Table.

Objectives

After completing this lesson, you will be able to:

*   Understand Vault Revision Table Supported Drawings and Prerequisites.

*   Enable the Vault Revision Table functionality.

*   Understand the Vault Revision Table settings.

*   Create a Vault Revision Table.

Vault Revision Table Supported Drawings and Prerequisites

Supported Drawings

*   AutoCAD® drawings (.DWG)

*   AutoCAD Mechanical drawings (.DWG)

*   Autodesk® Inventor® drawings (.IDW)

*   Autodesk Inventor drawings (.DWG)

Prerequisites

*   Autodesk Inventor is installed so that Inventor IDW and DWG drawings can be updated.

*   Revision Table functionality is enabled.

The system property 'Revision' is a key mapping and must be mapped to at least one of the column headers.

- The Job Server is enabled with the synchronize properties option selected for the required state transition(s).

- Suitable column headers are created and their property mappings established between the drawings' revision table columns and the Vault properties.

Once all the prerequisites are met, the revision tables for the supported drawings are automatically updated with specified Vault data whenever properties are synchronized with the Job Server. This way, you can be sure that the revision table in your drawing is always up-to-date with the appropriate information from the vault.

Vault Revision Table Administration

Administrators can configure the information to be displayed in the revision table of the drawings for standardization across vault through the Revision Table Settings.

The Vault Revision Table feature must be enabled before you can configure Revision table settings or use the Revision Table feature in the Autodesk Inventor and AutoCAD Vault add-ins.

Enable the Vault Revision Table

1. Click Tools>Administration>Vault Settings.
2. In the Vault Settings dialog box, select the Behaviors tab and click Revision Table.
3. In the Revision Table Settings dialog box, select the Enable Revision Table checkbox to enable the Vault Revision Table Functionality across Vault.

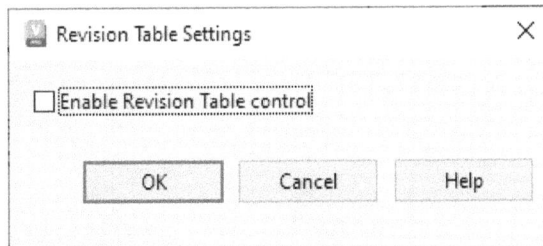

You can also open this dialog box from within the add-in by selecting Vault Options in the Vault ribbon and clicking Settings next to Configure Revision Table.

Revision Table Settings	×
☐ Enable Revision Table control	
OK	Cancel	Help

When this checkbox is selected, the full view for the Revision Table Settings displays.

Revision Table Settings Dialog Box

In the Revision Table Settings dialog box, you can configure how data displays, which Vault properties are mapped to the revision table, and the type of content displayed. You can also incorporate filters so that only the information you need displays in the revision tables.

Feature	Details
![icon]	Loads suggested settings.
![icon]	Loads the default settings for the dialog box.
![icon]	Restores all changes in the Revision Table settings dialog box to the settings used the last time the dialog box was opened.
Mapping Tab	In the Mappings tab, you can map Vault Properties to the Revision Table columns.

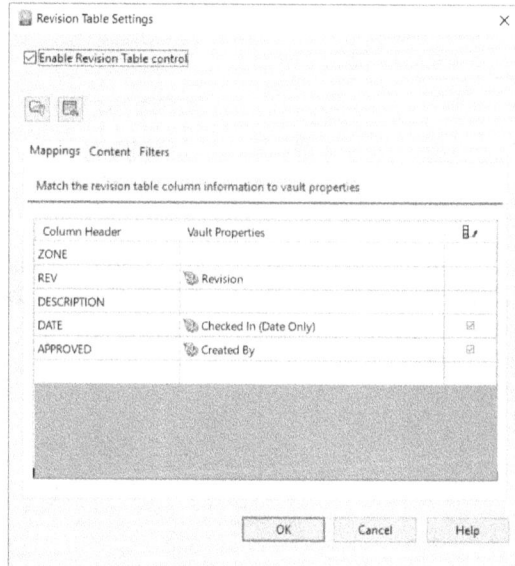

Column Header	Column name that displays in the revision table.
Vault Properties	The name of the Vault property that you have mapped to the associated revision table column.
	The value for this property will automatically display in the column field of the revision table for the drawing.

🗄✎	Released vs. non-released bias control.
	Select the checkbox for any row where you want the system to update the revision table with released only information. If the checkbox for a row is not selected, then the latest information from the vault is used.
Content Tab	In the Content tab, you can enforce the type of information that displays in the revision table.
Update rows using	Select version control.
	Select the version and the released state that you want to apply to revision history records.
Limit number of rows checkbox	If you want to limit the number of rows displayed in the revision table, select the Limit number of rows checkbox. Specify the limit for the number of rows that you want displayed by selecting a value from the value spinner.
	Note: When the Limit number of rows option is toggled ON, the exceeding records are deleted by default. In Autodesk Inventor drawings, you can also select to hide these exceeding records instead of deleting them.
Hide exceeding records for Inventor drawings checkbox	Select this checkbox to hide, instead of deleting, the additional Autodesk Inventor drawing records.

Update latest revision only	Select this checkbox to update the mapped values only for the latest revision row in the revision table. All other mapped values in previous historical revision rows do not get updated even if the data is non-equivalent in the vault.
	Note: Even with the Update latest revision only enabled, the Vault Revision Table feature continues to remove revision rows which are not found in the Vault.
Detect revision scheme change and remove previous revision history	If you are using multiple revision schemes, select this checkbox to ensure that the current revision scheme is used. Historical revision rows of an older revision scheme are replaced with the current revision scheme.
Filters Tab	In the Filters tab, you can further refine the data displayed in the revision table by applying revision level filters.
	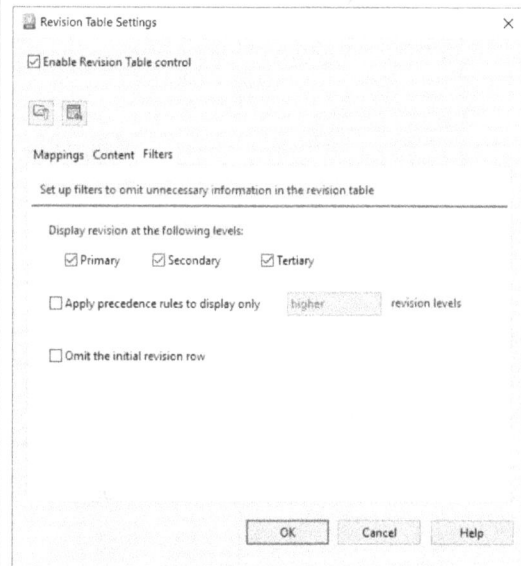
Display revision at the following levels	Select the checkbox for each revision level that you want displayed in the revision table. For example, if you have a drawing marked as revision B.2.1, and you only select the Primary and Secondary checkboxes, then only B.2 displays in the revision table.
	Refer to Revision Schemes for more information about Primary, Secondary, and Tertiary revision levels.

Apply precedence rules to display only X revision levels	When multiple revision levels exist in a revision group, it is important to identify the level of revision that you want to be displayed. Enable this checkbox and select whether you want the highest or lowest revision levels displayed in the revision table.
	This selection takes precedence over the Display revision at the following levels option.
Omit the initial revision row	Select this checkbox to omit the initial revision row from the revision table.
	Some users find that if the initial revision value (e.g., A) is already in the title block for the revision table, having it repeated as the first revision row is unnecessary. By selecting this checkbox, the first revision row in the revision table becomes the next revision value (e.g., A.1).

Practice 9d | Using Vault Revision Tables

In this practice, you will create a Vault Revision table in Grip.idw. Grip.idw is a drawing of Grip.ipt. These files are managed by the Flexible Release Process lifecycle definition. To permit the Job Server to run in the Released state, the default settings for Security for the Released state in the Flexible Release Process needs to be modified. For the Released state, change Modify and Delete for Everyone to Allow, as shown in the image below.

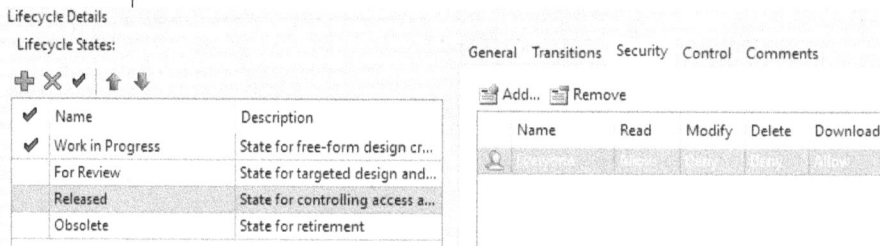

Also, ensure that the properties get synchronized using the Job Server for the transition of Work in Progress to Released, as shown in the image below.

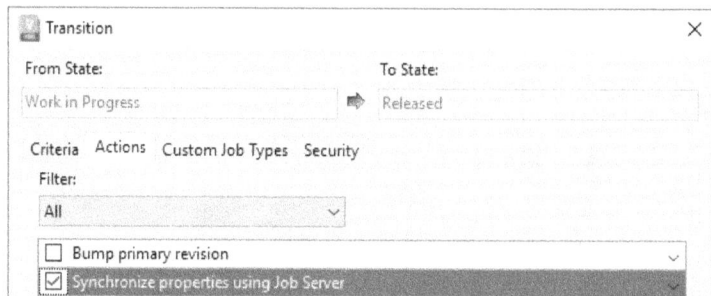

Task 1 - Enable the Vault Revision Table and map description property.

1. Start the Autodesk Vault Workgroup software. Log in using the information below and ensure that Designs.ipj is set as the Inventor project file.

   - User Name: **Administrator**
   - Password: **No password**
   - Vault: AOTCVault

2. Click Tools>Administration>Vault Settings.

3. In the Vault Settings dialog box, select the Behaviors tab and click Revision Table.

4. In the Revision Table Settings dialog box, select the **Enable Revision Table control** checkbox to enable the Vault Revision Table Functionality.

5. Click Yes to load recommended settings. The Revision Table Settings dialog box updates as shown below.

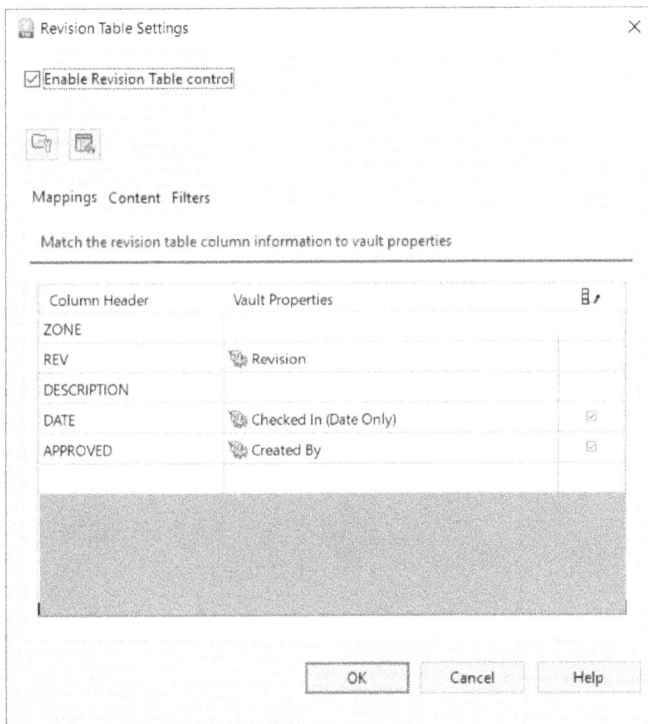

6. For the Description Inventor property, select the Comment system Vault property. Note that by default, the APPROVED property maps to the Created By Vault property. Click OK and then click Close to close the Vault Settings dialog box.

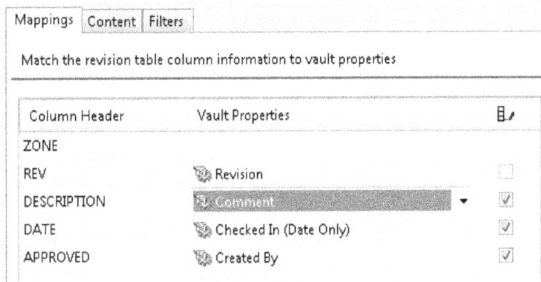

Task 2 - Add Vault Revision Table to drawing.

1. In Inventor, log in to Vault and from the Vault tab, click Open. In the Designs/Clamp folder, select Grip.idw.

2. In the Annotate tab, click Vault Revision.

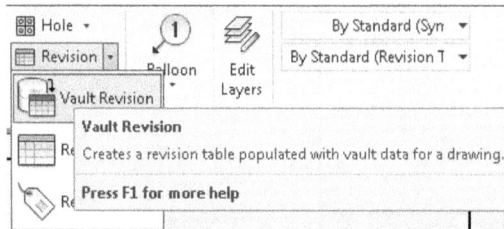

3. Insert the table in the top right corner of the drawing.

Task 3 - Edit Vault Revision Table.

1. To edit the table, right-click on the revision table and select Edit.

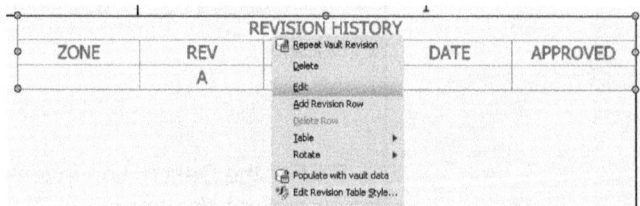

2. To remove the Zone column, right-click on a column header and click Column Chooser...

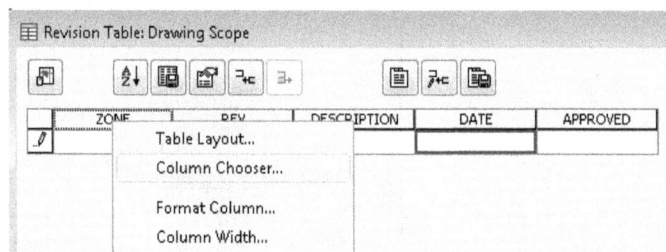

3. Select Zone in the Selected Properties list, click Remove, and then click OK.

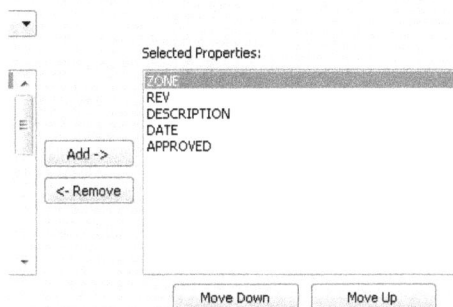

4. Click OK. The revision table in the drawing updates without the Zone column.

REVISION HISTORY			
REV	DESCRIPTION	DATE	APPROVED
A			

5. Save the drawing and check it into the vault using the Close files and delete working copies option.

Task 4 - Release the drawing.

1. In Vault, select Grip.idw, right-click, and select Change State. You can also perform a Change State in Inventor.

2. Select Released from the new lifecycle state drop-down list.

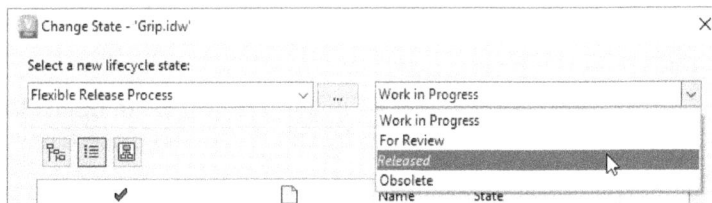

3. Update the comment to say Initial Release and click OK. The state updates to Released in the main table.

4. Now the Job Server will create the visualization files. To force the jobs, open Job Processor and select File>Pause then File>Resume.

Task 5 - Create a new revision.

1. Now you will create a new revision to make a change to the Grip.ipt. In Vault, select Grip.idw, right-click, and select Change State.

2. Select Work in Progress.

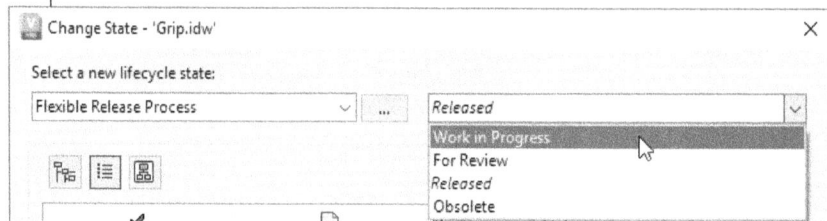

3. Click OK. In the main table, the state updates to Work In Progress and the revision changes to B.

Grip.idw	Work in Progress	B
Grip.ipt	Work in Progress	B

4. In Inventor, open Grip.idw from the vault using Open (Check Out All). Click Yes to All to update properties. Note the change to the Vault Revision table.

REVISION HISTORY			
REV	DESCRIPTION	DATE	APPROVED
A	Initial Release	5/10/2016	Administrator
B			

5. In the Vault Browser, open Grip.ipt and make a change to the length. Save and close Grip.ipt.

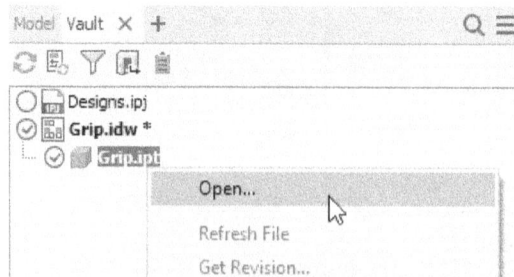

6. In the Vault Browser of Grip.idw, save and check in both the drawing and the part. Select the Close files and delete the working copies option.

7. In Vault, change the State of the Drawing to Released again. For the comments, enter Rev B - Changed Length.

8. Once again, the Job Server will create the visualization files upon Release. To force the jobs, open Job Processor and select File>Pause then File>Resume.

Task 6 - View Vault Revision Table.

1. In Vault, right-click on Grip.idw and select Open to open the drawing in Inventor.

2. The Vault Revision Table is updated.

REVISION HISTORY			
REV	DESCRIPTION	DATE	APPROVED
A	Initial Release	5/10/2016	Administrator
B	Rev B - Changed Length	5/10/2016	Administrator

3. The Update Properties feature is integrated with the vault revision table feature so that the revision block data is synchronized with the vault released information. The manual ways of updating properties if mapped properties are edited include using Update Properties in the Vault Browser, Vault tab, or right-clicking on the Vault Revision table and selecting Populate with vault data.

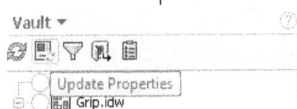

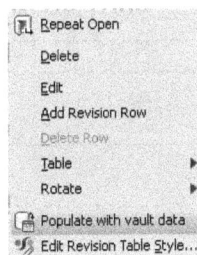

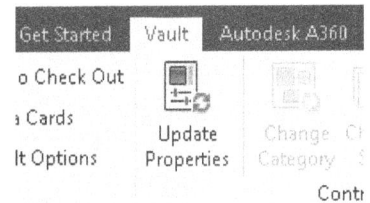

4. (Optional) If you would like to change the files back to a previous lifecycle state, in Vault, select the files, select Actions>Roll Back Lifecycle State Change, and follow the prompts.

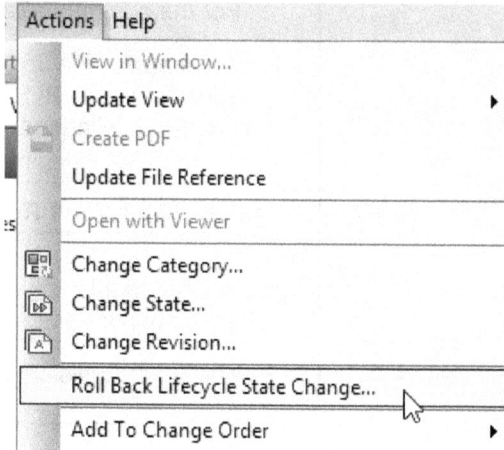

Actions	Help
View in Window...	
Update View	▶
Create PDF	
Update File Reference	
Open with Viewer	
Change Category...	
Change State...	
Change Revision...	
Roll Back Lifecycle State Change...	
Add To Change Order	▶

9.6 Backup and Restore

Overview

To prevent data loss, you can select Backup and Restore your Vault.

Objectives

After completing this lesson, you will be able to:

- Backup and Restore your Vault machine.

Back Up the Vault

1. Log in to Autodesk Data Management Server Console.
2. From the Tools menu, select Backup and Restore.

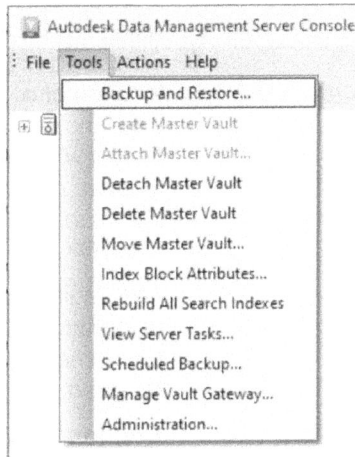

3. Select Backup in the Wizard. Before backing up the data, the server console validates the data to ensure that the file store and databases are synchronized. If the database is out of sync, a dialog box displays listing the files that are mismatched. You can cancel the back up to correct the files.
4. Select Full Backup or Incremental Backup. The Incremental Backup option will not be available if no changes have occurred since the last Full or Incremental Backup.
5. Specify the location to store the backed up data. To browse for a location, click the ellipsis (...) and then locate a directory using the file browser.
6. Toggle on the Validate checkbox to verify the archive is good once it is created.
7. By default standard Content Center libraries are included in the back up process. To exclude standard Content Center libraries from the back up, toggle off the Backup Standard Content Center Libraries checkbox.

8. By default a backup will wait until all files that need to be replicated are replicated before starting. Check the Ignore non-replicated files checkbox to start the backup without waiting for these files to replicate.
9. Click OK.

Restore a Vault

Access to the vault database is blocked during this task. Data management clients cannot access the database until the task is complete.

Access to the Incremental Restore option is available when no changes have occurred since the restore of the previous increment

Restore the Entire Vault

1. From the Tools menu, select Backup and Restore.
2. Select Restore in the Wizard.
3. Restoring a vault deletes the data sets and file store. You are prompted for confirmation before proceeding. Click Yes.
4. Select Full Restore or Incremental Restore.
5. Specify the location of the backed up data. To browse for a location, click the ellipsis (...) and then locate a directory using the file browser.
6. Select whether the database is to be restored to the default location or a different location. If you choose Select Restore Location, specify a target directory for database
7. Select whether the file store is to be restored to the default location or a different location. If you choose Select Restore Location, specify a target directory for the file store.
8. Click OK.

   The vault data is automatically migrated when it is restored using the server console. If you are restoring the data using the command line, you must migrate the data after it is restored.

   Caution: If you have another Vault on your machine where you want to restore a Vault you need to detach these existing Vaults prior to restoring the required Vault to avoid any overwriting! When you have finished the restore of the Vault you can attach the other Vaults.

Manually Restore Only the File Store

The file store can be manually restored by itself from a backup package to a remote location in a multi-site environment. This process should only be done by experienced vault administrators.

1. In the selected backup package, open the folder FileStores. The FileStores folder contains one folder for each vault in the backup. Each folder is named according to the vault to which it belongs.
2. Locate the appropriate file store folder and copy it to the remote location.

Back Up Vault Data

Backing up vault data is essential. The following are recommendations for backing up Autodesk® Vault.

Use the Supplied Backup-Restore Utility

Use the server console to back up all data required to restore a server if a failure occurs. In Vault Workgroup the users are blocked from accessing the vault during a backup. Vault Professional provides a 'hot backup' process, enabling users to continue to access the vault during the procedure. In addition, server console backs up or restores all vaults on the server. There is no way to select individual vaults to back up or restore.

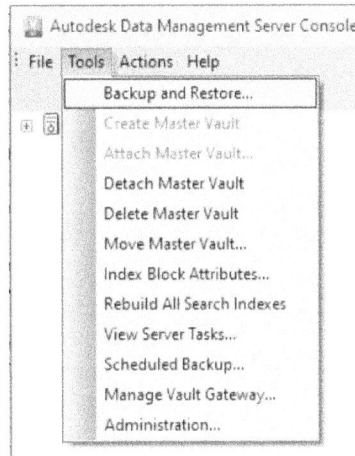

Develop a Backup Schedule

The next step is to automate the process. Two common methods are:

- Use Tools>Scheduled Backup. This process uses the backup tools included with the server console to create the backup script and task automatically.

- Include the backup as part of a tape backup set. This process uses a tape back up system to back up the vault directly.

The preferred and most reliable method for backing up a vault is to integrate the server console backup tools into your tape backup plan.

Scheduled Backup

1. From the Tools menu, select Scheduled Backup.
2. In the Backup Configuration dialog box, specify the location of the backed up data. To browse for a location, click the ellipsis (...) and then locate the directory using the file browser.
3. In the Vault Credentials tab, if using a Vault user account, for the Vault account name, specify administrator.
4. Select the Full Backup tab or Incremental Backup tab depending on what type of backup is being scheduled.
5. Select the checkbox for Schedule a full backup or Schedule an incremental backup depending on what tab in step 4 was selected.
6. Specify the Schedule name, Start date, time, and days for the backup.
7. Click OK.

   The batch file is created and a task automatically created in the Windows Task Scheduler.

Restore Vaults from Backups

1. From the Tools menu, select Backup and Restore.
2. Select Restore.
3. Restoring a vault deletes the current data sets and file store. This action cannot be undone. You are prompted for confirmation before proceeding. Click Yes.
4. In the Restore from directory field, specify the location of the backed up data. To browse for a location, click... and locate a directory using the file browser.
5. Select whether to restore the database to the original location or to a different location. If you choose Select Restore Location, specify a target directory for the database. This selection is sometimes required when restoring data to a different machine that does not have the same drive letters or locations available.
6. Select whether to restore the file to the original location or to a different location. If you choose Select Restore Location, specify a target directory for the file store.
7. Click OK.

   The vault data is automatically migrated when it is restored using Autodesk Vault server console. If you are restoring the data using the command line, migrate the data after it is restored.

Practice 9e

Back Up Your Vault

Back up your Vault as described above.

9.7 Chapter Summary

The Autodesk Vault Workgroup and Autodesk Vault Professional software provide the Copy Design feature that helps you save time by creating new designs based on existing ones. The Autodesk Vault Workgroup and Autodesk Vault Professional software also contain a powerful Job Server that manages a job queue for batch DWF generation and custom defined jobs. This job processor offloads DWF generation to another machine, helping to speed the check-in experience for end users. Common interactions from Vault leverage the Job Server, such as checking data in from CAD applications. In addition, the Job Server queue can be used to track job details and overall progress. With the bonus tool LifeCycleEvent Editor lifecycle transitions can be managed through automatic jobs that are generated on events. The Vault Revision Table feature provides powerful functionality to automatically update the revision table of a drawing with Vault data when properties are synchronized through the Job Server.

Having completed this chapter, you can:

- Create new designs from existing ones with the Copy Design feature

- Differentiate between the meaning of Job Server and Job Processor.

- Enable the Job Server in the Global Settings.

- Initiate a job.

- Work with the Job Queue.

- Configure Job Processor via UI.

- Understand settings in the configuration file.

- Use the LifeCycleEventEditor.

- Use the Job Server Log files for analyses.

- Enable the Vault Revision Table functionality.

- Understand the Vault Revision Table settings.

- Backup and Restore your Vault machine.

www.ingramcontent.com/pod-product-compliance
Lightning Source LLC
Chambersburg PA
CBHW080915220326
41598CB00034B/5579